PRAGMAT

MW01002539

CHARLES W. ANDERSON

Pragmatic
Liberalism

THE UNIVERSITY OF CHICAGO PRESS

Chicago and London

The University of Chicago Press, Chicago 60637
The University of Chicago Press, Ltd., London
© 1990 by The University of Chicago
All rights reserved. Published 1990
Paperback edition 1994
Printed in the United States of America

99 98 97 96 95 94   5 4 3 2

Library of Congress Cataloging in Publication Data

Anderson, Charles W., 1934–
    Pragmatic liberalism / Charles W. Anderson.
        p.   cm.
    Includes bibliographical references.
    ISBN 0-226-01801-6 (cloth)
    ISBN 0-226-01802-4 (paper)
    1. Liberalism.   2. Pragmatism.   3. Associations,
institutions, etc.   4. Community life.   I. Title
JC571.A498 1990
320.5′1—dc20   90-30177
                                                        CIP

*This book is dedicated to the people and the university
of the state of Wisconsin, the seedbed of many
of the commitments expressed herein*

CONTENTS

PREFACE

The political theory I shall call pragmatic liberalism emerged gradually in the American mind in the early decades of this century. Charles Sanders Peirce, Josiah Royce, William James, and John Dewey provided its philosophical foundations. Thorstein Veblen and John R. Commons were among the authors of its political economy. Pragmatic liberalism was once the basis of our public philosophy, and it was our dominant mode of social analysis. It shaped the distinctively American disciplines of political science and institutional economics. It greatly influenced our theories of philosophy, education, and law. Pragmatic liberalism formed part of the intellectual background for Progressive reform and the New Deal.

Today we have almost forgotten this method of practical political analysis and the reasons for our once strong commitment to it. Within the past generation, a striking change has taken place in our habits of public thought. Versions of liberal theory virtually unchanged since the Enlightenment, ideas that were once thought to be of no more than historic interest, have become, again, prescriptive models for political argument. A mechanical free market philosophy and a closely calculated utilitarian economizing rationality have for some time dominated our discussions of public affairs.

The academic disciplines have been greatly affected by this resurgence of historic forms of liberal thought. Economics now teaches a formal, axiomatic version of classic liberal theory, virtually to the exclusion of all other ideas. (I realize that economists normally speak of the "neoclassical" synthesis, but I am going to strenuously avoid the use of the forms "neo" and "post" throughout this study.) Philosophy has returned to the state of nature and the social contract as starting points for speculation on rightful order. Even in political science, that most eclectic and practical of the disciplines of social analysis, formal liberalism has become fashionable, in the guise of public choice theory.

Today, this small episode in the history of ideas has probably passed its prime. What I shall call "classic" or "orthodox" liberalism—to designate those forms of liberal theory grounded in the idea of the utility-maximizing individual, generally celebratory of marketlike arrangements, skeptical of public action—is no longer dominant or unchallenged in setting the tone of the public debate. People have begun to seek a more generous and carefully considered ethic of public responsibility and human purpose. However, they do not yet find it taught. The liberal arts and sciences, whose task it is to scan our heritage of ideas and remind us of our options, have not yet come to terms with the problem of formulating a workable alternative to the prevalent views. This book, then, is a small effort to rectify the imbalance.

Pragmatic liberalism is the logical alternative to orthodox liberalism in this country. Pragmatic liberalism represents a well-worked-out critical response to the excessive abstractness, the "impracticality," and the strangely mechanical view of human motivation and public effort of the classical tradition of liberal ideas. Rather than seeking a novel basis for the reconstruction of our public philosophy, I think we are better off picking up the thread of discussion where we left off, starting with a way of thinking that still comes naturally to the American mind.

My aim in this book is to provide a fresh statement of pragmatic liberalism as a political and political economic theory. I begin, as the early pragmatic liberals began, by stressing the collaborative nature of constructive human effort, while retaining the individual as the source of value. "Rationality" now becomes not calculated self-interest but the critical examination of customary methods and practices, the search for better, more reliable ways of "doing things." There is understood to be a close analogy between this method of practical reason and that of scientific discovery.

Pragmatic liberalism is a discipline of practical political reason. The problem is to relate "theory" to "practice," to invoke liberal principles of responsiveness to individual will, nonarbitrariness, social efficiency and economy, fairness in distributions and in distinctions of recognition and reward, to the critical analysis and reform of our diverse organized forms of cooperative human endeavor. For reasons that will become clear, I call these "rational enterprises" and "communities of practice." I have in mind not only business enterprise, as we shall see, but all forms of organized undertaking.

This mode of analysis yields a different vision of the relationship of the public and the private realms. The state is properly regarded as a party to the rational development of the enterprise. Its role is collaborative, not adversarial. At the same time, participation in the affairs of an enterprise is to be understood as an act of citizenship. Governance is not simply a matter that concerns the affairs of the state, for there is a public interest in the conduct of every significant organized undertaking.

This book is not a work of historical scholarship. I am not trying to reinterpret the writings of Dewey, Veblen, and the rest. I want to speak for the continuity of this tradition, but I see no reason to be bound by its texts. Many of the disputes and enthusiasms of the formative years of this intellectual movement are now completely beside the point. Perhaps, had I chosen a different name for this theory, I could have pretended to greater originality. However, the fact of the matter is that there is little novelty in political thought. The task of political theory is largely that of reassessing our current state of civic consciousness in the light of our total heritage of ideas, and recommending a different distribution of emphasis from time to time, or reminding us of neglected possibilities.

I write on behalf of a particular version of liberalism, but I also write within the larger liberal tradition. This is, as Karol Soltan would say, a "loyalist's perspective." This will not be a lament for the decadence of the age or a stern exhortation to restore ancient virtue or achieve "authentic subjectivity." This is rather a reminder of the source and value of our more commonplace convictions.

It is not that I believe that liberalism is the ideal state of civic consciousness. Perhaps it is an interim ethic that will be replaced in the course of time. But liberalism is what we have, and it seems the best of the available options. I believe it is compatible with the most revealing surmises of our intellectual and religious inheritance concerning human nature and its destiny. Liberalism is a durable and open habit of mind. Many moves are possible within it, and its implications are far from exhausted.

Acknowledgments

I would first acknowledge certain long-standing intellectual debts. The work of Albert O. Hirschman, Charles E. Lindblom, Brian Barry, and Willard Hurst has served as a continuing source of inspiration and orientation through the years. The reader will also sense the influence of many other contemporary political theorists, particularly James Fishkin, Alasdair MacIntyre, Philippe Schmitter, and Michael Walzer, though the appropriate acknowledgment, perhaps, is to all those who, following on the landmark initiative of John Rawls, reopened the argument about liberal political theory and began again exploring its many implications and possibilities.

Two books, Thomas A. Spragens' *The Irony of Liberal Reason* and Jeffrey Lustig's *Corporate Liberalism,* came along at just the right moment and helped me see a relationship among problems I had been working on separately for a number of years.

Early sketches and studies for some sections of the book appeared in different form in the following volumes: John Nelson, Allan Megill and Donald N. McCloskey, eds., *The Rhetoric of the Human Sciences* (Madison: University of Wisconsin Press, 1987); Frank Fischer and John Forester, eds., *Confronting Values in Policy Analysis* (Beverly Hills, Calif.: Sage Publications, 1987); Alfonso J. Damico, ed., *Liberals on Liberalism* (Totawa, N.J.: Rowman and Littlefield, 1986); Philippe C. Schmitter and Gerhard Lembruch, eds., *Trends Toward Corporatist Intermediation* (Beverly Hills, Calif.: Sage Publications, 1979); E. B. Portis and M. B. Levi, eds., *Handbook of Political Theory and Policy Science* (Lexington, Mass.: Greenwood Press, 1989).

Three trusted friends read early versions of the manuscript and provided invaluable advice. Booth Fowler displayed again his special gifts as scholar and teacher and provided a patient and remarkably comprehensive critique of the whole manuscript. Ira Struaber helped me clarify my purposes and pointed out where some of the land mines lay. But it was Stephen Elkin who had the penetrating insight to see clearly what was wrong with the original structure of the argument and the courage to tell me that I had to fix it.

Quite without knowing it, I am sure, my colleagues in the Integrated Liberal Studies Program at the University of Wisconsin helped restore my spirit, and provided an environment which stimulated me to see the matter whole and which helped me overcome narrowing professional inhibitions.

I gratefully acknowledge financial support provided by the Glenn L. and Cleo Orr Hawkins professorship and the Graduate School of the University of Wisconsin.

The staff of the University of Chicago Press were careful, thorough and thoughtful in the production of the book. They exemplify the kind of "good practice" about which much will be said herein.

Finally, for Jeanie, my partner in all things, this book has been another episode in a life together filled with many adventures and great blessings.

1

Introduction:

Practical Political Reason

Pragmatic liberalism is a hybrid term, and it is not obvious that the parts belong together.

In everyday use, pragmatism often connotes tough-minded practicality, a sense for the arts of the possible. Liberalism, on the other hand, stands for a politics of principles. Liberalism is, if nothing else, the belief that there are specific things that government must and must not do if individuals are to be free to act on their own responsibility.

In philosophy and political theory, pragmatism and liberalism have often seemed antagonists. Pragmatism took exception to the stark individualism of formal, classic liberalism and stressed the cooperative nature of human endeavor. Its image of reason was not the endless calculation of self-interest but the collaborative contrivance of workable methods of action.

For its part, classic liberalism thought pragmatism relativistic and unprincipled. The insistence of Peirce, James, and Dewey that inquiry should not be prefigured, that the quest for certainty was misplaced, that there were no independent foundations of truth or right, seemed to those who followed in the tradition of Locke and Kant a denial of rationality and morality itself.[1]

The two terms may define the main lines of partisan rivalry in the United States. Pragmatism is associated with a flexible, activist conception of law and state policy. This was the basis for progressive reform during the early decades of the century, at least through the New Deal. On the other hand, classic liberalism provides the foundation for the doctrine of free market capitalism and minimal government, and a jurisprudence of strict interpretation of fundamental law. Throughout the century, these positions have provided the point and counterpoint of our political argument.

Nonetheless, I think these terms belong together, and that taken together, they define a distinctive position in liberal thought.

Pragmatism is a much maligned and much misunderstood philosophy. The aims of Peirce, James, and Dewey were anything but the raw practicality with which pragmatism is usually associated in the public mind. Nor was pragmatism a simple attack on "foundationalism" in philosophy. The early pragmatic philosophers were grappling with the problem of truth. They were concerned with the question of how far and in what respects the mind could grasp the world. They were continuing the project of Hegel, as well as Plato. Their essential point—particularly apparent in Peirce though certainly true for Dewey as well—was that the reliability and durability of our ideas, their ability to "work well" in a variety of situations and to win the critical consent of a community of inquiry, was the best guarantee for finite minds that we were perhaps getting at the underlying order of things.

Nonetheless, when applied to politics, pragmatism needs liberalism if it is not to become a vague and indeterminate counsel, perhaps, in the end, a doctrine of sheer expediency. Pragmatic reasoning is supposed to begin in the face of a quandary of belief and action. Pragmatism can be understood as sheer instrumental rationality, the mutual adjustment of means and ends, resources and values. This is taken as a general conception of method: the aim can be anything. However, if one thinks of liberal principles as constituting the problematic situation to which pragmatic reasoning must respond, the matter is otherwise. Now pragmatic reason has essential point and purpose. And this is in fact how we do frame dilemmas that call for political thought and public choice. To say that a pattern of practice is unfair, or unresponsive to the interests of affected parties, is to set the question for pragmatic reason. In our society, liberal principles provide the normative structure for pragmatic method. Louis Hartz observed that pragmatism "fed" on America's commitment to liberalism and suggested that "It is only when you take your ethics for granted that all problems emerge as problems of technique."[2]

Pragmatism needs liberalism if it is to have moral and political significance. On the other hand, liberalism is empty and formal without pragmatic method. The abstract principles of liberalism require interpretation. The great values of freedom, equality, justice, and social efficiency may be, in a certain sense, "self-evident," but what they mean when applied in diverse circumstances is not at all clear. It is not, in fact, the philosophic grounding, or the ordering, but the *application* of the fundamental principles that generates the great disputes of liberal politics.

Thus, the method and the maxims are inseparable, and if we are to understand liberalism as a public philosophy, then we should understand pragmatism as a conception of practical reason that complements and completes it.

A Definition of Pragmatic Liberalism

What then, precisely, is pragmatic liberalism? Let me try, as succinctly as possible, to define the nature of my subject and the aim of this book.

Pragmatic liberalism is, first of all, a theory of practical political reason that applies not only to the state but to all forms of organized human endeavor: to industry and the professions, the crafts and trades, the schools and sciences.

Perhaps the most distinctive feature of pragmatic liberalism then is the proposition that the performance of the diverse functional associations that make up our society is a matter of public concern and that participation in them is a form of public responsibility and an act of citizenship.

Classic liberal doctrine seems to assume that the state should have no purposes of its own. Its function is to provide a framework of law and policy within which individuals are free to pursue their own ends. The state should endorse no specific conception of the human good. But in this case, the *character* of a liberal society will arise largely from the configuration of its dominant associations and institutions. Its ethos and philosophy, that which it honors and that which it deplores, the human potentialities that will prosper and those that will be thwarted, the artifacts that will be abundant and those that will be scarce, in short, the way of life of a liberal society, will be predominantly the product of those specialized, rationalized forms of organized action that arise out of the collaborative efforts of its citizens.

The conventional understanding of liberalism not only strictly separates the public from the private sphere but also insists on a sharp differentiation of the logics and languages that pertain to the diverse forms of human activity. Each institution should be guided by its own rationality. Political reason applies to the affairs of government alone. The productive enterprises are to be the domain of economic calculation. The churches take their bearings from their theologies, the crafts and professions from canons of technique, the sciences from their logics of inquiry.

However, for pragmatic liberalism, each human association has a political aspect and is part of the public life of the society. There is a public interest in the performance of each functional enterprise and in the composite performance of the pluralist regime as a whole. Orthodox liberalism holds that performance is best enhanced by stimulating competition among individuals. Pragmatic liberalism believes that creative effort is naturally collaborative and cooperative and is best promoted by systematic deliberation and argument about the purposes, practices, and responsibilities of a cooperative undertaking. For pragmatic liberalism, such discussion is necessarily a public matter, and it calls for the exercise of practical political reason.

Pragmatic liberalism is in some respects a political position and a political program. It entails a progressive conception of the relationship of state and society and of the public responsibility of "private" associations. In these respects particularly, it is different from classical or orthodox liberalism. However, pragmatic liberalism is, above all else, an idea of *method*. Our main concern is to understand how the fundamental principles of liberalism apply in practice. As we shall see, in pragmatic liberalism, these principles are tests not only of the performance of governments but of all kinds of purposive association. Pragmatic liberalism is a *discipline* of political judgment. Its principal norm of argument is that policy grounded in liberal principle must be shown simultaneously to serve the public good and to enhance the performance of some particular substantive enterprise. Pragmatic liberalism is concerned with the policy of the state: how it regulates, coordinates, promotes, and supports the configuration of organized ventures that constitute the larger public life of the society. It is also concerned with the governance *of* the enterprise—its "management," its internal political culture, its constitutional principles and political processes.

Pragmatic liberalism is a way of being "practical" about liberalism. But that is not its only object. The purpose of such a theory is also to add a needed dimension of substance and of community to liberal thought. And the point of focusing on the performance of the enterprise, as well as of the state, is to generate a political economy, a theory of how the world's work is properly done, at the same time that one develops a political theory, an ideal of rightful order.

Now let us go on to consider the principal characteristics of this method of applied liberalism, this idea of practical political reason.

The Problem of Practical Liberal Reason

Formal liberal political theory is normally written at a high level of abstraction. It is concerned with first principles and basic constitutional arrangements. It would have us regard the great issues of consent and obligation, of democratic process and individual right, of the relative priority of liberty and equality, as the essential questions of political thought. Liberal theory makes it seem that the first task of citizens, and the basic object of political deliberation, is to engage in a persistent reconsideration of the constitutive principles of the regime.

Formal liberal theory takes the point of view of the lawgiver, the constitution-maker. And it is this quality of formal liberal theory that makes it seem so remote from the problems of practical political reason. For we are seldom in a position to start all over again. We better understand ourselves as parties to an ongoing political project, one it would be imprudent, if not impossible, to unravel and recast along fundamentally different lines. Our public problems arise within a complex legacy of ideas and institutions, and the issues that call for deliberative action concern the fitting of that legacy to new contingencies and opportunities.

Questions of the regime are remote from practical experience. The significant problems of political judgment are immediate and local. They arise as much from the contexts of work and social function as from formal political responsibility. Even when the citizen functions as public official—as legislator, administrator, or judge—the focus of attention is not apt to be on fundamental principles in themselves, but on these only in relation to a set of concrete problems and projects.

Thus, we enter public life always in midstream, never at the beginning. We are seized with a particular project: the construction of a road, the location of a factory, the adoption of a land-use plan, a question of curriculum or research priorities in the university, a problem of doctrine for a church. We confront the dilemmas of public life from the vantage point of a specific role or position of responsibility. We are mindful of the expectations of those who will be affected by our actions. Our deliberations reflect conceptions of purpose, tradition, and normal practice of a particular going concern. And out of such partial, piecemeal decisions, the larger constitutive order of the liberal polity gradually emerges and takes on settled form.

Liberal Principles and Political Judgment

We do not tend to make up public problems. Rather, we are confronted by them, or charged with them, in a specific context and role of responsibility.

The issue, then, is to connect the immediate problem to the larger philosophy of the regime. How, in fact, do liberal principles bear on the immediate local decisions that are the essential tasks of citizenship, and which, in the end, define the spirit and temper of a people and their political order?

The art of judgment, of guiding the conduct of affairs in highly particular circumstances, is often said to depend on an experienced "feel" for the situation.[3] However, liberal theory requires that public decisions rest on known, general, and impartial principles. Liberalism is a long historic effort to reduce the degree of arbitrariness in human affairs.[4] The public official has no right to base public decisions on hunch or instinct. Liberalism is a language of justification, and it is not good enough to say simply that one "knew" the right thing to do or "had a sense" that one should proceed in a certain way.

Liberalism becomes a discipline of practical reason as one searches for a rule, a principled ground of choice. The search for principled justification becomes a corrective to initial impulse. The solution that "seemed right" may not stand up under scrutiny. One perfects a design for public action in contemplation of the reasons one must eventually give for it.

Liberal thought is a process of abstraction from particulars. Kin to scientific rationalism, liberalism assumes that we come to terms with discrete events and experiences by subsuming them under general categories and rules. We perceive significance and order in otherwise inchoate patterns of events by identifying them with the constructs of a logical system. This, we say, thinking scientifically, is an illustration of the principle of the conservation of energy, or centrifugal force, or symbiotic relation. This, we say, thinking politically, is a problem of market failure, or individual right, or distributive justice. To so identify a situation with a principle clarifies it in our mind, enables us to "understand" it, and, in liberal thought, also suggests how we ought to appraise it and act in relation to it.

To characterize a state of affairs in terms of liberal principles is to invest it with public significance. Once we invoke notions of right, or collective efficiency, or responsiveness to individual will, we are no longer dealing with a matter of strictly private concern. We are no longer talking simply business, or science, or neighborliness. We have given the question political significance, made it, potentially, a matter for public resolution, for law or policy.

Two Dilemmas of Practical Liberalism

Two basic problems become apparent when we try to apply liberal principles to practical problems. The first is that the method of formal liberalism does not yield a doctrine but a variety of competing and conflicting maxims of choice. The second problem is that liberal principles are expected to be impartial and general, neutral among particular human interests and, as it is said, "conceptions of the good." Yet any practical decision will require us to identify a "better" way of carrying out a specific project, and this will lead us to endorse some individual and community interests over others. Let us see how these problems arise and how we intend to deal with them.

Classic liberal political theory is normally written as axiomatic system. The project, historically, was Cartesian, an exercise in systematic doubt. Instead of *assuming* that humans were political animals, the Enlightenment liberals felt obliged to prove it, using a bare minimum of inherently contentious propositions about human nature. They thought it rationally indisputable, simple axiom, that individuals would seek what they thought good and avoid what they thought bad. From this starting point, they tried to infer what people standing apart from inherited beliefs and values would accept as a fair and legitimate basis for government. This was the method of Hobbes, Locke, and Rousseau, and in our times of Robert Nozick, John Rawls, James Buchanan, and others.

To picture individuals standing isolated from one another, stripped of tradition, emotion and social and cultural background, seems a very odd representation of the human situation—a point that has been made consistently, if somewhat monotonously, in Western philosophy for almost three hundred years. Nonetheless, this strange and mechanical form of thought is the source of some of our firmest political convictions.

Liberals do believe that the individual is the ultimate immanent source of value. They assume that only moral choice which is uncoerced is significant. And they believe that human nature is creative, and that for this reason the individual should have a broad array of options for practical action. Individual freedom is the presumptive case in liberal argument. The difficulties begin when we try to specify the principles of restraint, reciprocity, collective interest or public authority that freedom is to be measured against.

The great problem of liberal thought is that starting from essentially the same premises, it is possible to construct very different kinds of political theory.[5]

Thus, at one end of the spectrum, classic free market liberals such as Hayek and Friedman argue that free individuals ought accept no political authority beyond that necessary to guarantee rights that they cannot secure themselves. The task of the state is to protect life, liberty, property, and the probity of contract, and to secure "an exact administration of justice," for no one can be an impartial adjudicator in one's own case.[6] At the other extreme, perhaps, egalitarian liberals such as John Rawls presume that it is the first duty of the state to secure to all citizens equal liberties and opportunities for choice and creative activity. This is necessary if liberalism is to be a legitimate political order, one consistent with its own premises.[7]

In between are the varieties of utilitarian thought, in which social arrangements are to be judged by how well they contribute to the sum of satisfactions available to individuals. And formal democratic liberalism should be recognized as a distinctive variant in itself. Generally, democratic liberals contend that there is no independent rational foundation for ideas of individual right or public purpose. These then must be established by the will of the democratic community. However, if there is no basis *apart* from the political process for ideas of right, then there must be an idea of rights *for* the political process. For the will of the community to be authentic, there must be equality of voice and vote, offices open to all, periodic elections and periodic reconsideration of the public agenda. Thus, democratic liberalism, resting on a skepticism of the classic method of the rational, individual calculator, itself becomes a closed, self-reflective, axiomatic system.[8]

Now it is possible to adopt any one of these versions of liberal theory as a working ideology. Each yields a specific decision rule, a maxim of choice. Thus one could say that, at the margin and in the absence of other compelling considerations, one will adopt the policy which will best assure that the outcome reflects individual free choices registered through marketlike arrangements; or that which will yield the greatest aggregate social utility; or that which best reflects the deliberate will of the democratically constituted community; or that which will benefit the least well-off, without infringing on basic individual liberties. One *could* adopt any of these standards and thus commit oneself to a program for the gradual transformation of society toward a specific vision of the liberal ideal. And some would insist that this is precisely what we *must* do, for liberalism means acting on principle. However, the fact is that any such strategy would be no more than an act of personal commitment. One cannot demonstrate that any one of these rules is uniquely rational, beyond disinterested criticism or reasonable doubt.[9] Furthermore, any one of these rules, applied relentlessly, will, in extreme cases, produce results that are self-contradictory and illiberal, if not actually barbaric and inhumane.[10]

The first problem of practical liberal reason then is that formal liberal political theory cannot tell us which principle to apply to particular kinds of cases and controversies. This requires an act of judgment. The question then is whether these judgments can be made on a basis that is more than personal, in a way that is not willful or arbitrary. For if they cannot, liberalism cannot make good on its promise to provide a method of government that is based on impersonal, impartial principles rather than the will of rulers.

The second problem of practical liberal reason follows directly from the requirement that rules be general and impersonal, impartial among individual interests. In practical judgment, we are constantly making distinctions between the right and the wrong way of doing things, between better and worse performance. Such judgments of quality are part of any substantive, purposive human activity. If liberalism insists that it must be impartial on such questions, that issues of performance and effectiveness, excellence and merit, cannot be more than matters of individual preference, then liberalism cannot help us with our most important questions of practical reason.

There are those who would say precisely that because liberalism cannot give us guidance on matters of practical performance, it is inadequate as a public philosophy. We must give up the universal ideals of liberalism and base our judgments on specific, historic traditions and practices.[11]

My position is exactly the reverse. I think that it is precisely when we apply liberal principles to particular projects and enterprises that their meaning becomes clear and they become useful as guides to improved performance, to better practice. The problem now is to demonstrate how this can be done. My aim in this book is to describe a method, a discipline of political judgment, that shows how liberal theory can be applied to practice. This means not only that we have a very clear idea of what we mean by theory, but also a very specific idea of what we mean by practice.

Theory and Practice

"Being practical" can mean to act efficiently or expediently, to find a satisfactory or workable solution to a problem.[12] But "practicality" can also mean being guided by an idea of "practice," as when we speak of the practice of medicine or standard building practice. It is this stronger sense of the term that will be crucial in what is to come.

To follow a practice is to act in a disciplined, systematic, or customary fashion, to be guided by a collectively understood body of technique and method. It means that our conceptions of what is and is not a problem, of what will or will not count as a solution, will be measured by the legacy of skill and craft, the critical standards and the logic of inquiry of a particular community of good practice.

The communities of practice include industries that share a common legacy of productive techniques and operating rules. They also include, of course, the professions and crafts, those vocations identified with collectively established standards of performance and technique, as in accounting, architecture, law and medicine, or forestry, fire fighting, journalism, and computer engineering. The idea also embraces the frameworks of inquiry and appropriate method of the scholarly disciplines, as well as the doctrines of churches, the dominant styles of artistic endeavor, in fact, any activity that has been consciously systematized.

These purposive enterprises played a particularly important role in the tradition of pragmatic liberal thought which is the touchstone of our analysis. Dewey, Veblen, and Mead saw the public domain as a configuration of purposive associations as well as individuals. The sources of their thought lead back to Hegel and Durkheim as well as Locke and Mill. There are intimations of the theory of medieval corporate institutions in their idea of pluralism. Ultimately, their ideas are founded on an idea of practical reason and natural associations that derives from Aristotle.[13]

In this tradition, rationality was always understood as a collective product. It was the progressive, evolutionary refinement of practical technique through criticism, trial and error, and systematization. The individual "rationality" of calculated self-interest on which classical liberalism focused could not be the basing point for political thought, for personal preference could not be divorced from the collaborative, collective rationality of socially founded patterns of thought. Ideally, the pluralist communities of practice, as the state itself, was constituted as a perfect scientific society, self-critical and self-conscious, engaged in a continuing process of exploration and experiment, a constant search for improvements in practice.

It is in this sense that this is a theory of practical political reason. Essentially, I shall be concerned to show the ways we can, and do, use liberal principles to take the measure of the performance of substantive enterprise. I shall try to show that by thus appraising practice in the light of theory we create a clearer picture of the public character of various social undertakings.

In this analysis, I shall be weaving together themes from the liberal and the pragmatic philosophic traditions. In pure liberalism, a collaborative undertaking is regarded as legitimate to the extent that it can be shown to arise from the free choices of autonomous individuals, equally considered. For pure pragmatism, a community of practice is well founded if its organization and method are efficiently fitted to the end in view. For liberalism, consent is the fundamental standard of rightful collective action; for pragmatism, it is performance. The pragmatic criterion seems perhaps cold and technocratic unless combined with the liberal concern for individual needs and purposes. But pragmatism adds the substantive elements of craftsmanship and social responsibility in the pursuit of purpose to a liberal ethic which would otherwise be founded only on the norms of individual interest and impartial procedure.

The idea then is to avoid the excesses both of formal liberalism, where rigid abstract notions of right can themselves become inflexible and thus arbitrary in application, and of a pure subjective pragmatism, which may have no standard of public action other than simple effectiveness or an indeterminate idea of the public will.

The Outline of the Book

Pragmatic liberalism is an idea of political argument. My aim is to make explicit the standards of pertinence and soundness of statement that we apply in our workaday deliberations of public issues. My case will rest then both on the implications of acting on various kinds of principles and on what might be called "ordinary language," our common sense of what counts as a good reason for a public action and what does not.

In part 1, I focus on pragmatic liberalism's extended notion of the proper objects of political deliberation and of the public domain. To apply liberal principles to practice means to regard not just the state, but every form of organized human activity, as a subject for political discourse and political analysis. I first discuss how pragmatic liberalism applies *within* the enterprise, as a philosophy of its governance. I then consider pragmatic liberalism as a basis for public debate about the enterprise as a subject of law and policy.

In part 2, I develop a pragmatic liberal political economy. The object is to show how pragmatic liberalism, in its concern for the performance of *particular* enterprises (rather than the overall rhythms of economy and society), offers a distinctive approach to the management of the economy, the distribution of its product, and the sustainability of the productive system—its environmental soundness.

In part 3, we step back and reflect on pragmatic liberalism as a discipline of practical political judgment. I first explore the idea that principles are to be *discovered*, that they emerge from our efforts to come to terms with specific problems of governance. I then provide a somewhat formal statement of the organization and terms of political discourse and deliberation that pragmatic liberalism would encourage. I then go on to discuss the development of the liberal enterprise itself and how this is related to our efforts to reconcile liberal objectives with the aims of specific organizations. I conclude with a brief discussion of the philosophy of political education that would be compatible with the practice of pragmatic liberalism. Those particularly interested in pragmatic liberalism as an idea of method may wish to explore this last section first and then return to the opening parts of the book.

PART

1

———————

Liberal Principles, the Individual,
and the Enterprise

2

Liberal Principles and the

Performance of Enterprise

For pragmatic liberalism, the meaning and significance of liberal principles depend on an idea of purpose, on a clear conception of what we are trying to do. Freedom and equality, social efficiency and distributive justice, the rights of citizens to participate in the formulation of public purpose are, of course, ends in themselves. But they are also *qualities* we would see realized in any form of organized, substantive activity.

Classic liberalism was almost entirely concerned with the relationship of the state and the individual. Other associations—industries and professions, arts and sciences, trades and crafts—had a shadowy and uncertain place in traditional liberal theory. Classic liberalism drew a sharp line between the public and private spheres. What was not manifestly of public concern was exclusively the business of individuals. Presumably, then, associations other than the state were to be regarded primarily as forms of contract, of interest only to those who were parties to them.

For pragmatic liberalism, every association has a political aspect. The communities of practice have a public function, and there is a public interest in their governance and their performance.

This would seem a more realistic view of the political order and the problem of liberal reason. There are, of course, many different issues of the relation of the state and the individual which remain to be resolved in liberal theory and practice. But, increasingly, our most important, and most perplexing, public issues have to do with the relations of the individual, the state and the enterprise. The policies of industries, and the professions, determine our prospects and our conceptions of public purpose, surely as much as does the state. And increasingly, our ideas of individual right are linked to the performance of specific communities of practice. To declare a right to education, or to health care, is actually to say that all should have access to the organized practices of schooling or scientific medicine.

Similarly, it seems appropriate to think of the communities of practice as private governments.[1] These associations are a source of rights and obligations, backed by sanctions, that may govern us more intimately than does the state. The state may change our prospects or opportunities in marginal ways, but our corporation or university or profession provides the more exacting regulation of our daily activities. It can honor or disgrace us, secure our prospects or punish us, at least as certainly as can the state. Once this is acknowledged, we begin to sense the "strain toward consistency" that Philip Selznick once spoke of in the governance of the larger liberal regime.[2] Despotic authority, arbitrary rule, is no more acceptable in the government of the enterprise than it is in the state.

For pragmatic liberalism, then, liberal ideals and values do not apply to the state alone. They are general standards of rational performance, tests of how any socially significant task is properly done. The communities of practice become the subjects of political deliberation and discourse. Their performance is, potentially, a matter of public concern.

The Enterprise and the Organization

I chose *enterprise* over *association* as the main term to define these communities of practice. *Enterprise* is the more active word. It suggests that these are self-conscious, collaboratively organized ways of doing things. In pragmatic liberalism, it is purpose, more than solidarity alone, that matters.

A distinction should also be made between the enterprise and the organization. The organization is often the more tangible entity, easier to grasp and identify. However, in politics and political economy, the enterprise is more significant. It is the industry and not the firm that is essential in the formulation of public action. We have distinctive regimes of policy for agriculture, energy, insurance, banking, education, science. It is the technology, the normative culture of practice, our understanding of how an important social function is properly performed, that creates the important questions of public debate.

Nonetheless, the organization is also a source of public issues, and we will have occasion to move back and forth between these levels of analysis. When thinking about social performance we will more likely focus on the enterprise. When discussing private government, we will also take the organization into account, for the corporation, the union, the university, the guild, and the church are pertinent and often problematic elements of political order.

The Enterprise and the Idea of Citizenship

To regard the enterprise as the subject of practical political reason is to take a much broader view of the public realm than is conventional in orthodox liberalism and it leads to a more expansive view of the meaning of citizenship as well. For pragmatic liberalism, to engage in the ongoing perfection of a craft, skill, or science, as a member of a self-critical community of practice, is a form of public activity as vital and important as are the acts of voting or running for public office.

Thus, pragmatic liberalism, as a discipline of political discourse and practical judgment, has two applications. It first pertains to the responsibilities of the citizen of the enterprise. Pragmatic liberalism is a system of ground rules for political deliberation *within* the enterprise, a philosophy for its government.

Second, pragmatic liberalism applies to the responsibilities of the citizen of the liberal regime. It is a framework for thinking about the relations of the state and the communities of practice as a subject of law and policy.

From each of these vantage points, there are two problems to be considered. First, we must ask how the social function of the enterprise is best performed. Liberal principles become tests of product, technique, and performance. Then we must examine the political order of the enterprise, and of the state in relation to the enterprise. Liberal principles become tests of the political process of the enterprise and of the total system of relations between the state and the regime of enterprise.

The main purpose of this chapter is to describe how pragmatic liberalism applies to the appraisal of the performance of enterprise. We are thinking here from the perspective of the citizen of the enterprise. I begin with a discussion of the limitations of the more orthodox versions of liberalism in coming to grips with this problem. I conclude by examining certain objections to the method that might be brought by advocates of more conventional liberal doctrines.

In chapter 3 I discuss the image of organization, or political order, of the community of inquiry and practice that follows from this conception of practical political reason, and I contrast this with more orthodox ideas of the proper governmental form of the enterprise.

In chapters 4 and 5, I examine the same problems from the perspective of the citizen of the liberal regime. I take up first the problem of the role of the state in guaranteeing and enhancing the performance of enterprise. I then consider the role of the state in defining and structuring the political order of the communities of practice.

Thus, just as economists can see all associations in their economic aspect, and think of bargaining and the allocation of scarce resources in the family as in the firm, so we would see them in their political aspect, possessing the qualities of governments, making authoritative decisions for their members, and establishing rights and duties backed by sanctions.[3] And as the economist might think of rationality in all such associations as reciprocal calculations of self-interest, so we would see them all as locales for the exercise of political reason, for deliberation on shared responsibilities and on the desired course of development of a cooperative venture.

My view then is that the government of enterprise is a central problem of liberal politics and one that conventional liberal theory cannot come to terms with. The problem then is to recast and reconstruct liberal political theory to provide a more adequate framework for applied political reason. Let us see then how the problem arises and how pragmatic liberalism would deal with it.

The Emergence of the Enterprise

It is a first premise of any form of liberalism that the state should not be the architect of social order. Rather, the arrangements of production and culture, worship and inquiry, should arise from voluntary agreements among individuals.

For classic liberalism, all collaborative human projects are to be understood as forms of contract. They arise from individual will and interest, and they are legitimate insofar as they can be shown to be the result of free choices by equally competent individuals.

The close corollary of contract in classic liberal thought is the idea of the market. If contract provides a model of the statics of liberal society, the market describes its dynamics. If a perfectly competitive economic market could allocate goods and services so as to fit the expressed preferences of individuals, then, analogously, marketlike arrangements in the realms of scientific exploration, artistic endeavor, religious practice, and the like would lead to a pattern of social order that better expressed the deliberate wills of individuals than any conscious plan could devise.[4]

Pragmatic liberalism accepts the principles of contract and the market as a provisional ideal of associational legitimacy. But these ideas do not provide a complete conception of the liberal social order. The ideal conditions of contract and the market, if they exist at all, are exceptional and transitory. It is easy enough to see how a human project, in its incipient stages, could take shape as the product of negotiations among individuals each separately seeking to advance some personal interest. But once the bargain is struck, the situation changes. An institution comes into being with characteristics quite different from those of the simple contractual nexus. If the enterprise survives and succeeds, it takes on organizational form and a normative order of its own.

At this point, the relationship of the individual to the project changes. One no longer *creates* a relationship through contractual exchange. Rather, one *joins* an ongoing endeavor. One no longer bargains for goods, or patterns of social engagement, that fit one's particular wants and interests. Rather, choice now is between established, structured alternatives. Simple contract becomes, in the language of the law, a contract of adhesion.[5] One does not design one's own insurance coverage; one buys a standard plan. One does not spontaneously worship God; one joins a church and "practices" a religion. One does not simply study the natural order; one becomes a physicist and works within its program of scientific investigation. Practical reason is not the calculated expression of will; it is the adoption of a discipline. One no longer acts solely on the basis of reflective self-interest, but also as the agent of an organized form of practice.

Pragmatic liberalism takes these purposive associations seriously. It regards the evolution from contract to institutionalized going concern as a natural and a positive process of development. Such institutions represent forms of cooperative, intelligent, adaptive effort that are very congenial to its most fundamental ideas of human knowledge and action. The emergence of the purposive organization in all of its forms is one of the most significant achievements of the liberal order. However, this also constitutes one of its principal public problems.

The rationalization of practice is an essential interest of liberalism. The task of mind is to examine established usage and improve upon it, or transform it, if it can. The object is to universalize "best practice," to make it expectable and commonplace. The premise is that we are better off with comprehensive and *dependable* electrical systems, medical services, schools, and agricultural marketing arrangements. Rationalization implies standardization and system, which imply organization and control. In the end, the justification for the most significant associations of our age is not tradition, or solidarity, or democratic consent, but the systematization of technique.

Orthodox Ways of Appraising the Performance of Enterprise

Conventional political theory (and here we go a bit beyond the bounds of liberalism itself) offers us four basic grounds that can be brought to bear in appraising the performance of enterprise. As we shall see, none, in itself, is sufficient to the task.

1. Rational system and the standardization of technique is not by itself a very appealing ideal. We tend to associate it with assembly-line rigidity, numbing routine, and government by experts. Liberalism cannot accept a defense of performance based on an argument of "system for system's sake." In liberalism, technique must be shown to be responsive to the needs and interests of individuals, equally considered.

2. Nonetheless, contract and market processes do not provide an adequate basis for such appraisal. In the first place, competition is a paradoxical norm of organizational legitimacy. It is not that a form of practice that triumphs over all its rivals thereby

proves its right to prevail. Rather, the monopoly loses all legitimacy. Nonetheless, the presence of alternatives does not imply that all are equally worthy as forms of practice. The market requires *sustained* competition if it is to work as a test of performance. But rational analysis should lead to convergence around specific ideas of "best practice."

It is important then to distinguish competition *within* and *between* forms of practice. It is one thing to say that when a number of firms produce automobiles or fast food, there are some built-in guarantees of quality, price and service. But it is quite another thing to say that we require the widest possible range of technique to guarantee good performance, that, for example, the performance of medicine would be enhanced if standard practice were opened to competition by witch doctors and faith healing.

3. For some, the performance of the enterprise would be legitimate if it rested on consent, if it were democratically constituted, and if its aims, purposes, techniques, and procedures arose from free and unfettered political deliberation and discourse. But rational organization, the systematization of good practice, may imply a variety of forms of organization, and deliberative assembly is not necessarily the most appropriate. Furthermore, the natural constituency of the enterprise is not necessarily obvious. To whom should the auto industry, or the wheat growers, or the medical profession, or the universities be responsible?

4. Some would argue that there is no independent basing point for political judgment and that prescriptive tradition is the only appropriate ground for appraisal of the communities of practice. We must evaluate them only in relation to their own inherent norms and purposes, their paradigmatic structures. But liberal rationalism believes precisely that we can stand back from inherited system and technique, and evaluate its adequacy in the light of universal principles.

The Legitimacy of the Enterprise

None of these approaches to the appraisal of enterprise is sufficient in itself. Each identifies an important *element* in evaluation, but each also ignores important qualities that we would see achieved through collaborative projects of action. The problem then is how to reconcile them, how to bring such criteria into relation one to another in a practical scheme of political reason.

However, the problem is not only that these methods lead to proposals that we will not think practical or sensible but that, used exclusively and relentlessly, each tends to make our most important and characteristic institutions illegitimate, suspect in our own eyes.

"The corporation fits oddly with democratic theory and vision," the political economist Charles E. Lindblom writes: "indeed, it does not fit."[6] But if that is the case, the problem may lie with the theory as well as the practice. The relentless application of the liberal norms of contract and consent will eventually delegitimate any rational organization, render it suspect in our eyes. Pure contract presumes that all parties are equal in all significant respects, that there are no externalities and no dominant options. Pure democracy requires absolute equality of voice and vote, deliberation that is not constrained and not prefigured.[7] These are utopian conditions. Taken in this absolute sense, they are of greater value to those who would discredit liberal institutions than to those who would work for their continued development.

We do, in practice, draw back from the full logical implications of these norms. Especially when it comes down to cases, few enough accept the radical libertarian notion of a society in which all relations are reduced to primitive contract or, at the other end of the spectrum, the equally radical view that only a society in which all institutions are constituted as communal democracies is worthy of support.

It becomes apparent that contract and consent do not suffice as tests of the probity and worth of our dominant institutions. We need a way of reconciling these values with the specific ideas of practice, of rational performance, of the enterprise in question.

The Significance of Rational Performance in Practical Liberal Reason

The paramount rule of liberal politics is that public decisions must rest on impartial, general principles, consistently applied. This may be a maxim of natural justice. All the great Western philosophies have taught as much. But it is also a practical matter.

The basic reason for rational consistency in law and policy is that it is a condition of human freedom. The object of liberal politics, and of the rule of law, is to create a stable, comprehensible framework within which individuals can develop plans and personal projects, with some assurance that they can estimate their prospects for success. Lawful order is also a condition of morality, for without the capacity to foresee consequences, one cannot act responsibly.

This is the reason for liberalism's abiding hostility to tyranny in any form. Tyranny connotes arbitrary authority, power exercised without reason. The world becomes unpredictable, a strange and treacherous place.

Classic liberalism might apply this principle only to the realm of public law. Given minimum conditions of public order, the rest is open to personal expression and design.[8] But the pragmatic liberal is apt to press the point further.

The idea that rational consistency is a requirement of freedom is congenial to the pragmatic liberal temper of mind. This is not rationalism understood as an appeal to a priori principles or Cartesian criteria of proof. This is Kantian consistency, not as formal maxim, but in applied form.[9] And it is a sense of rationalism, from the pragmatic liberal point of view, which unifies the realms of politics and law, scientific inquiry and practical endeavor.

In each of these domains, the object is to reduce the personal, idiosyncratic, whimsical, capricious, random, and arbitrary to orderly system. The object of politics is the development of law. Similarly, the purpose of science is the generation of reliable knowledge. As the discipline of the policymaker is to subsume decisions under principles of rightful authority that can be applied consistently in like cases over time, so the discipline of the scientist is to subsume personal observations under lawlike statements that can be sustained, in experience, over time.

The function of science is to render nature comprehensible, which is to say, predictable, familiar, and routine. By the same token, the object of the various realms of rational enterprise is to render human performance knowable, systematic, orderly, and consistent, and in that sense, predictable, familiar, and routine. The virtue of rationally designed laws, scientific principles, airline networks, telephone systems, and motel chains is that they will work as they are expected to when one calls on them. In medicine as in manufacture, the object of rational inquiry is to create a standard, universal, and consistent product or performance, one that functions, as a rule of justice does, the same way "in all relevantly similar situations."

Rational enterprises, then, represent reliable ways of knowing and acting within the larger society. They provide a background of relative stability, an infrastructure of settled meaning, within the general atmosphere of transitoriness and flux that characterizes liberal society. The order that is so essential to freedom arises not so much from the marketlike arrangements that classic liberalism took to be the essential instrument of free commitment, but from the communities of good practice, the guildlike institutions that are embedded in and derivative from the skeletal ordering process of contract and the market.

However the justification for rational enterprise lies not in predictable routine itself but in the claim that standard practice is as well best practice, that it arises from a practical codification of the results of a collective, self-conscious process of trial and error, systematic critical analysis, a sustained scrutiny of how a particular function is properly performed. The goal of rational system is not to standardize custom or common practice but to make the exemplary case general and routine. Indeed, liberalism properly regards as equally arbitrary those public actions that arise from personal whim and caprice and those that rest on unexamined custom, dogma, or orthodoxy.

The Political Character of Rational Performance

The main point of pragmatic liberalism is that rational performance is not to be to judged by the aims and objectives of the enterprise alone. Rationality—which we can also call efficiency—has a larger political character. Thus, an appraisal of performance requires that we invoke the full array of liberal principles. However, this also implies that political considerations cannot be separated from substantive objectives. Let us now see how specific considerations of rational efficiency are related to other liberal ideals.

Efficiency and Economy

The first principle of rational enterprise is efficiency. Efficiency is not the same as economy. Efficiency, strictly speaking, means fittedness to purpose—that technique and organization are as appropriate as possible to the end in view. It also implies that a function is consistently repeatable, in a word, reliability. Efficiency connotes quality in relation to practicality, that a purpose is being carried out as well as possible, given the circumstances and intent.

Economy—that a function is performed at the lowest possible cost consistent with purpose—is an attribute of rational performance, but it is not identical to efficiency, as it is deemed to be in classical political economy. To distinguish between the two is a distinctive characteristic of pragmatic liberalism.

Thorstein Veblen, properly a forerunner of pragmatic liberalism, drew a similar distinction. He contrasted the "pecuniary interest" and the "instinct of workmanship" as psychological bases for liberal political economy. His point was that the "pecuniary" and "predatory" skills, which he associated with the more avaricious kinds of business leadership, with business perceived only as financial calculation, were parasitical on a productive system which was itself the product of "idle curiosity," or scientific inquiry and invention, a "parental instinct" which connotes management as good stewardship, and a "pride in workmanship" which was the foundation of rational, consistent performance, or efficiency.[10]

For pragmatic liberalism, efficiency is prior to economy in the order of liberal values. The public function of the firm is to make a useful product. Profitability is a test of its performance, but not the definition of its purpose. The aim is to make a given product as economically as possible, not to make those products that will yield the highest rate of return. The difference, when one thinks about it, is all important.

Nevertheless, economy is a principle to be weighed with efficiency in the appraisal of the rationality of enterprise. The public significance of the value of economy lies in its relation to social waste. A society that would open a broad array of opportunities for individual development must practice frugality.

The moral virtue of economy can be expressed in the economist's notion of opportunity costs. If I can perform my work more economically, the resources saved can be devoted to other socially useful purposes. In effect, then, not to scrutinize performance for gains in economy, to *fail* to remove waste and slack from the performance of an enterprise, is to deny resources to others unfairly. Economy is an aspect of the idea of justice. Exploitation by sloth may be as great a wrong in the liberal list of deadly sins as exploitation by avarice and predation. In any event, the presumption of liberal argument is that improvement is always possible, and the burden is always on the enterprise, or the individual, to demonstrate that function is being performed as economically as possible.

Yet efficiency is logically prior to economy. Economy is the secondary principle, basically a tiebreaker among options that have met minimum criteria of good practice. At the margin, considerations of efficiency trump those of economy. It is not good practice in medicine to achieve savings by impairing the health of patients, nor in manufacture to make a product less expensive by rendering it less useful. Economists can *ask*, through cost-benefit analysis, whether increased quality or reliability, or diminished risk, is worth the cost, but they cannot answer the question. Whether a given cost is worth paying, or a given economy worth achieving, depends entirely on a prior stipulation of purpose.[11]

Considerations of Justice

The rationality of practice is not defined by narrow calculations of utility alone. In the appraisal of the enterprise, the full spectrum of liberal principles is brought to bear. In the clear cases, considerations of fundamental fairness strongly constrain the pursuit of efficiency or economy. One cannot advance the purposes of an enterprise by force or fraud, by means that are demeaning, exploitative, or cruel, or by imposing costs on third parties. In the assessment of rationality, justice is the stronger principle. We only compare the efficiency and economy of alternatives that we believe meet fundamental tests of fairness. However, in the close cases, where judgment is required, there is an intricate interdependence between considerations of efficiency, economy, and fairness.

The "relevant reasons" which liberalism requires to support differences in the treatment of persons—in authority, honors, working conditions, compensation—normally have their source in the rationale of practice. To ask then whether existing distinctions are "fair" is also to ask whether they are "efficient," whether they are rationally related to purpose.

To justify wage differentials to the employee in terms of differences in skill, responsibility, or productivity in relation to the purpose to be served will probably be more satisfactory than defending them on the basis of "market forces." To say that someone deserves more because what they produce is of higher, more consistent quality is a more compelling reason for differences in reward than simple possession of a "scarce" skill. To say that someone with a specific set of qualifications was needed, and that there were many bidders, may win grudging acceptance, as a matter of practical realism, but those who felt themselves wronged will continue to ask, "Is it fair?" (I return to this question in chapter 7.)

To think of justice in relation to the efficient and economic performance of function leads us, inevitably, to reopen inquiry into the rationality of prevailing practices. When something seems unfair, it quite possibly also does not make sense. An industry that cannot provide reliable service on its products, consistently and as promised, is acting unfairly—and inefficiently. A university with a curriculum so disorganized that it cannot maintain consistent expectations and standards is neither fair nor efficient. A medical insurance system that gives doctors incentives to provide better treatment for those who are merely affluent seems neither fair nor efficient. An expression of outrage is a signal to look deeper at technique and system. It is often a sign of trouble with substance and method itself and not simply a problem of human relations.

Justice as fair treatment is intimately related to the idea of fittedness to purpose. The ancient image of justice as "right proportion" presupposed an absolute ideal with numberless variations, all dependent on the aim in question. The everyday pragmatic liberal ideal of justice finds fine expression in the opening arguments of Plato's *Republic* where the relationship of the sense of justice and the idea of craftsmanship is subtly and sensitively explored.

Responsiveness

Responsiveness might seem the most fundamental of liberal standards of performance. As I have said, all liberal theories share the principle that social arrangements must arise from choice. Hence, one might think that if one could show that a pattern of practice was freely chosen, that would be all that was required. But on close examination, responsiveness turns out to be a somewhat erratic test of the worthiness of performance and technique.

To be sure, liberalism implies diversity and flexibility. Products and performances should be adapted to distinctive individual needs and interests. There is something worth looking into when individuals have to do the adapting rather than the system. To invoke responsiveness as a test of rational performance is to check for pointless standardization for standardization's sake, routinization at the price of purpose, design that follows the interests of practitioners rather than clients.

However, ironically, it is also true that responsiveness can be invoked to defend the status quo against potential improvement. Those who support established practice can claim that they are "giving the people what they want." In some versions of liberalism this seems an irrefutable argument. The critics are cast in the role of elitists, imposing their preferences on the public.

In fact, of course, this is a poor defense of established practice. Liberal rationalism implies that ideas of improvement move in advance of public will. The ongoing inquiry into the rationality and reliability of practice is not simply a matter of ascertaining demand. Liberalism entails the criticism of widely accepted usage.

Liberalism implies an interplay between the formulation of patterns of practice through deliberate collective design and the *acceptance* of those activities, or their products, from among alternative opportunities for engagement. It is true that liberals wish to sustain a broad array of options, both so that individual differences can be accommodated and so that prevailing method is constantly challenged.

Nonetheless, in the hard cases, where the principle of rational action and that of diversity of possibilities do not neatly coincide, the mingled considerations of efficiency, economy, and justice weigh heavily against raw responsiveness. When one technology proves generally superior, how much effort must be given to preserving the residual alternatives sought and cherished by only a few? How few customers must still depend on the product before we drop the line? How few students must be left in the Department of Exotic Languages before it is disbanded? How much care should be taken to preserve craft skills displaced by mass production techniques? These are not easy questions to answer, for sometimes the intelligent reconsideration of practice calls for a revival of earlier methods, and this cannot be done if these techniques are lost. And concern for those whose ways are lost to "progress" is a continuing, and poignant, theme within liberalism.

But what is clear is that the principle of responsiveness does not resolve all quandaries of practical judgment and that individual choice is not the definitive test of the worth of practice.

The Pattern of Political Argument

There is a certain order and logic to pragmatic liberal argument. To invoke any liberal principle in criticism of prevailing practice is to open the process of deliberation. To assert that a pattern of practice is unjust, or socially wasteful, or unresponsive to the interests of those it is intended to serve is to signal that there is a potential problem in the performance of enterprise which must be considered and, if possible, remedied. This is simply a quality of our political language. Claims based on liberal principles cannot be dismissed as irrelevant or beside the point. They are always germane to the appraisal of the performance of an enterprise. A serious person will weigh them, and a critic will feel obliged to respond.

However, such claims are not automatically compelling. We are, I think, quite reluctant to endorse reforms based on contract or consent when these conflict with the manifest purposes of an enterprise. It is not a dictate of practical liberal reason that the university should be guided primarily by the will of its students, that the hospital should be responsive, first of all, to the interests of its employees, that the worth of a religion is tested mainly by its ability to attract adherents, or, for that matter, that a corporation is to be judged solely by how well it meets consumer demand.

The promotion of collective rational action is a fundamental purpose of liberal politics. The aim of liberal reason is, in effect, to *enhance* the performance of enterprise.

Most protagonists in the public debate seem to recognize the inherent assumptions of our thought. Thus, advocates of workplace democracy may protest, as Robert Dahl does, that "if democracy is justified in governing the state then it is also justified in governing economic enterprises." Their main point may be that hierarchical, managerial authority in the firm is incompatible with our basic political norms, and that submission to such authority is destructive of the sense of self-esteem and civic virtue that is essential to the democratic political order. But they also take pains to argue that such reforms would be compatible with sustained productivity, investment, and reliable performance and that, in fact, increased job satisfaction, initiative, and responsibility would be the products of industrial democracy.[12]

And, of course, Milton Friedman's celebrated school voucher plan was based on the assumption that market choice in schooling was not only good in itself, but that it would enhance the efficiency and economy of the educational system.[13]

To be sure, the requirement that principle be consistent with practice cuts both ways. If no compelling reasons of reliable performance can be adduced, then improvement lies in making the enterprise more compatible with the fundamental norms of the liberal political order. It is not good enough for the advocates of prevailing practice to say simply that "employees don't make production decisions" or "students have never participated in curriculum planning." Unless there are reasons of good practice at stake, enterprise *should* be made progressively more responsive to liberal norms.

Hard Cases

In the ideal case, we discover ways to reconcile performance, contract, and consent. However, in practical reason, we often have to weigh the respective force of claims of practice and principle. This is the source of many of the hard cases, the tragic dilemmas of our public life.

The epic example, of course, was the American resolve to abolish the practice of slavery, as incompatible with the values of human dignity and equality, though it meant fratricidal war and the extinction of an established political economic system. However, such dilemmas are also characteristic of the everyday acts of citizens of an enterprise, of the politics of a community of practice. Would more marketlike arrangements in medicine diminish the quality of medical service or enhance economy and responsiveness? Would more participation in the church strengthen or threaten doctrine? Would more economical methods of air traffic control jeopardize safety and reliability? These are empirical questions, questions of consequences. But they are also questions of the priority among values, and many of them cannot be resolved until we define that priority or find a course of action that resolves the tension better than present practice.

Such dilemmas are characteristic of our public life. Consider the claim of the Old Order Amish that their religious practices would be imperiled if their children were required to attend public schools, for the integrity and continuity of their faith requires strict insulation from the appeals of secular artifacts and ideas. Consider also the countercontention that the responsibility of the state runs to each and every child, and that the Amish have no right to enforce a political regime that effectively denies Amish children the opportunity to pursue any way of life other than that of the Amish. Is it not the duty of the liberal state to ensure to all citizens that education which cultivates criticism and skepticism of established ways—that which might loosely be called a "liberal education"—and prepares citizens for choice between alternative possibilities in an open society? The Supreme Court, in *Wisconsin v. Yoder*,[14] ruled for the Amish on First Amendment grounds. But that is not the only answer possible within liberal theory.

Consider also the problem of affirmative action. Obviously, nondiscrimination is an essential liberal norm, for disparities of opportunity based on accidental or irrelevant characteristics— race or sex—raise questions of whether the regime actually reflects autonomous individual choices and whether the differential rewards produced by the system are in fact merited. There are good instrumental grounds for supporting quotas and other means of preferential treatment in, for example, selecting among applicants for professional education. Simple norms of equal treatment are hard to enforce unless the onus for compliance is on the institution, and active policies may be necessary to overcome deeply ingrained prejudice.

Yet the object of a medical school, one supposes, is to eduate doctors, not rectify social wrongs. The relevant criteria for admission measure prospective ability at this task. To mandate otherwise is not only inefficient in that it jeopardizes rational performance, but, significantly, we regard it as unfair as well, for it introduces criteria which are irrelevant to function.[15]

But once again, the burden of proof need not be always on the reformer. The argument cuts both ways. Arguments from purpose become strong cases against discrimination. In recent years, much of the struggle for equal treatment has involved constant reiteration of this theme. Thus, strength may be a relevant consideration in selecting firefighters, but sex, in itself, is not. Questions of rational purpose and performance focus the mind admirably on the question of relevant distinctions. They thus enhance and support liberal concerns for equal treatment and differentiation on the basis of merit alone.

The Social Responsibility of the Enterprise

Pragmatic liberalism holds that the enterprise is *answerable* for the quality of its product, for the impact of its actions on communities and on the environment, for fair treatment of employees and the public. The basic requirement of liberal argument, again, is that officials show that their actions serve a reasonable public purpose, that they are not arbitrary, capricious, or self-serving. In extending this idea of political reason to the enterprise, we are saying that its decisions must be similarly justified. This doctrine gives little comfort to those who believe that the enterprise is strictly a private affair, that those who control resources can do with them precisely as they please.

On the other hand, pragmatic liberalism provides scant encouragement to those who think that nothing more is required of the social critic than to point up the power and the characteristic foibles of large enterprise. Our public discourse—and our academic analysis—too readily dissolves into a contest between those who take their task to be that of demonstrating that public action is generally inept and those who would show that large enterprise is, on the whole, venal and overbearing. None of this is particularly helpful to the cause of practical political reason in a society which relies on the impersonal norms of liberalism for its framework of public order, and on a diverse array of complex, rationalized institutions for the content and the character of its way of life.

Pragmatic liberalism holds that the performance of dominant institutions is properly measured by the same norms that inform public life generally. But pragmatic liberalism also requires that the *application* of a liberal rule must be compatible with best practice, with the sustained performance of the enterprise in question. Thus, this discipline of political reason requires social responsibility on the part of both the citizen of the enterprise and the citizen of the polity. It enjoins the protagonist of the enterprise and its critic to search for common ground.

A Response to Critics

It is time now to anticipate certain objections that advocates of other conceptions of practical political reason will bring against pragmatic liberalism, to respond to them, and thus to refine our understanding of pragmatic liberalism itself.

Pragmatic liberalism is a theory of political argument. It presumes that public life will be well conducted if it is based on a general acceptance of certain fundamental principles of political deliberation and decision making. This is a characteristic it shares with many other versions of liberal theory: with Lockean, Kantian, and utilitarian liberalism. And it seems fair to say that those liberal regimes have fared best and prevailed longest which have rested on a widespread assent to certain fundamental affirmations about the right conduct of public life.

However, liberal theory can take another form. There are liberal theories which assume that the proper conduct of public life depends on the institution and maintenance of certain mechanisms, procedures, and processes. In these theories, the logic of political argument is unimportant and, in fact, protagonists of these theories often assume that any effort to prescribe norms for the pertinence or significance of political statement, any effort to stipulate standards for the appraisal of public life, is misguided. What is important is to secure the greatest unpreordained freedom possible—either for individual choice or for individual expression.

The principal objections to pragmatic liberalism we will want to consider come from the protagonists of liberal theories that take this latter form. To the right of pragmatic liberalism are those who assume that free market processes will serve to secure the core values that we would promote by extending the notion of political reason to the realm of enterprise. For those who hold this view, political deliberation is a cumbrous and uncertain process compared to the automatic operation of the market in promoting the realization and reconciliation of liberal values.

To the left of pragmatic liberalism are those who would see public life ordered as pure procedural democracy, based on unconstrained personal expression and common discussion. The objection of participatory democracy to pragmatic liberalism lies both in its stipulation of substantive rules of discourse and decision, and in the privileged place it gives to the notion of "good practice" as the touchstone for debate on the performance of enterprise.

I will discuss these two main lines of criticism in turn, then conclude this section with a brief comment on a third source of objection to pragmatic liberalism. While the participatory democrat thinks that pragmatic liberalism entails, potentially, a conservative bias, the conservative or traditionalist suspects that pragmatic liberalism, with its emphasis on rational order and rational performance, might be "perfectionistic" and, perhaps, technocratic.

There are sources of potential misunderstanding of what pragmatic liberalism actually entails in each of these positions. Hence, what follows is less a defense against critics than an opportunity to clarify what pragmatic liberalism does and does not stand for. The point is to use the perspective of alternative versions of liberalism to clarify and refine our understanding of pragmatic liberalism itself.

The Role of the Market

The orthodox liberal political economist is disposed to think that the aim of reconciling liberal principle and practice can perfectly well be achieved through market processes, without the antagonisms and uncertainties inherent in political argument. Political deliberation, Milton Friedman says, is a "cumbrous" process. Individual choice from among competing alternatives is a far more direct way of expressing approval or disapproval of performance than participation in public debate. Political deliberation is only resolved by authoritative public decision. The market permits a variety of diverse, decentralized possibilities.[16]

According to orthodox doctrine, an ideal market outcome represented a perfect reconciliation of liberal principles. The system is efficient in that it tends to produce that which individuals want and need in their own estimation, at whatever level of distinctiveness and differentiation is required, so long as it is within the capabilities of existing resources and technology, and demand is at least sufficient to support profitable production. For in the market, neither producer or consumer is coerced. A market solution is socially economic in that there are strong competitive incentives to constantly lower production costs, to eliminate waste. The market similarly provides maximum incentives for the continuing reappraisal of rational performance, for the perfection of technique, as measured by suitability to individual want and interest. And the market is just, it is said, in that it distributes rewards according to the social contribution of each, as every individual, through voluntary purchase and contract, measures the worth of the contribution of each other to personal interest. All problems of appraisal, and continuing rational development of the enterprise, are resolved by the invisible hand. There is no need to resort to the more arcane processes of political deliberation and judgment.

For pragmatic liberalism, politics and markets, exit and voice, are complementary processes in perfecting the performance of enterprise. Neither is sufficient alone. Political deliberation implies the consideration of alternative ways of doing things, and these can only be generated through pluralistic, marketlike arrangements. However, market forces without political deliberation provide no opportunity for the conscious examination and perfection of practice and technique.

The pragmatic liberal tends to look at the market as a form of social experiment rather than a conclusive demonstration of the relative worth of various patterns of enterprise. Rather it is assumed that a market outcome can itself be subjected to critical scrutiny and perfected through conscious action. This is a principal distinction between orthodox and pragmatic liberalism.

In fact, we do not normally insist that people must be "free to choose" until the unsafe medical procedure, the fallacious scientific theory, and the less durable and suitable industrial product pass from the scene. Neither scientists nor car makers insist that all their ideas for new models be submitted to the test of the market. They presume they can make some decisions on behalf of the public on what works well and what does not.

We do not insist that all proposals for more rational practice be demonstrated by revealed preference. Rather, we assume an individual preference for the more useful and serviceable. Basically, we invoke market tests as definitive only when we are indifferent among options on intrinsic grounds of performance.

All of this implies that a public distinction be made between those technologies and products that we establish as standard practice and those that we merely add to the market array of options. We permit the state itself to arbitrate some choices. Others

we invest in the communities of practice. Only in the most frivo-
lous pursuits—cosmetics, the popular press, the lighter entertain-
ments, gadgets and gewgaws—do we actually assume that the
market should be the ultimate arbiter of taste and performance.

The Dilemmas of Orthodoxy

The defenders of pure consent, of democratic process, will
raise objections to pragmatic liberalism equally as significant as
those of the defenders of pure contract, or market process.

The distinctive feature of pragmatic liberalism, in the family of
liberal theories, is its emphasis on practice, on the importance of
traditions of conscious, collectively devised technique. For the
pure participatory democrat, this represents an inherent bias in
the system of thought. In such pure democratic theory, the ideal
is discourse that is completely open, unprefigured and "undistorted," absolutely neutral among potential ends and purposes.
For such a theory, any methodological prescription, save that
which is necessary to assure that expression is free and genuine,
is unwarranted.

This is an important issue, and I want to explore it fully. The
discussion will lead us to consider further the analogy between
politics and scientific reasoning and the inadequacy of pure market processes in the evaluation of practice. And the discussion
forces us to confront a fundamental paradox that arises in pragmatic liberal, perhaps in any form of liberal, thought. I call this
the dilemma of orthodoxy.

In the first instance, all forms of liberalism are committed to
the widest, most diverse freedom of expression and action compatible with minimum requirements of order. In liberal politics,
there is no place for censorship, for *prior* restraint on individual
imagination.

At one level, this is a maxim of fundamental individual right. At
another, it is a condition of rational enterprise and rational understanding. It is fundamental to all modes of reason that follow from
the Enlightenment tradition. Thus, neither science nor liberal
politics can block the consideration of unconventional ideas. As
science, at the outset, must encourage the greatest possible range
of speculation and conjecture, so liberal politics must endorse the
emergence of a broad array of collective undertakings, systems of

belief, solidarity and action, so as not to foreclose opportunities for human action.

However, this initial agnosticism and tolerance are not based on the premise that all ideas have equal worth and merit. There is no extreme skepticism, no relativism here. Rather, open-mindedness at the outset is a condition of the search for truth, for public purpose, for improved performance. Tolerance is necessary to ascertain which ideas are in fact more sustainable and reliable. This implies that a wide range of ideas must be tested. And this means that for the worth and merit of a project to be fairly evaluated, it must be experienced in something like fully developed form.[17]

All of this would seem to be most compatible with the spirit of pragmatic liberalism. Pragmatic liberalism is both resolutely tolerant and inherently skeptical of novelty and unorthodox ideas. It commits itself to but little in advance. Its crucial test of the worth of an idea or project is how it works out in practice. And this implies that the experiment must be conducted, the project set in motion, the product developed and marketed. The thousand flowers must actually bloom, the hundred schools must be seen to contend.

Of course, some a priori judgments are both possible and imperative. It is not necessary to test all the unjust and inhumane alternatives in order to prove their injustice or inhumanity. It is not necessary to encourage the growth of authoritarianism to demonstrate the value of freedom. (By the same token, science cannot condone research that violates the fundamental rights of humanity.) However, within that broad array of options that are open to liberal society one cannot evaluate serviceability and inherent worth save on the basis of experience.

All of this leads to a problem of practical reason that is peculiar to pragmatic liberalism. Pragmatic liberalism cannot really approve or disapprove a project that is not obviously contradictory to liberal values until the results are in.

But the inherent problem with this method of analysis is that by the time a judgment can be rendered on the worth of a project, the enterprise may already have become a dominant option, and other opportunities and alternatives may have been neglected or foreclosed.

A project that has developed far enough for us to fairly assess its consequences may be very hard to reverse. The going concern has momentum and support. People have come to rely on it; it forms part of the structure of settled expectations that makes the free life possible and comfortable. Standard practice seems right and natural; it is hard to urge the fundamental transformation of what is so eminently "workable."

This is the dilemma of orthodoxy. Reliable knowledge and reliable performance are the goals of inquiry. But the *achievement* of reliable knowledge and performance implies prescriptive methodology, consensus on basic standards among practitioners.

I have identified rationality with discipline, with the development of an internal normative order in a human undertaking. However, for those who believe that only totally unfettered discourse can be "authentic," it is precisely the association of rationality with rules of good practice that inhibits discovery and the free flow of the mind and imagination.

The philosopher of science Paul Feyerabend argues that great scientific advances come not from following a prescribed system of rules and standards, but by violating them. Science progresses not so much by testing a single theory as by proposing a wide variety of contrasting hypotheses, sometimes wild conjectures. It is the proliferation, not the uniformity of theory, that is the condition of fruitful inquiry. All novel scientific advances (Copernicus, Galileo) rested, initially, on partial and incomplete theories, assumptions that seemed naive and irrational by orthodox standards. Often, important scientific advances required the revival of traditions discarded and discredited by the scientific communities.

Hence, any effort to impose rules of good practice on a science—or analogously, on any rational enterprise—may inhibit its development. Science—and presumably politics—should resist all efforts to create prescriptive methodology, to lay down canons of correct procedure, or to enact demarcation criteria that define what is science—or good politics—and what is not. The only appropriate methodological dictum is "Anything goes." [18]

Such methodological anarchism, with its rough and ready defiance of proprieties in the name of results, may seem like the purest pragmatism. In fact, it is the direct opposite of pragmatic liberalism, with its root metaphors of craft, guild, and workmanship, its Peircean conception of science as an evolutionary tradition of understanding and inquiry.

Let us admit that there is a time and place for the revolutionary reconsideration of practice. The issue is one of presumption, of the general rule. Rationality normally entails acting in accord with the tenets of best practice. Our quarrel here is with the attitude that, as a general rule, one should *resist* the discipline of standards and rules.[19]

There is a problem here with "pure" liberalism, one that is shared with pure positivism and pure nihilism. In the absence of standards, preference becomes the test of value. The language of science, for that matter, all rational endeavor, is seen as no more than persuasive argument, and the test of the worth of a theory is simply its ability to win adherents in the marketplace of ideas. The rule is that of caveat emptor. The community of inquiry assumes no collective responsibility for the quality of its product.

I have argued that the continuing collective reappraisal of standards of practice is a defining characteristic of the rational enterprise. Rationality itself is the critical process of appraising the merit of projects and proposals by appealing to principles of propriety and good practice that are inherent in the endeavor at hand.

But such rational criticism is not a distinguishing feature of marketlike arrangements. Such discourse as does take place in markets is largely a matter of purveyors advertising their wares, and here, rules of rhetoric rather than rational criticism apply. Consumers, for their part, need give no reasons for their choices. They may say that they *like* Kant better than Hegel, *prefer* Copernican to Ptolemaic astronomy, much as they might prefer Pontiacs to Toyotas. Or they may say, as significantly they do, that they find a certain theoretical scheme "interesting," "provocative," or "stimulating," appealing to what are, in essence, hedonistic norms.

We are obliged to give reasons for our judgments, it would seem, only when we are recommending, or justifying, an authoritative choice made on behalf of a community. Rational criticism is always public-regarding in character and, at least implicitly, legislative in intent. It is essentially political, not economic, in form, for politics implies deliberation on common commitments for the promotion and control of the undertakings and activities of a community.

Rational criticism has always been assumed to be essential to science as it is to politics. The purpose of scientific criticism may be to advance systems of knowledge, but it is also a form of quality control. As the political critic asks whether policy is compatible with individual rights, so the scientific critic asks whether a given approach to inquiry can be certified as reliable. And in doing this, the scientific critic must, of necessity, invoke some rules of appropriate method, as the political critic must ground judgment in some principles of rightful order.

It is often said that the liberal state should be impartial among human goods and purposes, and that this is best accomplished when there is broad latitude for self-regarding market choice. Yet in the highly organized, complex industrial societies, we do in fact have to deliberate on the "rationality" of our transport and energy systems, our established practices for getting housing, medical care, personal security, and legal justice to people. We do believe that the efficiency, economy, equity, and responsiveness of such arrangements have to be debated and decided. These are not matters to be determined by only the rhetorical appeals and mute revealed preferences of the market.

Like it or not, we have to make authoritative choices on behalf of others. In everyday life, we must reason politically as well as economically. In the university, it will not suffice to say simply that a diversity of approaches to the study of economics or mathematics should be encouraged. This may be a preliminary aspect of inquiry, but it is not the whole of it. Once competing approaches have been established, it is necessary to make discriminating judgments between them. Somehow, collectively, a curriculum and research priorities will be set. To say that the university should simply practice mutual toleration, letting professionals do precisely as they please, seems to the wary outsider little more than the self-satisfied corruption of the guild. The members of the university would seem to have a collective responsibility for the quality of their product, and this implies continued scrutiny of performance on the basis of general and clear criteria of scholarly excellence and the reliability of knowledge.

Pragmatic liberalism shares the strong affirmation of free expression that is fundamental to all liberalism. However, it also respects skill and workmanship, disciplined performance that is the product of rationally considered experience. Most of the distinctiveness of pragmatic liberal theory, its specific method of thought, its apparent commonsense moderation when contrasted with more axiomatic systems of liberal thought, is a product of trying to reconcile these two values.

Thus, in pragmatic liberal political discourse, the case must always be made for the going concern, for the rationality inherent in established ways of doing things. At the same time, pragmatic liberalism regards all rational frameworks as contingent. It is wary of what Veblen called the "trained incapacity" of the expert, the tendency of professionals to apply technique beyond its proper sphere or to invoke the authority of the guild to discredit promising new approaches. As we shall see in detail a little further on, there are a variety of parts that must be played, diverse voices that must be represented, if political discourse is to be coherent, balanced, and undistorted.[20]

The Problem of Overpractice

There is a final objection to pragmatic liberalism that should be considered here. This one comes from the prescriptive traditionalist, and it is precisely the opposite of that of the pure participatory democrat. The issue here is that pragmatic liberalism, like all forms of Enlightenment rationalism, is too intent on the persistent criticism and rational perfection of technique. It is insufficiently respectful of custom and usage that develops, unselfconsciously, over time.

This is a fair caution. The pragmatic liberal should respect workable anomalies. For a human enterprise to work well, people must find it trustworthy, familiar, and comfortable. Pragmatic liberalism should resist the grim systematizers, the perfectionists of technique.

There is a special issue here that requires comment. I call this the problem of overpractice, of the technologically baroque. I think this is a product of the excessive competitive zeal, the very concern for high standards of performance, of a society that has most fully assimilated the Enlightenment virtues of rational analysis.

The problem manifests itself in the design of electronic gear far too esoteric for ordinary use, in the multiplication of ingenious methods of "creative finance" that display stunning virtuosity in the pursuit of gain but have no redeeming social function, in the self-absorption with methodological sophistication that marks much contemporary scholarship.

All of this requires hard work. Great energy, forethought, conscientiousness, and effort are brought to such undertakings. Families are neglected, health is broken, in the relentless quest for a more subtle display of virtuosity. Yet, in the end, what we have is the excess of the virtue of rationalism itself, a caricature of the distinctive excellence of practical reason.

After a while of this, simplicity, functionality, conceptual directness, and elegance become rational imperatives, indicated criteria for the criticism and improvement of technique. In this sense, the rational development of practice is not unidirectional but cyclical, for we are constantly correcting for excess. Thus, the Victorian is replaced by the functional in architecture. Today, much of our high technology, gadgetry, many of our economic and financial systems, much of our law, will need rethinking in the name of simplicity, parsimony, the clear line of functionality that we still admire in design. Not too many years from now, we will probably think the artifacts of our era, material and social, considerably overstudied, and the intelligent reappraisal of established practice will be understood, in some measure, as a process of uncluttering.

3

The Community of

Practice and Inquiry

To think of the enterprise as a political forum, to understand that political deliberation takes place *within* the enterprise, leads us to reexamine our ideas of the organization of enterprise, of its proper constitution as a political order.

Orthodox liberalism provides us with three images of the proper organization of such purposeful associations.

First, if we think of the enterprise mainly as a source of reliable performance, we emphasize order and control, and see the enterprise ideally constituted as a rational hierarchy. The aim of hierarchy, of bureaucratic organization with a clear chain of authority and a well-defined division of labor, is to secure maximum responsiveness to command and maximum predictability of performance.

Second, if we think of the enterprise as legitimate only to the extent that it reflects the free choices of individuals, then we see it ideally constituted by contract. Reliable performance is secured by the promises and commitments that contract entails. However, basically, the enterprise has no inherent purposes. It is, as Hayek suggested, a self-organizing system. Its aims are set by the bargains struck by those who are parties to it, and its aims may change as it gains new adherents, or as members leave.

Third, if we think the enterprise should be constituted on the same lines as the democratic polity, we then emphasize full and open participation in determining its aims and purposes and see it, ideally, as the product of the manifest, collective will of its members, deliberately decided.

None of these images is fully compatible with our ideal of

practical political reason. All are examples of what might be called "mechanical liberalism." Classical liberalism often saw itself as an engineering discipline. Thus, hierarchic organization serves to constrain and coordinate individuals in efficient pursuit of a designated end. Adam Smith's market as well as Madison's vision of the constitution as a system of checks and balances were institutional contrivances intended to channel self-interested persons toward the achievement of a common good. The ideal conditions of democracy are designed to assure neutrality, that public purpose will be the genuine expression of community will.

In political architecture, form follows function, and we are not trying to achieve pure efficiency, pure contract, or pure consent. Rather, we are looking for a form of political order that would be appropriate to the exercise of practical political reason, one in which the aim is deliberation on how liberal ideals apply to the enhancement of the mission of an enterprise.

Politics and the Model of Scientific Community

The precursors of pragmatic liberalism thought of politics as ideally constituted not on the basis of consent or contract alone, but along the lines of the institutions of scientific investigation. Thus, Dewey regarded the state as analogous to an ideal scientific society, engaged in an ongoing, experimental search for an increasingly durable conception of public order. In doing so, Dewey drew on Charles Sanders Peirce's notion of science as reliable knowledge forged by agreement and consensus within a "community of inquiry." Jurgen Habermas drew on Peirce to create his vision of "undistorted communication" which many contemporary democratic theorists find suggestive as an ideal of democratic communication.[1] (In chapter 11 I have more to say about Peirce's philosophy and its relation to pragmatic liberalism.)

In the same spirit, Friedrich Hayek's defense of free market liberalism rests on an idea of experimental process, on the generation of social knowledge and the perfection of social performance through a process of spontaneous collaboration, trial and error, conjecture and refutation, very much in keeping with Karl Popper's image of scientific discovery.[2] David Braybrooke and Charles E. Lindblom describe incremental decision-making as an experimental process in which policies are tested by successive iterations of appraisal, in a process that rests on the "concurrence of investigators."[3] And Thomas Spragens argues for a reconstruction of liberal politics along the lines of Stephen Toulmin's conception of science as an evolutionary, collaborative, "rational enterprise."[4]

To be sure, the pursuit of truth is not quite the same as the pursuit of public purpose. Politics *requires* decision as science does not. In politics, one must opt for some course of action (for not to decide is to opt for the status quo as policy), while in science judgment can be suspended indefinitely. And the citizens of the communities of science are specially qualified and selected, while democratic citizens are not. Nonetheless, the image of the political order as a community of practice and a community of inquiry is peculiarly compatible with pragmatic liberalism as an idea of practical political reason.

The main reason for this is that pragmatic liberalism requires *disciplined* discourse, discourse in which there are substantive as well as procedural tests of the worth of statement.

The object of procedural democracy is that all voices be heard, all interests considered. However, in any field of science, or practical activity, there are standards that determine what problems are important, what forms of analysis are acceptable, what interpretations are legitimate. Discourse in science, and in practice, is not "undistorted." Nor is it "neutral" in the classic liberal democratic sense. Science is not a free-form investigation of all conceivable ideas about the world. Rather, all scientific investigation is guided by certain presuppositions and concepts of explanation. Explanation in physics will inevitably take the form of laws of force and motion. But in biology, explanation will have to do with ideas of the development of organism. This is what explanation in physics or biology *means*. Such core presuppositions of a discipline are not really subject to criticism or experimental analysis. They are rather constitutive principles of the enterprise. The same is true of any practical activity.[5]

The object of impartial procedure in pure democracy is to show that policy in fact reflects the sum of individual wills. However, the point of unconstrained discourse in scientific or practical investigation is to show that knowledge or practice is in fact reliable. These are not the same thing.

To demonstrate the trustworthiness of scientific statement or practical technique, it is never enough to point to the consensus of investigators alone, or to the freedom all had to speak their minds. Rather, one recounts the history of a critical analysis, citing the efforts made to think otherwise, the tests made to try to prove the hypothesis wrong, the repeated confirmations that the idea worked in practice, from all sorts of angles, in all kinds of applications. This is the case for the durability of knowledge, or technique.

Thus, scientific discourse, like practical political discourse within any purposive enterprise, requires a certain structure for argument beyond sheer rules of impartial procedure. And this requires a conception of the political order that is different from the orthodox models of rational hierarchy, contract, or democratic community.

The ideal scientific society is both radical and conservative. On the one hand, it must encourage subversive defiance of established truth. It supports creative impressions, wild surmise. However, it is not uniqueness of vision, simple originality, or eccentricity that it honors. It requires that novelty be shown to contribute to an established structure of problems and methods. Thus, Michael Polanyi says, "Science fosters a maximum of originality while imposing also an exceptional degree of critical rigor." There must be "a unity between personal creative passion and a willingness to submit to tradition and discipline."[6]

The ideal of political order that is uniquely compatible with pragmatic liberalism is that of the enterprise that is simultaneously a community of good practice and a community of inquiry. This ideal entails a very specific vision of citizenship and civic responsibility, of participation, and of the normative order of a political community. To be sure, in practical application the ideal will take many forms. In some, hierarchy and reliable knowledge will be emphasized. In others, creative participation will be at center stage. Many mixtures of the basic elements are possible, depending on the task to be done. And again, the balance among the elements should always be a subject open to continuing debate and deliberation.

As we shall now see, this ideal is not a utopian construction, but a very familiar part of our everyday experience.

The Community of Practice and the Community of Inquiry

In any science and in any profession, the practitioner is understood to play a dual role. In the first instance, the professional is responsible for reliable performance. The doctor follows prescribed procedure, the craftsman standard practice; the scholar teaches calculus in the orthodox manner, English literature through the canonical works. However, the professional is also a contributor, potential or actual, to the discipline. As a citizen of a community of practice, the practitioner is expected and entitled to take part in the continuing scrutiny of method and technique, in the search for innovation and improvement. It is in understanding the relationship between these two roles that we may come to a better understanding of what the historic pragmatic liberal quest for the "democratic community" looks like, realistically considered in the context of the enterprise and in relation to the spirit of our age.

In the first role, the professional is expected to subordinate individuality to a system of collective norms and methods. But in the second role, professionalism implies self-expression, creativity, a propensity to "think otherwise," and a vision of the whole beyond specialized function.

From the first perspective, a profession is a collective responsibility. One has no right to practice law, electrical engineering, or plumbing "just as one pleases," as a matter of personal inspiration, taste, or conviction.

It is not assumed that doctors invent the operations they perform, or that political scientists or chemists are the sole authors of their teachings. Rather, the professional is expected to act on behalf of a community of practice, as a representative of it. All professionals are, in important respects, presumed to be interchangeable. We expect essentially the same technique to be used, the same advice given, the same doctrine taught, by any certified specialist.

Professional knowledge is not tacit knowledge. Understanding and skill, of course, derive from intuition as well as reason, but it is not good enough for the practitioner to say that he or she "just knew the right thing to do." The justification for any professional action must rest on the accumulated knowledge and the canons of practice of a discipline. In principle, such knowledge is public knowledge. The professional should be able to recount, at least in summary, the process that led to collective agreement that a specific practice was good practice. Only on this understanding is "expert judgment" compatible with the larger logic of liberalism.

In the first instance, the profession is collectively responsible for reliable performance, for the maintenance of standard technique. However, as we have seen, that is only half the story. The community of practice is also community of inquiry. The practitioner is expected to participate also in the sustained scrutiny of established method.

This Janus-like image of the professional, at once faithful to established routine and iconoclastic and creative, is less paradoxical, more a commonplace of our experience, than we might at first suppose. Most of us understand full well the constitutional conventions of our callings, the time and the place for simply applying skill to the task at hand and for discussion, dissent, and rethinking. The two attitudes are not that hard to reconcile. Outside a narrow band of specialized heresy, the views of the scientist are likely to be prosaic and orthodox. The craftsman is expected to follow instructions, but if asked, is likely to have a clear notion of how the job might be better done.

The individual element in rational performance may first be expressed as style. Style is a matter of personal approach and interpretation within a system of standardized performance. Style is not, as the romantics might wish it, pure "authenticity" or self-expression, unencumbered by any discipline. Style is an act of responsibility toward a discipline, and it is a necessary adjunct to any rational performance. Style arises as reaction to, or adaptation of, a dominant system of standards. It is not merely individual. It is a collaborative matter as well. Whether in art or music, in business management, judicial philosophy, or automobile body work, style can be understood only in relation to some classical conception of how a job is properly done.

The appraisal of style, and its justification, must be understood in relation to the purpose of a rational enterprise. Style may begin as no more than personal inclination. It is rational to the extent that it can be expressed as a matter of personal philosophy. At the outset, style is individual. But personal style is available as a potential standard of collective action. Style is ultimately a form of entrepreneurship or innovation. It is the equivalent of hypothesis, or conjecture, in science. A profession develops through the continuing appraisal of alternative conceptions of style, their diffusion, potentially their universalization and enforcement as the distinctive mark of the enterprise.

However, ideally, the practitioner contributes not simply through personal interpretation and style, but as a citizen of the enterprise. The policy of the enterprise does not merely evolve: to some extent, it is consciously deliberated and chosen. The functions of citizenship then are the same as those in the formal political community: to propose, debate, and critique, to participate in collective decisions on actions that might be made authoritative for the community.

Despite the tendency to develop separate castes of researchers and operatives, the ideal of the practitioner as potential contributor is alive in most of the professions, in a surprising number of trades and crafts, and certainly in the arts and sciences in the university, where such contribution is normally understood as a *requirement* of practice. To be sure, in any profession or craft, the number of active participants is apt to be small, as the number of active citizens in a polity is apt to be a fraction of the whole, and such participation may be sporadic. In fact, ideally it is disbursed and sporadic, as ideas for improvement and issues that need to be joined occur to different members at different times.

Pragmatic liberalism assumes that this ideal applies not only to the professions, but to the factory, the store, and the office as well. And it would appear that the historic view of progressive management theory—that industry is better off with less rigid hierarchy, and with more participation, collective problem-solving, and entrepreneurship within the firm—is once more making headway. The stern systematizers have often intimated that universities should be run more "efficiently," on the model of corporations. Today, it is equally fashionable to suggest that corporations might be more productive were they organized on the highly decentralized, entrepreneurial model of the American university.[7]

The goal of such industrial citizenship may be job satisfaction and employee morale. It is also human development, perhaps the cultivation of civic virtue, at least consistency with fundamental liberal democratic values. But it is also, for pragmatic liberalism, simply a condition of rational performance.

Such a philosophy will not satisfy those who regard all normal work as stifling and repressive, imposed by the hegemonic demands of capitalism, technology, and rationalist values.[8] But then the demands of romanticism against the modern world cannot be easily satisfied. The fact is that all worthwhile endeavor implies tedium and toil. Pragmatic liberalism is distinctive in suggesting not that this fate can be overcome, but that work is made meaningful when it represents full engagement in a collective effort and responsibility.

Of course, the customer or client should not be considered simply a passive recipient of service. That reduces the quest for rational performance to simple "consumerism," a position more at home with market or utilitarian than with pragmatic liberalism.

Ideally, patients participate in their treatment, students are members of the university, the skill and ethos of the driver is understood as a crucial element in the community of practice of the transport system.

Here, however, we reach the frontiers of our thought. Our tradition gives us little guidance on how such parties might best be incorporated into the political order of the enterprise. The prototype of the professional guild, which has served us well in other respects, does not help us here. Too easily, in such matters, we settle for questionnaire democracy and interest group advocacy. It would be better if those who use as well as those who create a product or performance were understood as parties to an enterprise.

But the simple fact is that we cannot define the full constituency of the enterprise, cannot account for all the parties affected by its actions. The performance, and the political order, of the enterprise has become a matter of general public interest.

The Theory of Plural Citizenship

At this point, we must shift our focus. As I said at the outset, there are two vantage points for the political appraisal of enterprise. The first is that of the citizen of the enterprise itself. The second is that of the citizen of the liberal regime who must now consider the performance and organization of the enterprise as a potential subject of law and policy.

The implication of this idea of plural citizenship must be made clear. Orthodox liberalism teaches that the citizen should be concerned first of all with matters of the public good, that lesser loyalties should be subsumed under civic commitment. However, I have argued that the political decisions of everyday life, those acts of governance of firm and family, profession and association, are at least as significant as the acts of voting, attending meetings, and writing legislators—those acts with which the more simple crusaders for effective citizenship seem so often to be exclusively concerned.

There is an inevitable tension, and no necessary priority, I would argue, between the claims of citizenship in the polity and the enterprise. One can legitimately be with one's church and against the state, with one's trade union and against the state, with one's profession and against the state, in certain circumstances.[9] Liberal political theory presupposes such rightful defiance and seeks to preserve the possibility of resistance in the name of communities other than the state.

Nonetheless, in our age there is an inevitable tension not only between the roles of citizen of the regime and the citizen of the enterprise, but there may be tension between the diverse communities of practice as well.

In a practical and moral order constituted as a pluralist system of enterprises, the practitioners may come to inhabit different worlds and find the ways of other crafts strange and suspect. There is a wary mutual hostility, we all know, between businessmen, professors, and medical practitioners. The subcultures created by these invisible colleges may become more important than the ties of ethnicity, class, or region, and the folkways of each—manners and morals, clothes and family relation, hobbies and recreations—are quite identifiably distinctive and separate.

Simply to live successfully in a culture dominated by these complex communities of practice requires that the individual penetrate and comprehend something of their specialized languages and customs. To function competently today means not only to have a working knowledge of domestic appliances and the internal combustion engine, but to somehow comprehend the strange rituals of modern medicine and the airline system, and the more arcane mysteries of mortgage finance and estate law.

There are other tensions that arise from such plural citizenship. The community of practice is not the same as the organization or firm, and within any enterprise there are apt to be various factions or schools of thought. The individual must somehow sort out diverse obligations and loyalties. The automobile designer must somehow reconcile responsibilities to the profession, to the "state of the art" of the industry as a whole, and to the specific company, the employer. The scholar's obligations may be similarly complex and divided. The historian may be "medievalist" and "economic determinist," or the physicist "cosmologist" and proponent of "continuous creation," against theorists of the "big bang." Each is, as well, a member of the faculty of a particular university and perhaps also, in his or her own mind, of a universal "community of letters." At the moment of truth, which of these commitments should prevail?

Nonetheless, the principal tension that concerns us is that between the roles of citizen of the regime and citizen of the enterprise.

From the point of view of the citizen of the regime, the perspective of the citizen of the enterprise may seem parochial and self-serving. On the other hand, the criticisms of the performance of enterprise brought by the citizen of the regime may seem high-handed, uninformed, and "impractical" to the citizen of the enterprise. There is always some prospective loss of efficiency or autonomy to the enterprise in any program of civic-minded reform. To require the enterprise to further larger public interests may seem a diversion of resources, a distraction from the pursuit of essential purpose.

The problem is to reconcile the two perspectives. Without the social criticism of the citizen of the regime, the enterprise may become complacent and insensitive to the larger implications of its actions. Without the concern for practice of the citizen of the enterprise, the institutions of everyday life may become politicized, corrupt, or ineffective. Good government requires a sustained dialectic between the claims of theory and the claims of practice.

The Enterprise as Subject of Law and Policy

For the citizen of the regime, the critical question of political judgment is that of the regulation of enterprise. Robert Dahl describes this as a dilemma of autonomy and control:

> Independent organizations are highly desirable in a democracy . . . they are necessary to the functions of the democratic process itself, to minimizing government coercion, to political liberty and to human well-being.

Yet . . . independence or autonomy creates an opportunity to do harm. Organizations may use the opportunity to increase or perpetuate injustice rather than reduce it, to foster the narrow egoism of their members at the expense of concerns for a broader public good, and even to weaken or destroy democracy itself. Like individuals, then, organizations ought to possess some autonomy, and at the same time, they should also be controlled. Crudely stated, this is the fundamental problem of pluralist democracy.[10]

To this point, I have been discussing pragmatic liberalism as a philosophy for the governance of the enterprise. Now we must go on to see how pragmatic liberalism applies as a philosophy of public policy, as a basis for deliberating the relations of the state to the enterprise. In the next two chapters I will discuss first the role of the liberal state in the improvement of the performance of enterprise and then its role in the development of the constitutional order of the enterprise.

4

The State and the

Performance of the Enterprise

The routine convention of American partisan rhetoric is that one must be either with the state and against business or with business and against the state.[1] The Progressive legacy out of which pragmatic liberalism grows, the tradition of Croly and Commons, Dewey and the Roosevelts, presumed no such antagonism. One could be with *both* the state and business, *for* the autonomy of enterprise and activist public policy.

The problem now is to communicate the nuances of a position that does not rely on a stark separation of the public and private realms. In this chapter, I try to describe such an idea of the role of the state in relation to the institutions of economy and society, of the standards to which we might appeal in deciding when public intervention is warranted and when it is not. In doing so I appeal more to historic experience and practice, and to our ordinary language of political deliberation, than to formal doctrine. My point is that we have evolved a more subtle view of this problem than is expressed in orthodox liberal theory, a repertoire of possibilities that we can work with in defining the relation of the state to the communities of practice. The problem of practical political judgment then is that of deciding which of these possibilities to exploit in determining how public action might enhance the performance of a *particular* human enterprise.

Liberal Political Theory and the
Relation of State and Enterprise

Liberalism is, above all else, a theory of limited government. Yet perhaps the most perplexing problem in liberal theory is that of stipulating precisely when the state may intervene in economy and society and when it may not.

Many stand by fixed and immutable principles that turn out, on close examination, to be ambiguous. Most liberal maxims could justify either a highly constrained, laissez-faire government or an activist, consciously interventionist state. All depends on interpretation. It is a matter of whether we are more concerned about state or private power, about the defense or the establishment of rights.

Locke's doctrine was that state action is only legitimate when it protects individual rights better than the individual could protect them alone. Yet even Locke's paramount right of property, or estate, provides no sure test of the propriety of state action. Locke may seem to suggest that we will intuitively recognize any appropriation of "that with which one has mixed one's labor"—whether by another individual or by the state—as theft. However, taken seriously, Locke's qualifying principle of scarcity, that one must leave "enough and as good" for others, could serve as a mandate for the radical redistribution of wealth.[2]

For some, the utilitarian test, that a policy is good if it increases total social utility, implies noninterference in market processes, for this is the best way to generate wealth and personal satisfaction. For others, it means simply that a public project should be approved if it can be shown to yield positive public benefits. It is a recipe for an activist state.

And John Stuart Mill's contention that the state act only to restrain individuals from doing one another harm turns out to be not a sure guide to appropriate policy but an open and porous ground of argument. It is not clear what kind of human action is reasonably construed as a harm and what is not. Does any act count that seriously offends another, or that constrains opportunities? We may debate endlessly, then, whether "victimless crimes" (public smoking, pornography, seat-belt use) entail significant social costs and consequences.[3]

Classic liberalism presupposes a sharp distinction between public and private life. Pragmatic liberalism assumes that all purposive enterprises have a public character. Yet are the two positions really at odds? The classic argument is not that enterprise has a right to "privacy," nor that self-interest is good in itself. Rather, the whole point is that self-interest and private property must be *shown* to serve the public good if they are to be regarded as legitimate. This is what the theory of the market attempts to do. Pragmatic liberals only contest the sufficiency of this answer.

The essential difference, of course, is that classic liberalism is primarily a theory of individual action, and of individual rights against the state, while pragmatic liberalism is primarily a theory of the relation of the state to individuals engaged in and affected by various forms of collective action. Hence, pragmatic liberalism is a theory of how individual right is to be realized in a regime of complex organizations and undertakings. And again, in this theory, it is not only the control but the *development* of rational enterprise that is a legitimate aim of government.

The Legitimacy of Intervention

In all forms of liberal thought, the presumptive case is for the autonomy of practice. It is the advocate of government action who has to give reasons. For pragmatic liberalism, the grounds for state intervention are not general but specific. They arise from the sense that there is a particular fault or failing in the conduct of an enterprise.

Pragmatic liberalism does not assume that there is a single rule that defines the public interest in an enterprise. Rather, there are a variety of liberal principles. They function not as categoric tests of the propriety or impropriety of state action, but as a source of claims against practice.

Thus, to invoke ideas of right or free choice, of social efficiency or distributive justice, is basically to point to some discrepancy between theory and practice, some problem, as measured by liberal standards, in the performance of an enterprise.

The question then is to determine which claim, if any, is sufficient to warrant public intervention. Like the common law, pragmatic liberalism assumes that the pertinent principle arises out of a consideration of the "facts of the matter." It is a process of weighing the importance of such claims grounded in liberal principle against the rationale for practice itself.

The initial assumption is that the enterprise is a self-correcting mechanism. For classical liberals, the adaptation and evolution of the enterprise, its responsiveness to new demands, arises out of competitive market forces. For pragmatic liberals, it is primarily the product of ongoing, cooperative critique and assessment, and a matter of conscious control.

The critique and correction of the performance of an enterprise do not have to come from the state. The enterprise is, in the first instance, a system of governance within the regime. Thus, initially, the critique of practice is addressed to those authorities: the managers of firms, the leaders of scholarly or professional guilds, the influential practitioners.[4]

To override the presumption of autonomy, the case then must be made that state action is indicated to improve or perfect the conditions of practice. It need not be shown that the enterprise has committed a wrong. Liberal principles are, after all, in the broadest sense tests of the rationality of enterprise. Hence, the claim that a form of practice could be made more efficient or economic, or could be distributed more equitably, or made more responsive to those associated with it, signals a potential public interest in the enterprise.

Thus the object of state action need not be an infringement of rights, an act of deceit or domination, a demonstrated harm to some person or interest. Pragmatic liberalism assumes no adversary relationship between the public and the private realms. The relation of the state to the enterprise is ideally one of collaboration. Hence, state action may serve simply to enhance and perfect the conditions of good practice in a specific undertaking.

From this point of view, the state may choose to improve the performance of an enterprise by subsidy or support, regulation and direct control, or by opening the enterprise to competition. The choice between "politics and markets" is not a choice between total regimes, but simply of remedies. And the choice depends on the specific nature of the enterprise and the particular nature of the claim brought in relation to its performance.

Any of the following considerations, then, may define the public interest in an enterprise. The problem for political deliberation and judgment is to determine whether the discrepancy between theory and practice is sufficient to warrant intervention and whether the failure is best corrected or the opportunity for improvement best realized through state action.

The Public Interest in the Integrity of the Market

In liberal convention, economics is natural, politics artificial. The propensity to exchange and the recognition of property exist in the state of nature. The state is created by calculated consent. In fact, of course, the market was the historic creation of law and policy.[5] It was the product of conscious and comprehensive plan, imposed by the emergent liberal states, from the late eighteenth, to well into the nineteenth and twentieth centuries, depending on the nation.

The market expanded the domain of individual freedom and voluntary collective action. The state withdrew from the detailed regulation of human concerns. But the market itself required close supervision to secure its integrity.[6]

Some might think that market institutions set in motion were perfectly self-correcting, like a celestial machine. However, most believed that they required a good deal of sustained correction and support. Adam Smith recognized that the market required "an exact administration of justice." Market liberals, perhaps precisely because of their preoccupation with the pecuniary instincts, are prone to a certain skepticism of human motivation. They presume not honor but a propensity toward theft, deceit, and collusion. Smith's lugubrious view that "people of the same trade seldom meet together, even for merriment and diversion, but the conversation ends in a conspiracy against the public, or in some contrivance to raise prices"[7] does not lend support to the idea that an invisible hand would always properly arrange things. Rather, it pointed to a flaw in the machinery, something that had to be watched. Over time, the dominant wisdom of legal experience and public policy, if not of classical doctrine, was that the market required constant superintendence if it was to achieve its ends.

Hence, it is presumed legitimate for the state to intervene in the affairs of individuals and enterprises if its action can reasonably be shown to work toward the perfection of the regime of markets. The various schools of liberalism do not divide fundamentally on this point. They all support the same criteria for determining when state intervention is warranted. The differences are ones of judgment on the extent to which theory and practice can diverge before a market regime stands in need of correction by state action.

The narrow view calls for minimum intrusion by the state to secure the conditions of the market. Apart from defense, a monetary system, and certain indispensable public works, the most important task of government is to provide the elements of the criminal and civil law. There is need for security of person and possessions, and for a clear stipulation of the rights and exposures that attach to transactions. The state must provide what Hobbes and Locke would have called an "impartial adjudicator," for self-interested parties cannot be expected to construe their own contracts in a spirit of disinterested detachment.

On the narrow view, any state policy beyond a strict and limited fulfillment of these functions would distort the natural operation of market forces, There would be a bias in favor of particular interests over alternative prospects and possibilities. Thus the conditions of liberal neutrality would be violated.[8]

The broader view, which is characteristic of pragmatic liberalism, agrees with this fundamental program, but construes it differently. It sets more demanding requirements for the legitimacy of market transactions. At the margin, it opts for the conscious ordering of markets rather than their protection from the "distortions" of public policy.

We have already commented on the stringent requirements of the ideal conceptions of contract and the market as they appear in the logic of liberal thought. Any disparities of power or opportunity, of information or access, cast doubt on the integrity of the contractual nexus. Yet a degree of dominance can be discerned in almost every transaction. All markets fail in some respect. Few choices are from among truly costless options. The problem then, as John R. Commons put it, is one of determining "the permissible degree of power" in contractual relationships.[9]

The law contemplates transactions among individuals. The emergence of rational enterprise automatically complicates the problem of fashioning law compatible with liberal principles, for rational organizations, by definition, constitute dominant options in economy and society.

The reconciliation of the enterprise and the market then becomes a persistent theme of liberal thought, law, and policy. Liberalism develops as a philosophy, though the changes are largely ignored in orthodox doctrine. Since *Munn v. Illinois*,[10] U.S. law has recognized that centralized organizations could constitute "virtual monopolies" and that their regulation was an appropriate public function. The transformation of the labor union from un-lawful conspiracy to privileged organizational form was a delib-erate recognition of the need to develop institutions that would redress the imbalance in bargaining power between the corpo-ration and the individual if the integrity of the market was to be preserved. By a similar logic, it was thought essential to ad-dress the balance between the interests of large firms and con-sumers, large firms and suppliers, and large firms and small business as well.[11]

Markets can fail in various ways. As the growth of rational en-terprise made it more difficult to assure equality and impartiality in the contractual nexus, so the development of complex tech-nologies made it harder to limit the effects of action to those who had freely consented to them. Industry could impose its costs on those outside the contractual bonds by polluting water and air, by extracting resources or disposing of waste in ways that destroyed the beauty of the land, or worse, in ways that rendered the earth useless from that point on. The burdens were simply passed on to the public at large, or to future generations, and the price of present goods made that much more attractive.

Policies aimed at requiring enterprise to "internalize" such costs of production have been promoted by progressive liberals throughout the century, with growing intensity and controversy in recent years. The obvious rationale for such interventions in the realm of the market is public health and safety; increasingly, it has been seen as a question of the inhabitability of earth itself. How-ever, when we speak of such environmental degradation in the language of market failure—as "externalities," costs imposed on the public or on unwilling third parties—we suggest that the in-tegrity of the market system is also at stake, and that the interven-tion of the state is intended to secure not only the future of the habitat but that of the political economic order as well.

Many policies which we associate with progressive or reformist liberalism are justified, in our conventions of discourse, as means to secure the integrity of the market. Laws that would outlaw dis-crimination on the basis of "accidental" characteristics, such as race or sex, like positive measures designed to create equality of opportunity for those disadvantaged by reason of background or poverty, have as their end the legitimation of an order in which all choosers can be presumed equal, and hence all outcomes cer-tified as fair.

Pragmatic liberalism has maintained a stubborn conviction that the relations of the enterprise to the market could be worked out. In this, it has reflected the dominant temper of American opinion, which has steadily resisted appeals to abandon the market in the name of the enterprise, or the enterprise in the name of the market. The political problem was understood not as one of overcoming the "inherent contradictions" of the system by installing a new order, but of finding policies that would make the market work better, or those that would support and enhance the performance of enterprise.

Public Support for the Reliable Performance of the Enterprise

Reliable performance is the legitimate aim of the enterprise. But the state is its guarantor. Efficiency, in all its aspects, from the engineering of the automobile or aircraft to the minute details of food preparation and service, is a product of collaborative design in which technologist, entrepreneur, and public official each have a part to play.

Sometimes in public debate we argue regulation of the enterprise as a response to market failure. We say that the complexity and sophistication of modern manufacture make it impossible for the individual to appraise the quality and efficacy of products and services. The rule of caveat emptor no longer applies. Competition is no longer a sufficient guarantee of performance. However, for pragmatic liberalism, such measures are not only designed to protect the consumer. They are also intended to promote the rational development of enterprise. The state is not merely a regulator, but legitimately a party to the productive activity as well.

The state has at its disposal a variety of instruments that may be used to secure the quality and predictability of the performance of an enterprise.

Occupational licensing and certification were the earliest response to the proliferation of specialized professions and trades. The state took the place of the guild. The state might set minimum qualifications for practitioners, or empower the professional organizations to monitor performance, or link practice to a prescribed course of professional preparation or study. (Perhaps the most dramatic, if unacknowledged, of such policies was to entrust the pursuit of knowledge and systematic technique specifically to the learned professions in the public universities. It is virtually impossible, in this century, to practice any of the liberal arts or sciences without professional license and university affiliation. The contemporary university is an exemplary corporatist institution in a market society.)

The state may license the enterprise as well as the practitioner. It may establish specified industries as public utilities, in areas where performance is deemed vital to the total political economic order, prescribing price and conditions of service, controlling entry into and exit from the market.

And, of course, the state may directly intervene in the design of products and the provision of service, stipulating the requirements of good practice, securing the public interest in health and safety, and in the fidelity and reliability of the organized productive undertaking.

To underwrite reliable performance, the state may also act to rationalize markets, to secure an enterprise against certain foreseeable disruptive consequences of competition which the participants, acting alone and on the basis of market principles, cannot prevent.

Rapid entry into markets for new technologies or a rapid increase in productivity can distort or destroy rational performance. Late in the last century, it became apparent that unrestrained competition among railroads, with their fixed plant and capital costs, their inability to move easily among markets, could disrupt the provision of a necessary service. It is true, as revisionist historians always point out, that the railroads actually sought government regulation as protection against "ruinous competition."[12] But it is also true that the railroads were, from the beginning, deemed a crucial public service and that the regulatory regime was primarily intended to secure the reliable provision of that service, at rates that were reasonable and fair.

In the same way, seasonal fluctuations in crops and markets, as well as overall increases in agricultural productivity, could lead to disruption of the highly decentralized and market-oriented agricultural sector. Here the incentives of the market were perverse, for the more productive the enterprise, the more meager were the returns, and failure had little to do with competitive mettle. But apart from questions of fairness, and the perpetuation of the sociopolitical institution of the family farm, the manifest rationale for public intervention was to regularize and routinize performance in a vital area of productive activity.[13]

And, of course, the same logic led early to the regulation of radio communications in the United States, where it was recognized that without control of the broadcast band, stations would interfere and overlap, and competition would quickly defeat the purposes of the enterprise itself.

The perils of government regulation in support of reliable performance have become a major fixation of orthodox political economy in recent years. In fact, much of the current doctrine of both political science and economics reflects this rather intense contemporary reaction against the longer legacy of public policy in all capitalist nations.[14] The theory of free market liberalism tends here to be stated in extreme terms. The lines between the various schools of liberalism in this area are rather sharply drawn.

The critics charge, in effect, that any state action in support of enterprise is necessarily corrupt and uneconomic. It is corrupt in that any form of state licensing or certification can become a privilege granted present practitioners against potential competitors. In fact, the extreme position, taken mainly by those who conceive of no form of human intelligence save that of calculated self-interest, is that there is *no* rational reason for regulation except conspiracy by present members to limit new entrants into an industry.[15]

In the same spirit, it is argued that government regulation is characteristically uneconomic. It inhibits entrepreneurial energy and innovation. In the end, we will expect too much. The demand for reliable performance will become too costly for society to bear. One must weigh the expected gains in predictability, or risk reduction, or environmental protection, against their costs.[16]

The implication is that every regulation must meet a utilitarian test. The regulation must be shown to contribute as much to aggregate economic benefit as any hypothetical free market alternative. We have become accustomed to the idea that one weighs the value of a human life, calculated by the shamelessly utilitarian standard of "discounted future earnings" against the costs of straightening a road or removing asbestos from a factory or school. We have learned to evaluate the worth of a wild river in "user days." To be sure, we cannot assign an infinite value to every potential victim or every historic church. But given the bizarre character of the calculations that inevitably enter into cost-benefit analysis, is this the point on which a justifiable public decision could conceivably turn?

The view that would be more characteristic of pragmatic liberalism is that it is possible to draw clear distinctions between the legitimate public interests to be served by regulation and the abuses to which it is subject. Like any other aspect of enterprise, the regulatory regime is open to ongoing critique and scrutiny. It is of course important to assure that licensing requirements are demonstrably pertinent to the task at hand. Excessive requirements can be taken as a symptom of professional self-protection. As Walter Gellhorn observes, most states now "insist that recruits in the hair-cutting profession receive institutionalized instruction in bacteriology; histology of the hair, skin, nails, muscles and nerves; diseases of the skin, hair, glands and nails; and other matters about which one ventures to guess few barbers are consulted."[17]

In the same vein, pragmatic liberalism would hold not that a regulation be shown to yield more economic benefit than any free market alternative, but simply that the public objective in question be pursued as economically as possible. The aim, after all, is the most rational performance possible—in all senses of the word *rational*. Social economy is one measure of that performance, but it is not the exclusive, or necessarily even the most important, consideration.

It is also pertinent to ask whether the aim of regulation is to protect against fraud, deceit, and incompetence or whether it is to assure that standard practice is best available practice. Pragmatic liberalism again takes the view that the state has a legitimate interest in the rational development of enterprise, not simply in protecting individuals against criminal harms or wrongs. It is associated with the general trend of policy in this century that aims at improving standards as well as setting minimums. Thus, where it was once sufficient to prove that a product was not harmful, now it is more commonly necessary to prove that it is efficacious. Jethro Lieberman speaks of the gradual development of a "fiduciary ethic" in U.S. law and policy—an expectation of care and concern on the part of the practitioner beyond the minimum conditions of compliance with contract: "The fiduciary rule does not circumscribe the range of choice of either party to a transaction except to say, 'That which you undertake to do, do well.'"[18]

Again, rationalism is not always rational, and we can debate the point at which it is counterproductive to prevent contingency and risk, to seek ever higher standards of perfection. But such prudential analysis can proceed from two quite different basing points. For pragmatic liberalism, it is understood that the enhancement of the performance of enterprise is an appropriate public aim. This is quite different from the point of view that the goal is simply to minimize the impact of government in human affairs.

The Public Interest in the Improvement of Practice

It is a function of the liberal state to underwrite the rational order of enterprise. Government serves to secure the conditions of good practice. At the same time, there is a public interest, fundamental to liberalism, in assuring that established practice is always open to challenge, reconsideration, and change. This is the essence of rationalism, in our tradition, since the Enlightenment.

One might think that pragmatic liberalism would want the state to guarantee the openness of the government of the enterprise and thus ensure that the community of practice was also a community of inquiry. This would seem to follow quite naturally from pragmatic liberalism's strong sense of the relationship of democracy and rational performance and its belief that the values of public life ought to extend to all forms of purposive collective effort as well. I discuss the liberal state's role in prescribing the constitution of enterprise in more detail in the next chapter. However, in fact, in seeking defense against unwarranted orthodoxy, the more common practice of the liberal state has been to structure the environment of action of the enterprise rather than its internal political order.

The most characteristic policy of the liberal state in assuring that established practice is always open to reconsideration has been to try to secure the conditions of competition. Immediately, this suggests the prevention of monopoly. To be sure, Smith and Marx both agree that there is an inevitable tendency in capitalism toward collusion to protect dominant technologies and those who control them and that this condition is not self-regulating: it requires conscious state intervention and control. However, antimonopoly policy is probably the least significant of state policies to secure the openness of enterprise.

Since the Enlightenment, the liberal state has been itself a prominent party to that critical reexamination of practice that is the hallmark of scientific and liberal rationalism. The liberal state has not been merely the neutral monitor of the market but also the protagonist of innovation and the patron of change. In agriculture and manufacture, education, medicine and transport, its role has been to take the side of innovation against established doctrine, entrenched technique, and traditional usage.

It has been characteristic policy for the liberal state to support promising improvements in the critical passage from raw initiative to organized going concern. It supports the incipient enterprise through subsidy or tax advantage, or the temporary licensed monopoly of patent. It underwrites research and development expenses—and encourages systematic skepticism—through its public universities and research institutes. It may create privileged organizational forms (nonprofit corporations) or it may legitimate and assist in the maturation of new alternatives through government contracts (the use of airmail subsidies in the organization of the American airline industry). It may assimilate the radical new undertaking into the regime of direct public services (as in the case of the psychiatric hospital). It may try to simply *transform* practice, using its full repertoire of capabilities and powers, as it has, most conspicuously, in the case of agriculture.

It might be argued that such policies of preferment to innovation are actually to be understood as means of redressing imbalances in market power between established method and promising alternative, that here the state does nothing more than protect the "neutrality" of the market so that individual choice, in the end, may dictate the option that becomes, rightfully, dominant. However, in fact, the liberal state has more often simply been the champion of "improvement" over "orthodoxy." It has taken the side of innovation, presumed that the public interest lay in supporting progressive developments in method against traditional approaches. The myth of the neutrality of the liberal state cannot really be sustained. The state, historically, more often simply takes the side of the more "rational" option.[19]

A fundamental question in dispute between classic and pragmatic liberals is whether the aims of securing reliable performance and of ensuring that established practice is always open to challenge are compatible objectives of policy. The orthodox view is, of course, that when the state regulates to guarantee quality and stability, it also automatically generates rigidity. In the stylized liberal debate, governments are associated with bureaucratic routine and markets with innovation and flexibility. In fact, of course, historically, the state is as often vigorous entrepreneur and champion of creative innovation, while the invisible hand has sometimes guided the firms in an industry toward tranquil acceptance of the tried and true.

Regulated industries may be leaders in research and innovation. The American telecommunications industry long gave testimony to this. Nonetheless, in its efforts to secure reliable performance, the state may indeed cement a specific technology in place, or endorse a particular conception of good practice, for longer than it should. At some point, it may be good policy to open the enterprise to reorganization from the foundations up through a conscious policy of deregulation.

Classic and pragmatic liberals see the process of deregulation quite differently. Classic liberals suppose that removing regulatory restraints is in itself sufficient to revitalize an industry. The market *replaces* regulation. The natural order is restored, and sustained performance balanced with receptivity to change is assured.

Pragmatic liberals see the market as a consciously chosen instrument of policy. The object is to open an enterprise to general reorganization, where the problems are complex and no certain alternative to present practice is in view. The market is an experimental process. But it is not a self-sustaining state of affairs. At some point a new pattern of dominant organization will reemerge, and this will require a new policy of state support and regulation.

The deregulation of the American airline industry in the 1980s is a case in point. A series of changes in technology and practice—the short-range jet, the "hub and spokes" route concept, and computer technology which transformed the possibilities of scheduling and market analysis—combined to make the carefully structured system of noncompetitive or semicompetitive linear routes, modeled in imitation of the railroad network in the 1920s, seem increasingly irrational.

Deregulation did in fact produce a general restructuring of the industry. But its product was not the sustained, robust competition pictured by its early proponents. Rather, the industry rationalized along new lines. Mergers and consolidations led to a new pattern of stable concentration. One system of rational organization and standard practice replaced another, through an interim period of Schumpeterian creative destruction. And it became evident, in time, that the new order would generate problems of public concern of its own and that, at some point, state action would be necessary to resolve them.

The relationship of state to enterprise is not defined in a single, one-time settlement. The working order of an open, pluralist system is in a constant process of change and reconstruction. There are initiatives to promote new forms of collective action, and older enterprises are redefining direction, capability, and purpose.

Ideally, governance is a continuing process of monitoring the performance of enterprise, in which the public policymakers, the officials of enterprise, the practitioners and citizens, are commonly engaged. At any point, shifts in the direction of enterprise, or in the configuration of the pluralist order of enterprise, may suggest that the state's role be recast. Either opportunity or difficulty may suggest the desirability of public action.

The Promotion, Diffusion, and Universalization of Practice

When a new enterprise that represents a clear improvement over customary usage emerges, it is in order for the citizenry to ask whether it should be made more broadly available than the normal processes of market distribution might permit.

In recent U.S. history, there has been public support for libraries, rural electrification, medical and health services, higher education, public transport, culture and the arts. All are examples of efforts by the state to extend a form of systematic practice beyond the marginal point of commercial profitability. The rationale may be equity, that accidents of wealth or location should not determine access to an important social capability. Or it might simply be supposed that the practice ought to be generally available to all citizens. In many cases, such intervention is intended to enhance the rational design of the enterprise itself. It is assumed that a telephone system is better "fitted to purpose" the more global its coverage.

To assure universality, the state may simply constitute the enterprise as a public service, an agency of the government, as it does in the case of police or fire protection. The option is to establish the enterprise as a public utility. In American practice the object of controlling price, conditions of service, and entry and exit in an industry is to secure not only reliability, but universality of service, as well. Given this objective, monopoly is desirable and competition counterproductive. The goal of new entrants into the industry would be to "skim off" the more lucrative services, leaving the "common carrier" at a marked disadvantage.

The fullest exercise of the state's power, however, is to make a form of practice not only universally available, but compulsory. Education, of course, is the prime example. Throughout most of Western history, schooling was simply one of many potential forms of human activity, an optional engagement. (It is not without significance that we consider religion discretionary, education obligatory, while earlier ages put the matter the other way around.) For the liberal polity, however, education was a fundamental prerequisite of citizenship. Perhaps "natural man" could reason his way into the social contract, but he could not be expected to make his way in a working free society. Universal and compulsory education was the necessary guarantee of the integrity of the liberal order, the condition of equal opportunity. Only with universal "liberal" education could we show that institutions were the outcome of free choice. It was not only instruction in basic skills that was required. The more important objective was that the skeptical and analytical mode of reason, traditionally the specialized method of scholars and scientists, be widely, if possible, universally known and used. This was the essential condition of individual competence in free markets and free relationships. Thus the enterprise of the school, hitherto an adjunct of the church or the guilds, or an autonomous institution with purposes and a program of its own, became a central agency of the liberal state.

Social insurance is a second example of the transformation of a "private enterprise" into a function that the state makes compulsory. Historically, insurance is no more than a complex financial mechanism for purchasing security against risk. It was fundamentally an adjunct of commerce and trade, an affair of shipowners and merchants. Later it became a bourgeois means of protecting family fortunes against calamity. However, the risk-sharing characteristics of insurance were suggestive as a response to certain persistent quandaries of the liberal state in dealing with poverty and dependency. How protect the individual, and the family, against destitution due to age, illness, accident, unemployment, or other circumstances beyond individual control? How, at the same time, sustain incentives for each to assume responsibility for securing a livelihood? How create institutions that would not make public dependency a "rational choice?" Perhaps one had to make welfare so degrading and miserable an option—the subsistence-level dole or the Dickensian workhouse—that no one would voluntarily opt to live from public support rather than accept the meanest employment.

The point of social insurance was to require individuals, in partnership with employers and perhaps the state, to secure themselves against dependency. Social insurance essentially imposed an obligation on individuals to secure themselves against becoming public wards, against choosing to act as "free riders," assuming the ratepayers will pick up the tab if they imprudently failed to provide for themselves.

The idea of compulsory social insurance, understood along these lines, first emerged in Bismarck's Germany, where the collective character of insurance, its risk-pooling nature, was understood as a way of revitalizing guild consciousness. But the idea also appealed to the liberal imagination on other grounds, and social insurance became the foundation of the modern welfare state.[20]

We tend to take the existing array of public services for granted. We assume that there is some underlying rationale that distinguishes those services provided through states and those provided through markets. However, there are really no *natural* public goods. Neither schooling nor social insurance, nor police or fire protection, parks, sewers, or street lighting, actually has to be provided by the state.

In fact, the historic pattern is that a new technology or a new form of practice first emerges autonomously as a potential improvement in established usage, as an incipient enterprise. The decision on which of these shall be assimilated to the functions of the state is situational and piecemeal. It reflects no overriding plan, no set of categoric rules. The considerations that influence what shall be regarded as public service and what shall not change from time to time and nation to nation, as the enterprise of liberalism itself progressively evolves. As we know, in Europe, medicine, air and rail transport, telecommunications, energy production, and other complex technologies are generally thought to be appropriate public functions. And the specific history of how such functions came to be so regarded varies greatly from nation to nation and era to era.

The composition of the public and private sectors in any nation reflects different emphases among the criteria that may be used to define a public interest in an enterprise within liberalism. However, it is also a product of the vagaries of how entrepreneurial energy emerges and is applied at different times and places.

Though formal economics seldom acknowledges its presence, there is a form of public entrepreneurship that is as vital in shaping the contours of the political economy as is the private kind. Thus, the U.S. system of national parks owes as much to the entrepreneurial initiative of Gifford Pinchot and John Muir as the design of the auto industry does to Henry Ford and Alfred Sloan.[21] Robert Moses promoted public parks, parkways, and public works as Harriman and Hill consolidated railroads.[22]

As there are always ideas for incipient enterprise emerging spontaneously in the pluralist regime, so there are always proposals for the public support or development of enterprise to be discussed and debated. By what standards, then, should we judge which proposals for public services to support and which to deny? The extreme view of contemporary orthodoxy, that the only legitimate public goods are those whose costs cannot logically be divided among beneficiaries, is far too narrow, theoretically arbitrary, and historically indefensible.[23] Adam Smith took a far more expansive view, regarding it as the "duty of the sovereign" to erect and maintain "those public institutions and those public works which, though they may be in the highest degree advantageous to a great society, are ... of such a nature that the profit could never repay the expense to any individual or small number of individuals."[24] Smith had education and works that would serve trade and commerce, such as harbors and bridges. However, a literal reading of Smith's criterion would mandate state support for *any* incipient enterprise that is regarded as socially valuable and does not find sufficient private support to make it generally available.[25] There is a case for public support for mass transit, let us say, simply *because* it is undercapitalized.

For pragmatic liberalism, public support for the diffusion and universalization of vital enterprises is viewed as a duty of the state, one consistent with the general aims of liberalism itself. The very point of any version of liberalism is to assure that the benefits of civilization are not reserved to an arbitrarily designated few. It is a concern of justice that the distribution of education, medical service, open space, transport, energy, or the protection of the law not depend on accidents of location, income, or similar attributes. It is a matter of relevant distinctions. One might assume that the proper criterion for determining, say, the distribution of medical care, is the state of a person's health not level of income or place of residence.[26]

Nonetheless, there are important distinctions to be drawn between various forms of state support. Some processes of distribution will obviously take care of themselves. Implicitly, we assume that mass production assures adequate access to the automobile or television set, artifacts that today are arguably essentials of the free life. We seem to feel differently, however, about food and housing, both of which we subsidize in various ways.

It is also important to distinguish between those services we would establish as a matter of right, those we define as public utilities, and those which make income or other disadvantage a test of public support.

The strongest, and costliest, universal services are those established as rights. As Arthur Okun once noted, when we designate access to an enterprise to be a matter of right, we do not count the costs. Rights are removed from the economizing calculus of market transactions.[27] The right to vote, and to free speech, is exercised without charge.

(Of course, it would be perfectly possible to put any of these rights on a fee-for-service basis. One could analyze the costs incurred by representatives in listening to constituent complaints, answering mail, attending meetings and public hearings, and establish a compensatory user fee for exercising the right of petition. Such a policy might have beneficial effects for democratic government. At least it might lead the protagonists to weigh their words more carefully and thus elevate the general tone of public debate. To make free speech other than a free good might make it more valuable. However, to my knowledge, not even the staunchest advocates of public sector frugality have gone this far.)

By a similar logic, one is entitled to police and fire protection on demand and without charge, without regard to remoteness, value of property, or complexity of the case. In effect, in establishing access to the enterprise as a matter of right, we would have standard practice available to all, as required. As a matter of policy, we introduce no incentives to economical use. We would have no one "think twice" before calling the police or the ambulance. This is the crux of the matter when we deliberate service as a matter of right.

The alternative is to define an enterprise as a public utility. Here users are expected to bear some or all of the costs of service. Incentives to economizing are intended, but the enterprise is constituted as a cost-sharing community. One object of regulation is to reduce the disparity between fees that might be charged remote and proximate users, high- and low-volume customers, in the name of universal accessibility. We have done this traditionally in electric power, telecommunications, and transport. (We can mix user fees and direct support in many ways to secure wide access to a service, as we do with parks and universities, thus combining the features of the direct public service and the cost-sharing utility.)

The dedicated adherents of unencumbered markets of course think the "cross-subsidization" of less economic by more economic users fundamentally unfair. Their point seems to be that if people want airline or bus service, quality education or adequate health care, they should go to places where these services can be rendered economically, but that the citizens of, let us say, Chicago, should not be obliged to pay extra to support the few in the privilege of living in, let us say, Duluth or Fargo. In recent years, these advocates of calculated individualism have worked hard to discredit the historic idea of the public utility. At the same time, large concerns have displayed their consummate sense of public responsibility by opting out of public utilities as quickly as possible, shifting business to operators who deal principally with the more profitable segments of the market, as in telecommunications, and competitors of the postal service. These forces have done much to undermine a good idea, for the public utility remains a unique instrument, one of the most useful ways of securing universality, incentives to economical use, enterprise autonomy, and reliable performance.

The third possibility is to make public support contingent on income poverty. In effect, the state is relying on the market for general distribution and compensating only for marked distortions in the scheme of income distribution. This is the form of universalization of access we try to secure through food stamps, rent subsidies, scholarships based on need, and many other policies of the same kind. In liberalism, the market is a perfect distributor only where there is relative income equality. This is a matter to which we shall return.

In the end, it is on the question of the state's role in promoting universal access to enterprise that classical and pragmatic liberals most sharply divide. Classic liberals acknowledge the persuasiveness of the pragmatic liberal case. In fact, they think it irresistible, beguiling, and that followed to its logical conclusion, it would spell the end of the liberal order. Virtually every worthwhile enterprise can be defined as a vital service that should be generally available. Politicians have an interest in offering a constantly expanding array of services to constituents and practitioners in extending the scope of their operations and their clientele. The end of all this will be a burden of public expenditure greater than the economy can bear; it will increase bureaucratic rigidity which will imperil the productive functions of the market. The only remedy is resolute self-control, a determination to resist any entreaties to establish public support for enterprise beyond that minimum required to secure the elemental integrity of the market.

The pragmatic liberal response to this is, again, that it is perfectly possible to distinguish between legitimate public purposes and abuses and that one can account for the objections of orthodoxy in the design of programs by assuring that measures taken to universalize access to enterprises are as economic as possible and include incentives to economic use.

But here we reach an unbridgeable gulf in the argument, for it is one based on differing primary assumptions. The classical liberal, operating from a basic psychology of calculated interest, assumes axiomatically that citizens will prefer apparently costless public services to commodities priced in the market, and that the inevitable result of unrestrained democratic choice in this regard will be economic ruin. The pragmatic liberal, believing in the efficacy of intelligent collaborative action, assumes that it is perfectly possible to distinguish those enterprises whose availability is a prerequisite of the free life from those that are discretionary engagements.

By the same token, the classical liberal presumes that any public service is to be regarded as a withdrawal from productive activity, for wealth can only be generated by private endeavor. The pragmatic liberal simply denies this distinction, assuming that public action in support of the rational development of enterprise generally enhances productive capability.

In the end, the dialectic of liberal argument does proceed, though in an asymmetric way. Pragmatic liberals regard the concerns of orthodoxy to be legitimate. They are to be weighed in the balance in the deliberation of policy. Universalization is costly. It obviously becomes increasingly expensive as one tries to reach the most remote, or oblivious, citizens. The presumption of liberalism is in favor of free choice and self-support. Thus, the case for public action must be strong. But these are considerations of prudence, not grounds for reducing the public services offered by a society to the meanest minimum.

The Public Interest in Religion, Science, and Culture

Throughout, I have spoken of religious practices, the organized forms of science and scholarship, culture and the arts, as rational enterprises. These have then, presumably, a political and public dimension, as do economic enterprises, and we should consider the nature of the public interest, and the part the state should play, in their development.

Americans, despite their strong views on freedom of thought and expression, do admit a public role in the cultivation of science and learning, and support for the arts. However, Americans, by law and tradition, take a categorical position on the separation of church and state. The idea that we should consider the "public interest" in religion along the lines we have been following so far will seem to many dangerous counsel, illiberal, perhaps sacrilegious. Nonetheless, let us pursue this line of thought simply to find out where it leads.

In fact, of course, the American position is idiosyncratic. Many liberal nations, Great Britain and the Scandinavians in particular, do support established churches even as they practice religious toleration. In such nations, there is at least a historic residue of the idea that the diffusion of faith is, in part, a public responsibility.

It might then be observed that American "free market" arrangements seem to have led to a more robust and vital expression of faith than has been characteristic of nations where the state has underwritten the religious enterprise. The differentiation and diffusion of religion in the United States has been an overwhelming success. Every nuance of doctrine is available, and access to the church is at least as universal as access to the post office, the newspaper, the doctor, or the school.

However, the American position has other consequences. It is forbidden to seriously question the condition of faith as a public issue. Critical public discussion of the *quality* of religion provided by the institutions of worship is sharply discouraged. Sanctimonious laments for the decline of faith are of course customary, but one does not ask, in the spirit of rational criticism that we apply to other endeavors, whether current practice in the churches is in fact best practice, and whether there is some public interest in assuring the competence of the establishments of religion.

We live in a peculiar and most unrepresentative moment in Western history. We take it for granted that the claims of faith and those of reason are distinct, that science and religion are separate, perhaps hostile, enterprises. Of course, in the larger Judeo-Christian tradition, faith and reason were presumed to be complementary, and science, or rational inquiry, was normally understood to be a sacred vocation. Its task was, as Saint Augustine put it, "to justify the ways of God to man."[28] Liberalism itself, of course, rests on the historic affirmation that the order of nature, and of human nature, can be known by reason, that the will of the Creator, in matters of human conduct, can be discerned by "common sense," at least in its rudiments. In this it follows the ancient intimations of the Judeo-Christian tradition, of Plato, Aristotle, and Roman Stoic thought as well.

It is true that the Roman Catholic church, some Protestant denominations, and some elements of Judaism are constituted as communities of inquiry and communities of good practice. They assume a responsibility for the ongoing critical scrutiny of doctrine and for the quality of the teachings and observances of their practitioners. However, in the larger free market of American popular religion, there is much opportunity for charlatanism and fraud.

Is there a public interest in the standards of good practice of the religious institutions? All of our American instincts rebel against the thought. We understand that we live with a political settlement, with a historic rule designed as much to secure civil peace as to ensure freedom of conscience. Thus, the question of how reason and faith should speak to one another in the public forum, in the interest of the progressive development of each, simply does not arise. The result is that Americans generally assume that science is a progressive and developing force, while religion is a finished product, an inheritance to be preserved, but not to be nurtured, or explored, through the processes of inquiry that we apply to all other undertakings. We do not think it possible to come to a better understanding of the ways of God. In the interest of public peace and toleration in a pluralistic society, we have given up all hope that rational deliberation and analysis might yield a more perfect understanding of the will of our Creator. In this, our liberalism is quite unlike historic liberalism, and our science quite unlike historic science

The Enterprise and the Public Household

The idea that the state should support the rational development of enterprise is distinctive to pragmatic liberalism. Orthodox political economy is, in fact, largely indifferent to the specific nature of the thing produced, the character of the practice, or the service rendered. For orthodox political economy, the public interest lies not in the actual usefulness of the product or the activity of an enterprise, but in its indirect effects. It is the contribution of the enterprise to economic growth, employment, trade, and public revenue that matters.

The goals of policy, then, are taken to have to do with the overall performance of the economy and not with its specific content. The purpose of the unencumbered market, for Smith, was to promote the "wealth" of nations, as are the various measures of Keynesian or post-Keynesian interventionism. The object is straightforwardly Benthamite—to increase the sum of satisfactions available to the community, without regard for its specific composition. The goals are also implicitly mercantilist. The point of policy is to improve the economic position of one's jurisdiction in competition with rivals. The goal is, bluntly, to distort the conditions of the open market by suitable incentives and restraints on trade to achieve local advantage. These are the policy aims of nations and increasingly, of U.S. states and cities.

Such objectives justify a wide range of state actions, and some are directed toward specific enterprises. Thus, the state "targets" specified industries, subsidizing research and development, or providing taxation or marketing incentives. The benefits of such policies are calculated in terms of public revenues generated, jobs created, the revitalization of regions, exports over imports.

We have become so accustomed to this as the language of policy and public debate that we do not realize quite how extraordinary it is. However, for pragmatic liberalism, this exclusive preoccupation with the macroeconomic consequences of the performance of enterprise is disturbing doctrine. It places undue emphasis on the economic rather than the substantive qualities of the performance of enterprise. In Veblen's terms, it exaggerates pecuniary interest over workmanship and neglects the essential problem of social provision. When states begin to see their universities primarily as a source of support for "high-tech" industry and when we come to regard fast-food franchising as the leading edge of economic development because of the jobs it generates, something has obviously gone wrong with our whole way of thinking about the management of the public household.

CHAPTER

5

The State and the Constitution

of the Enterprise

For pragmatic liberalism, the diverse human associations have a political character. They are institutions of political order. They are part of the greater regime. In what respects then are their political form and structure a constitutional question, a matter for public deliberation and decision?

There are three questions to be considered. First, what is the role of the state in defining the aims and purposes of the enterprise, its legitimate social function? Second, what part should it play in establishing and guaranteeing its internal system of government? Third, what role should the liberal state play in structuring the entire system of relationships among the enterprises, and of these with the state?

Each of these questions, as we shall see, raises a problem of autonomy and control, and of theory and practice. It is a matter in each case of striking a balance between the particular aims of enterprises and the general values and interests of the liberal commonwealth.

The Stipulation of Purpose

If practical political reason depends on finding a relation between principle and practice, how do we in fact construe the aims of an enterprise for purposes of public action? This is a difficult question, and the dilemmas involved in answering it are immediately apparent. First, there is the difficulty of securing agreement to *any* particular definition of the essential aims of an organization or undertaking. But even should we resolve this, the issue arises of whether such a definition should be imposed on the enterprise as a matter of law and policy.

It is obvious that the aims of the corporation, the church, the profession, or the school can be viewed differently, from the distinctive vantage points of different interests and constituencies. For some, the purpose of the business enterprise is to create profits; for others, it is to make useful products. For some its aim is to secure employment, for others, to generate public revenues. Perhaps the idea of the purpose of an enterprise is what the philosopher W. B. Gallie called an "essentially contested concept." Like democracy or equality, it is a crucial idea, where the parties recognize contending usages, but where each insists that its own use is correct and where there is no standard for settling disputes.[1]

My own view is that the definition of purpose is a necessary function of public deliberation and decision. It is not an affair of the parties to the undertaking alone. In fact, it is probably true that normally a conception of the public purpose of an enterprise only emerges as a product of public scrutiny of its performance or its internal order.

In the evolution of enterprise, the conception of purpose is often inchoate and unspecified. To secure collaborative action among people of diverse views and inclinations, it is often best not to put too sharp a point on things. A certain irresolution about essential purposes is also essential to sustaining the enterprise as an open community of inquiry, one which is capable of reexamining its fundamental preconceptions and usages.

The initial formulation of an idea of essential purpose probably is needed only under conditions of public critique and challenge. It is when a community of practice is asked to *justify* its ways that the need to construct a rationale based on essential function and purpose arises. The task of formulating this defense of practice first falls to those most clearly identified with prevailing method—the conservatives, the loyalists.

This case for the "prescriptive constitution" must be made. It is an essential basing point for further judgment. (Later on, in chapter 10, I try to spell out in detail the relationship between the various "cases" that must be made if political deliberation is to be considered and complete.)

Of course, the case for prevailing usage is not in fact prescriptive. It is subject to criticism and reconsideration in the light of general standards of good performance that apply to any enterprise within the liberal order. And this is a function of public deliberation. It is not the concern alone of the members of the community of practice and inquiry.

It is a maxim of formal liberalism that the state should be neutral among human interests, that social arrangements are legitimate if they arise from voluntary, contractual consent. Liberal associations are formally construed as self-organizing systems, which take their aims from the convergence of individual interests of those who are parties to them. Yet, in practice, we have to draw public distinctions between the various *forms* of enterprise, and sanction these distinctions through law and policy.

We do invoke ideas of institutional purpose in practical political argument. We advocate policies on the ground that they will "advance science" or "strengthen the family." We use arguments from essential purpose to make distinctions in law and policy. We take exception to comprehensive models. Thus, we say, a university cannot be treated as though it were a corporation, and a family farm is not exactly like a factory. We thus maintain a sense for what Michael Walzer has called the "art of separation."[2] We discern that there are different "spheres of justice," that different institutions require particular policies, different public treatment.

We may acknowledge that practical political discourse requires some stipulation of institutional purpose. But does this imply that it is the duty of the state to *enforce* such conceptions of purpose on the relevant communities of practice?

We here enter into an ancient controversy.

The issue that was posed in the theory of classic pluralism was whether the association was to be regarded as a "legal fiction" as Savigny thought, or whether it had "real personality," as Gierke and Maitland insisted. The language now has an antiquated sound. Nonetheless, the stakes were real. The historic corporation was a specific grant of state power, which conferred legal form, rights, and authority, Yet, if this was *all* it was, it followed that the association was merely a creature of the state, and that the definition of the associational regime was a sovereign prerogative. The alternative was to take the view that the human enterprises and associations were "natural" products of society which the state was obligated to protect and support.[3]

The concern is still fundamental in ordinary liberal thought. Liberals define totalitarianism precisely as a regime that would use the factory, the union, the school, and the family as instruments of political indoctrination and control. We think it a corruption of public authority for the state to subvert an autonomous association, or transform it into an instrument for its own ends.

The notion of academic freedom is perhaps particularly instructive as an indicator of this dimension of our thought. Academic freedom is not, in fact, derived from liberal rights of freedom of expression, for not everyone has an equal entitlement to speak in the forums of the university. For liberal democrats to insist that the university should *not* teach as the legislature directs, they must, it would seem, repair to a notion of distinctly medieval lineage, that the state should support and protect an institution dedicated specifically to free and systematic inquiry.

The stipulation of function for an enterprise is not, then, properly the prerogative of the state. Nor do I think we believe it exclusively the affair of the contracting parties. I do not believe we are willing to say that a family is anything to which consenting adults decide to apply the term, or that it is up to the owners to determine what a corporation *is*, how it is entitled to act and how it is properly constituted.

We do draw fundamental distinctions among the various forms of association. Despite the universalizing ambition of classical liberalism to reduce all kinds of affiliation to the basic terms of contract, we in fact do have separate realms of law for the corporation, the trade union, the family. Our conception of each of these forms of organization rests on concrete historic deliberations and choices among alternatives. Thus, the business corporation came, in the early nineteenth century, to be understood not as a specific grant of privilege for the performance of a particular public purpose—to found a bank or school, to build a bridge or canal—but as a standardized method of organization, a "general utility" open for the expression of entrepreneurial energy.[4] Conversely, in the late 1800s the municipal corporation, the chartered "city" of colonial and early national times, came to be seen primarily as an instrument of state administration, an agency charged with the delivery of particular public services and the performance of specified regulatory functions.[5]

In everyday legislation, public administration, and legal interpretation, we have to make clear distinctions between the various forms of association. We have to determine what a school, or a church, is and is not, for such categories convey legal rights and responsibilities.

At this point, my concern is simply that we acknowledge the constitutive character of our deliberations on the idea of the corporation, the university, the club, the family. Out of such efforts, the specific character of our civilization emerges. We sanction certain possibilities for human engagement, to the neglect of others. This is a concern of liberal politics as important as the precise definition of individual rights or the specification of a just and representative process for the election of public officials. To the question of whether the state should play a role in defining the purpose of enterprise, then, I have answered that this is a practical necessity. I have also argued that the critical analysis which leads to a formal conception of function must arise out of an appreciation of the rationale for prevailing practice. Once again, this is a problem of the relation of theory and practice.

The State and the Constitution of the Enterprise

Like the stipulation of purpose, in pure, formal liberal theory the internal political order of the enterprise is of concern only to its members. So long as the conditions of free contract and free association are met, the state is indifferent to its political form. Presumably, the individual is free to choose hierarchy or democracy, equal rights or prescriptive status, critical deliberation or settled doctrine, in church, guild, or occupation. (Of course, one is not free to assent to slavery, indentured servitude, or other inherently exploitative relationships.)

In principle, the political structure of the association evolves autonomously. Yet in fact the liberal state remains the residual framer of its political order. It invests the enterprise with legal form. As Willard Hurst writes, "A statutory charter had content beyond a mere license for private will: in its details it was more like a constitution, fixing the internal structure of the corporation."[6]

There are, in fact, three different ways in which we can understand the constitution-making responsibilities of the state in relation to the enterprise. We can see it as a matter of securing the rights of contract and free association. Or we can understand it as a matter of guaranteeing a democratic form of government within the enterprise. Or we can think in terms of extending to the government of the enterprise the basic norms of the legal order.

Contractual Voluntarism

It is not true that the liberal state, historically, has been indifferent to the political order of the enterprise. In fact, the objective of the newly emergent liberal states in the eighteenth and nineteenth centuries was to rationalize and standardize the total structure of associations and institutions within the regime. The public purpose was to break the grip of ancient particularistic rights, rules and arrangements, the pattern of medieval feudalities, orders and statuses, and to reconstitute society on the basis of a universal norm of contract. As Wolfgang Friedman observed, "The evolution from status to contract, from immobility to mobility, gradually pervaded all spheres of life, beyond the fields of commercial and labor contract. It invaded family relations and the law of succession. It became the basis of club and union membership."[7]

Thus, there is an expectation that the liberal state will act as the guarantor of the political order of enterprise, and of the broader institutional framework of the total liberal regime. At the very least, it must maintain the conditions of contractual voluntarism; it must protect against force and fraud in such relationships. This expectation alone empowers the liberal state to stipulate, in some detail, the political forms that private government may and may not take.

Democratic Process

Explicitly or implicitly in establishing the legal form of the association, the state stipulates a constitution for its governance. The corporation is made responsible to its owners—a notion of "sovereign authority" as disputable in liberal logic as the idea that it should be responsible to the workers alone. Many recent changes in family and property law are intended to redefine the constitution of the family, to democratize it, to remove the expectations, and the sanctions, of paternal authority.

When we come to recognize the enterprise as a private government, as an institution that participates in authoritative decision making, it might seem incumbent on the liberal state to assure that it rests on consent, to guarantee a democratic form of government within the organization. However, as we have already seen, it is by no means apparent, as a matter of liberal democratic theory, how the constituency of the enterprise should be stipulated, to whose interests it should be made responsible. Furthermore, as a matter of historical experience, we have been quite reluctant to impose a particular vision of democratic order as a norm for the constitution of enterprise.

The more general view has been that the political order of the enterprise was an internal matter, so long as basic conditions of contractual probity are met. Mr. Justice Frankfurter's words that courts have "a duty to enforce the rights of members of an association . . . according to the laws of that association . . . Legislatures have no obligation to adjudicate and no such power"[8] seems to capture our basic spirit about such matters.

However, when the association becomes in some significant sense involuntary, in the liberal scheme of things, democracy may be a requirement of legitimate governance. In our experience, the most evident case is the law of industrial relations. When the collective contract replaces individual bargaining, the rights of individual action are sharply curtailed. The corollary is the imposition of democratic practice on the union. The entire scheme of industrial relations becomes, in fact, a matter of public concern, and an issue of prescribing constitutional frameworks and norms for the union, and for the institutions of collective bargaining. In the United States, by the time of the Landrum-Griffin Act, most of the procedural standards associated with constitutional democracy, including periodic elections, the secret ballot, free speech, the right of nomination and opposition, were imposed on the trade union by law and enforced by public authority.[9]

Similarly, the political party has been seen as a distinctive case, an institution where the state must oversee internal democratic processes. In part, this is because the function of the party is integral to the democratic political process as a whole. In part, however, this is because the party system is regarded as less than a product of full and free contractual association. The Progressive legislation which "rationalized" the U.S. electoral process after the turn of the century was intended, in part, to institutionalize the two-party system. It provided special advantages to the dominant parties and hampered the development of new partisan formations. In effect, the dominant parties were to be regarded as "public utilities" with a quasi-monopoly status, and this implied that their internal political order was a proper object of public regulation.[10]

To some extent, contractual voluntarism and democratic process are alternative means for securing the responsiveness of organizations to individual will and interest. As Albert Hirschman observes, "exit," the power to leave the association, and "voice," participation in its governance, are two general processes that individuals can use to deal with unsatisfactory institutional performance.[11]

For the liberal state, then, the creation or maintenance of marketlike arrangements normally seems as pertinent to securing legitimate government for the enterprise as requiring democracy within the institution. To break up monopolistic arrangements is as relevant a course of public action as reconstituting them along democratic lines. To create "choice" in schooling may be a more effective means of securing responsiveness than enhancing the autonomy of local school boards. As Hurst has noted, the legitimacy of the business corporation in the law of the United States depends less on the rights of shareholders to elect officers and participate in assemblies of owners, and more on their ability to exchange their shares quickly and efficiently in a regulated stock market.[12]

In present context, the important point is that the definition of the relationship between contractual voluntarism and democratic process in the constitutional arrangements of any enterprise is a persistent theme for practical political reason, and for public policy-making in the liberal state.

Due Process of Law

In recent years particularly, we have come increasingly to see the organization as a source and realm of law, and we have moved to make its internal order more consistent with the higher-order norms of the legal process. Thus, the state has required corporations, universities, and professions to acknowledge basic rights of fair procedure and due process in cases that involved the termination or discipline of employees or members. Similarly, rights against discrimination are increasingly being enforced against enterprises and associations, wherever a plausible public interest in the functions of the organization can be found. Thus, private clubs that can reasonably be considered as serving as "forums" for business negotiations and civic deliberations may be said to have a public character, and membership in them cannot be determined on arbitrary or exclusionary grounds.

In normal day-to-day transactions, "rights" may be more important than "participation" or "choice" for the citizen of a modern, complex society. For the consumer, it is the expectation of good performance and fair treatment rather than the ability to go elsewhere or be heard at a meeting that matters when things go wrong. For the employee, protection against arbitrary authority on the job, in hiring, promotion and termination, probably means more than the possibility of changing jobs, or workplace democracy. In these respects, the extension of legal rights and procedures to the enterprise is part of that process of underwriting rational performance and good practice which, in my view, is a central aim of the liberal state.

Nonetheless, we must recognize that extending the domain of legality is not entirely compatible with increasing democratic participation or providing a richer diversity of pluralistic, marketlike arrangements. The more one refines one's notions of what the individual is entitled to expect from the enterprise, the less scope it has for autonomous action, the less diverse its forms are likely to be.

For example, industrial democracy might provide more employee participation in determining the hours, organization, and rhythms of work. But it is hard to see how the democratic autonomy of the shop could extend much further. Beyond this, rights of other parties begin to appear. The autonomy of the shop is limited by obligations to consumers and suppliers for the reliability and quality of its performance, and there are rights of the citizens against the government of the industrial democracy, to fair treatment and to due process of law.

Pragmatic Liberalism and the Constitution of the Enterprise

The sustained scrutiny of the political order of the enterprise, the continuing critical analysis of its system of government, is congenial to the spirit of pragmatic liberalism. In the deliberations of the liberal public, there should be a constant tension, a concern that all forms of governance be brought into closer conformity with the basic values of the regime.

Yet pragmatic liberalism takes issue with those who would universalize a certain model of institutional legitimacy simply to make the liberal regime uniform and consistent in all its parts. Thus, the aim is not merely to extend the domain of free markets, or democratic participation, or that of rights, for its own sake. To be sure, these are the causes zealously championed by many orthodox liberal theorists. But, rather, the object is to *orchestrate* the institutions of contractual voluntarism, democratic process, and legality, so as to create an institutional design that fits the specific purpose, and the traditions of practice, of a particular enterprise.

I earlier suggested that the constitutional model for pragmatic liberalism was not pure hierarchy, democratic assembly, or market contract—any more than it is pure adjudication—but the ideal of a community of inquiry that is also a community of good practice.

For purposes of law and policy, this is an ideal to be construed flexibly. The enterprise constituted as community of inquiry needs a charter stipulated in general terms. An enterprise open to the persistent reexamination of practice, technique, and the terms of its own internal political system must have substantial rights of autonomous development. This is the basic norm. Hence, the ideal charter of firm or family, university or profession, stipulates purpose no more narrowly than is necessary to prevent identifiable abuses or corruptions (as in using the special status of a "church" for profit-making activities).

However, the community of inquiry is also the community of good practice, and we have noted before, the state may identify a public interest in the reliability or universalization of a certain performance. The enterprise then is constituted as a public utility, and its scope of action is restricted by more detailed considerations of public purpose. The problem of practical reason, again, in defining the constitution of any enterprise, is to strike a balance between the claims of flexibility and of reliable performance, between substance and procedure. And once again, this is an issue that cannot be settled by abstract principle, but only in consideration of the characteristics of a particular human undertaking.

The Pluralist Regime

Let us now return to the question with which we began. What is the place of the enterprise in the liberal regime? Liberal political theory is primarily concerned with the relations of individuals and the state, and liberal constitutions rarely define the place of the critical associations in the political order. We have talked of the constitution *of* the enterprise. But where do such associations fit *in* the constitution of the liberal political order?

The forerunners of pragmatic liberalism, very much aware of the importance of the complex organization in the changing civilization of this century, tried to envision an open and democratic regime that would be an order of associations as well as individuals. This early pluralist thought had a variety of sources. Hegel described an idea of the state as an organic order of associations.[13] Fichte, von Gierke, Maitland, Comte, and many others advocated some form of pluralist doctrine.[14] Durkheim taught that organizations and professional associations might serve as a new source of community and that an occupational ethic might replace lost traditions of morality in a world where historic ties had broken down in the face of the specialization and the rationalization of technique.[15] Many of the early pluralist theorists harked back to a medieval ideal of an order of self-governing guilds and corporations.[16]

Classic pluralist thought is interwoven with the legacy of pragmatic liberalism. Thus, John Dewey taught that the state "was a distinctive and secondary form of association, having a specifiable work to do." A good state "renders the desirable associations solider and more coherent; indirectly, it clarifies their aims and purges their activities."[17]

In fact, we tend to forget how widespread pluralist ideas were in the early decades of the century, at that point when the frame of mind we associate with pragmatic liberalism was taking shape. The position was general, even commonplace. In 1926, John Maynard Keynes could write that "progress lies in the growth and the recognition of semi-autonomous bodies within the state ... bodies which in the ordinary course of affairs are mainly autonomous ... but are subject in the last resort to the sovereignty of the democracy expressed through Parliament. I propose a return, it may be said, towards Medieval conceptions of particular autonomies."[18] In Britain, G. D. H. Cole and Harold Laski taught a doctrine of guild socialism, in which a confederation of functional associations would serve as a sovereign legislative authority for a comprehensive order of industrial democracy. In the United States, Mary Parker Follett proposed a similar ideal for the "New State."[19]

The view that the state was one association among many, its task to harmonize relations among the rest, influenced not only the pluralist theory that became a major teaching of political science but public policy as well. The Progressives thought that relations between business, labor, and the state could be cooperative rather than adversarial, that the object of policy was to organize, coordinate, and stabilize the industrial order. Such convictions, more than Populist discontent, underlay the early regimes of industrial regulation, such as those created by the Interstate Commerce Commission and the Federal Communications Commission. They may be associated with early antitrust, consumer protection, and wages and hours legislation. However, the pluralist ideal appears most clearly in Hoover administration efforts to empower trade associations as institutions of industrial self-regulation, a movement that found further expression in the National Recovery Administration of the New Deal and in various institutions of wartime planning.[20]

Given this heritage, it might be thought that a reconstructed theory of pragmatic liberalism would culminate in some idea of functional representation, some vision of a pluralist or corporatist regime. However, as we shall now see, it is very difficult to reconcile any general scheme of interest or associational representation with the basic norms and principles of liberal democracy.

Interest-Group Pluralism

For political science, interest-group pluralism was long the dominant conception of how the associational order could be reconciled to the political process of a liberal regime. The basic idea is that group representation serves as a proxy for "pure" democracy under modern conditions. The true conditions of democratic participation can only be approximated in small and homogeneous groups and communities. The modern state is remote, and interest associations provided immediate and highly differentiated forms of political engagement for the citizen. The coalition formed from group negotiations represented the closest feasible approximation of the aggregate public interest. As Robert Dahl argued, the result would be a system not of majority rule, but of "minorities rule."[21]

The usual critique of interest-group liberalism is that some interests are systematically neglected or disadvantaged in the competitive struggle. There is an inherent bias in favor of the wealthy, the socially competent, and the organizable over the poor, the uneducated, and the disbursed.[22]

However, as a theory of the regime, the problem of interest-group pluralism lies deeper. To say that a policy "represents a configuration of group demands" does not constitute a justification for public action in any known form of liberal democratic theory, save interest-group pluralism itself. To be intelligible as a ground of liberal political argument, the interest-group liberal would have to show that some configuration of interests reflected a pattern of individual wills, equally considered, and this interest-group theory cannot do.

In the formal theory, marketlike qualities are imputed to group process. The invisible hand of competition guides the system toward the creation of "countervailing forces" and long-run "equilibrium." Leaving aside all questions of intrinsic disparities in group power, there is a question of the formal validity of the principle. How does the "configuration of interests" at any time authorize public action? How does it obligate the citizen to comply?

Interest-group pluralism cannot provide a theory of the regime. It contains no criteria for defining the interests to be taken into account, no grounds for the inclusion or exclusion of any association, or for the weighting of appropriate influence among interests. Any group that forms autonomously has a claim to representation equivalent to any other group. For that reason, any policy attributed to group process can be challenged by pointing to some interest not accounted for in the definition of policy. Democratic majoritarianism, for all its faults, is at least definitive as a rule of legitimacy. Interest group pluralism does not have that attribute.

Corporatist Representation

The logical alternative to interest-group pluralism is generally thought to be some scheme of corporatist representation. *Corporatism* is the term properly applied to a structured system for the representation of functional associations. In pluralist systems, groups are multiple, voluntary, and competitive. They have no official status as part of the state structure. In corporatist systems, interest groups are, in effect, "licensed" by the state. They are granted a formal representational monopoly, and membership in them is normally compulsory.[23]

It is true that institutions with a corporatist flavor exist in all liberal nations. Proposals for structures of this type are a feature of the ongoing public debate. Most schemes of industrial policy or economic planning rely on structures of this type, as do most forms of professional regulation and licensing. In the composition of councils, committees, and boards of directors, whether for public agencies, corporations, or universities, representation of "affected interests" is a principle frequently appealed to or applied, and at times, some such system of representation is required by law.

But it is extremely difficult to justify any scheme of interest representation through liberal principles. We may say that a commission on mental health should include representatives of the practitioners, the clients, the community—but who else? How does one show that such a scheme is legitimate, that it is logical and exhaustive? In economic planning, the triune relationship of business, labor, and the public seems, intuitively, to make sense. There is a pleasing symmetry about the relationship. But what in fact does it mean? Business, presumably, is interested in profit, and labor in wages. What then of the "public" interest? Perhaps the "public" interest is to be construed as the "consumer" interest, and consumers are assumed to be interested in prices. This may be the underlying logic of the arrangement—that out of interest-group tugging and hauling, some sort of economic equilibrium will emerge, rather as in the market. But if we take the "public" interest to be the consumer interest, is not the state's interest identifiably distinct? And if, in fact, the state is to represent the public interest in the serious sense of the term, how defend minority status for what is, one would think, the only legitimate basis of public policy? And what of the "interests" of the environment, or of generations yet unborn? Should such interests have equal standing with those of labor and management? If so, why? If not, why not? By virtue of what principle can one defend any such scheme of interest representation and the proportionate weight of its members?

Of course, any system of functional representation must have an underlying rationale. Classic Catholic corporatism could appeal to Aristotelian and Thomist theories of "natural associations" in defense of its conception of the critical interests to be represented, but liberalism cannot. Liberalism cannot prefigure the relevant distribution of interests. The state cannot fix the regime of purposive associations. That must evolve by itself, from voluntary association and the self-reflective development of the communities of practice.

Furthermore, any convincing justification for a system of functional representation would have to include guarantees of the authenticity of representation. How does one show that a student representative on a university committee actually reflects the views of the constituents in question, or that a "public" or "consumer" representative on a corporate board mirrors the attitudes of those for whom they are designated to speak? How devise a democratic process for every such instance of interest representation that would guarantee even a minimum of fidelity to democratic precepts?

In fact, the case for corporatist institutions in liberal societies is usually argued in practical, instrumental terms. The collaboration of labor and management is presumed necessary to give effect to public economic policy, and their participation in the formulation of policy is a useful inducement to cooperation with public aims.

While the creation of privileged positions of influence for powerful groups is offensive to liberal democratic sensitivities, this is in fact a case for functional representation that is compatible with liberal principles of political design. Interest representation is seen purely as a mechanism of administration. The problem is to devise institutions that will elicit the support, and coordinate the efforts, of interests that have a vital role to play in the execution of policy, or to provide forums that will bring presumably hostile or competitive parties together, to cause them to deliberate and arrive at common policy.

Such systems can be defended within the liberal regime because they supplement, but do not displace, the legitimate forms of authority. The interests that are represented are those whose participation is essential to effect a democratically defined purpose, or those whose overt conflict would be socially destructive. The relevant grounds for contesting such policies, then, bear on the efficiency of the institutions in achieving designated ends, and also on the question of whether such institutions do in fact become dominant over those of formal, representative democracy.

Form Follows Function

It becomes apparent that the issue of the constitution of the enterprise cannot be settled through a theory of representation alone. There is no way in which pure liberal or democratic principle can yield a solution to the problem of the proper political order of the complex organization.

Once again, some notion of *purpose* must be introduced if we are to find sensible grounds on which to evaluate the political order of the association. Liberalism is primarily a theory of impartial procedure. But a theory of political design must include a substantive element as well. Our notions of how an association is properly constituted follow from an idea of what that institution is expected to *do*. The motto of the modernist movement in architecture applies to liberal political engineering as well. Form follows function in the design of political institutions, as well as buildings.

I think we can see the point of hierarchic arrangements in armies, aircraft cockpits, and operating rooms, where precise, coordinated action is paramount and unconstrained deliberation a handicap. I think we also find a qualified version of such authority defensible, if not obligatory, in a church, or a science, where fundamental understanding is at issue, where error matters greatly, and where all opinions do not count the same.

Nonetheless, it is the iron law of liberalism that deviations from freedom and equality, from choice and vote, and from full and free discussion must be justified. Thus, it is always in order to scrutinize existing arrangements, repeatedly to reopen the question of whether such deviations from the strong force of liberal principles are necessary at all.

In the end, the pertinent defense of the particular political arrangements of any enterprise is to show that they are well suited to purpose. In effect, the burden falls to the enterprise to show that its authority structures and the sanctions it exercises are appropriate to the promotion of reliable performance and the maintenance of standards, and that its internal procedures of deliberation and decision are designed to ensure the continuing critical reevaluation of technique. To the extent, then, that an enterprise is constituted as a community of inquiry and a community of practice, its political order is properly regarded as compatible with that of the larger liberal regime.

Classic liberalism searches for universal norms and principles. It seeks to abstract from particulars, to "rationalize" by subsuming specific cases under general rules. Thus there is a tendency in liberal theory to understand *all* associations as undifferentiated instances of a single norm, such as voluntary contract or democratic process, and to suppose that the relation of the state to the enterprise, and the structure of the internal order of the enterprise, can only be legitimate if it is consistent with one of these forms.

However, for pragmatic liberalism, it is appropriate that each enterprise have a particular relationship with the state. The relationship of the state to the total associational order ought to be differentiated and diverse. The state ought to have a different relationship to the business firm, the churches, the universities, the labor unions, and the professions. The proper ordering of the regime of enterprise calls for even finer distinctions, for the proper governance of the auto industry is not the same as that of the insurance business, and the government of wheat is not at all like that of dairying. This is the view, I would argue, that is most appropriate in defining the total framework of the liberal regime. And it is also a view that is consistent with pragmatic liberalism's longer continuities, with its historic instinct that there was something in the medieval tradition of an order of functionally specific guilds and corporations, each with its own distinctive charter, rights, and duties, that was peculiarly compatible with the terms of liberal democratic politics in a complex industrial society.

Now, as we shall see, to insist on a specific fit between theory and practice defines not only pragmatic liberalism's position on the constitutional question, on the issues of form and structure, but also its political economy—its conception of the role of the state in the productive process and in the distribution of the social product.

A Pragmatic Liberal
Political Economy

CHAPTER

6

The Management of

the Economy

In the next three chapters, I outline a pragmatic liberal approach to political economy. I try to show how this method of analysis might be applied to some of the more important public issues in that area where the work of the world and the processes of government meet.

First we consider the role of the state in the overall management of the process of production. Then we discuss issues of the just distribution of the social product, focusing on incomes and welfare policy. Finally, we examine environmental or ecological policy which, on this view, is concerned primarily with the sustainability of man-made systems, their reliability as part of the order of reasonable expectations that makes freedom possible.

In each case, we begin with a short discussion of how liberal theory frames the problem of policy. We examine the orthodox liberal responses to these problems and then present the position that would seem most naturally to derive from a pragmatic liberal analysis.

The distinctive pragmatic liberal position usually flows directly from its central concern with "practice"—with the various dimensions of the public interest in a specific industry or technology. For pragmatic liberalism, the central political economic phenomenon is the enterprise, not the market. As we shall see, this makes a great deal of difference for the kinds of recommendations that this version of liberal thought is able to generate.

Liberal Theory and Political Economy

Our ideas about the proper management of economic affairs reflect the basic presuppositions of liberal political philosophy. Yet we are seldom fully cognizant of these deeper roots of our conventions of everyday practical thought.

Again, the first axiom of formal liberal political theory is that the state should govern only through impartial rules. Ideally, the liberal state is neutral. It must not give preference to any particular way of life or conception of the good. It should not provide advantage to any industry or favor one form of art, science, worship, or culture over another.[1]

From this it follows that the state should be concerned only with the aggregate performance of economy and society, with the sum of satisfactions available to individuals. The utilitarian rule becomes the effective test of policy, and the familiar tone and temper of classical political economy begin to emerge. The interest of those who manage the economy should be only with the abstract total well-being of society. The state is concerned with nothing in particular, only with things in general. It must not define the substance of the economic product, the specific array of goods and services available, their quality or distribution.

Classic liberalism, as we have already seen, regards any structured relationship between the state and an enterprise as necessarily suspect. To subsidize an industry, or regulate its product, can only be understood as a tawdry exchange of privilege for power. Furthermore, any selective intervention by the state in the economy will divert resources from their "best use." To underwrite housing, or to impose a tax on depletable energy resources, only makes goods cheaper or dearer than they ought to be and diverts investment from its most attractive opportunities. The end result of any such policy will be, in a word, uneconomic.

Thus do the formal liberal maxim of impartiality, the utilitarian criterion of want satisfaction, and the instrumentality of the market lock together in a system of impressive logical completeness.

Thus also arises the peculiarly abstract and unworldly language of conventional political economy, which provides, more than we perhaps fully realize, the dominant imagery for political discourse in our times. In this language, we speak only of composite qualities, never of things themselves. "Consumer durables" exist and are far more essential than refrigerators. It is a world in which only the fate of indexes is cause for concern and the end sought is a kind of harmony of aggregates. If indicators of growth, employment, monetary stability, and trade all point in the right direction, all is, in effect, right with the world. In this *Weltanschauung*, only ideas of "inflation" and "recession," the "marginal propensity to consume" or a disembodied "investors' confidence," have real essence. To introduce other kinds of considerations—to ask, for example, whether we might have too many shopping malls, to question the desirability of clear-cutting native cedar, or to inquire whether plumbers should be paid more than police—is, we quickly learn, regarded as somewhat irrelevant and vaguely indiscreet.

Pragmatic liberalism shares the concern of orthodox doctrine for the overall rhythms of the economy. However, again, pragmatic liberalism's view of the relation of theory to practice is distinctive. Every technology, each productive process is an appropriate subject for public discussion and, potentially, for reform. Thus, pragmatic liberalism tends to pursue issues of the health of the economy as a whole to their source in the practices of particular sectors or industries. It is led to disaggregate the abstract concepts that orthodox political economy uses to represent the world, to ask how they apply to different productive processes.

This is more than a difference in levels of analysis. As we shall see, the two approaches yield quite different recipes for economic policy. We first examine the implications of conventional political economy and then point up the respects in which pragmatic liberalism is distinctive.

Keynesianism and the State's Responsibility for Management of the Economy

Our present conception of the state's role in managing the public household is, if not specifically the product of the teachings of John Maynard Keynes, then certainly the result of the broader movement called Keynesianism. The basic proposition of Keynesianism is that it is the state's responsibility to secure the reliable performance of the economy as a whole. This represents a marked change from classical doctrine, where the state was expected to adapt to and reflect the general conditions of the market.

We do not yet fully recognize how greatly Keynesian assumptions have affected our *political* thought, how they have reshaped our ideas of the legitimacy of the state and the terms of our political argument. We have in practice adopted a set of economic indicators as tests of the performance of governments. We now assume that some combination of economic growth, full employment, price stability, and balance of trade equilibrium defines the goals of public life.[2] These indexes have, in some good measure, displaced the classic principles of liberal theory as standards for measuring the legitimacy of the state. Today it is probably as essential that governments do well in international rankings of economic performance as that they rest on consent, respect the rights of citizens, or refrain from taking political prisoners.

These major indexes of political economic achievement have a certain perverse quality about them. They almost never all point in the right direction. Hence, they provide a persistent theme for social criticism and political controversy. In all democratic nations, the major parties now divide primarily on which of these indicators should be emphasized at the expense of the rest. Keynesian liberals, historically, have been inclined to accept some inflation in the interest of full employment and growth. Free market liberals are more apt to array other objectives around a core commitment to monetary stability .

To be sure, the measures of macroeconomic performance have a strong affinity to central liberal values. Full employment is, in effect, a proxy for the liberal commitment to equality and social justice. To regard employment as a right as well as a duty becomes a specific response to the historic problem of proper policy toward labor and the poor. The goal of relative price stability is a consideration of lawful order. To count on the value of money is part of that frame of reliable expectations which, like the integrity and consistency of law, is a condition of rational plan and effective freedom. To set balanced trade as a goal of policy follows, of course, from the classic liberal commitment to free trade.

However, economic growth is perhaps the paramount index of economic achievement for conventional political economy. This is the accounting convention for the utilitarian rule that that state is best governed which provides the greatest sum of satisfactions to its citizens.

Economic Growth in a Mature Liberal Society

The goal of sustained economic growth is central to the discipline of political economy as we understand it today.[3] Many think continuous growth a necessary condition for the survival of liberalism. Lester Thurow, for example, represents the prevalent view in arguing that we are unprepared to face the implications of an economy without growth.[4] As long as the total product is increasing, there is enough to go around, and the claims of different groups and interests can be met. In a steady-state economy, priorities have to be set and some will have to pay the costs for benefits that others receive. But liberalism really has no theory of distributive justice that is equal to this task. Conscious political decisions will have to be made, judgments about who is to receive and who is to be denied, and more than a few analysts feel that modern governments have no basis for such decisions. The result of a zero-growth economy would be a loss of political authority and support, conflict and hostility between classes and interests.

Some go so far as to proclaim that all of this implies an inherent contradiction in the idea of democratic government itself. Politicians must promise expanded benefits to diverse groups to get elected. Thus governments must maintain ever-increasing levels of material prosperity if they are to succeed in mediating among competing demands. To achieve this, governments must constantly induce the economy to perform at unnaturally high levels. Unless this is sustained, democratic government will break down.[5]

Even apart from such lugubrious considerations, the logic of growth seems impeccable and irrefutable. Growth fulfills the mandate of the liberal state to improve the human condition yet endorse no specific conception of human ends. Growth is the means to all other good things. It is the critical variable in the equation, the key to full employment, a strong and stable currency, and revenues sufficient for the array of public services that should be provided to all in a decent society.[6]

Nonetheless, many of the great political economists taught that growth is not a sustainable condition, that growth automatically slows down at higher levels of prosperity, and that this is a desirable outcome, the culmination rather than the decline of the capitalist venture.

At a certain level of sufficiency, one enters the economics of the stable state. The object then is to maintain this condition rather than to continue a process designed to overcome scarcity and which, at higher levels of well-being, begins to seem irrational.

Thus, Marx taught that the stern economizing logic that rendered capitalism legitimate and historically irresistible becomes unnecessary as scarcity is overcome. The very achievements of capitalism make it possible to pass beyond it, into a new historic stage, in which the extraction of surplus value through the private ownership of the means of production would no longer fulfill a useful social function.

John Stuart Mill, similarly, saw the steady state not as decline, but as the fulfillment of liberalism. Mill thought that with declining rates of return, capitalists would voluntarily sell their assets to worker cooperatives. As the market reached stasis, they would be better off with fixed incomes, and the workers had every incentive to acquire the fruits of their labor. The steady state would then be potentially a regime of social justice, in which it would finally be possible to reconcile the libertarian and egalitarian themes of liberal value.[7]

And John Maynard Keynes too had an optimistic view of the era when economic growth would decline and end. He wrote, "If I am right in supposing it to be comparatively easy to make capital goods so abundant that the marginal efficiency of capital is zero, this may be the most sensible way of getting rid of many of the objectionable features of capitalism."[8]

Finally, of course, there are those who warn that the idea of sustained growth, carried relentlessly to its logical conclusion, inevitably means the exhaustion of the resources of earth.[9]

These are not considerations actively pursued in contemporary public debate. The animating motif of capitalist as of Marxist political economic thought today is the maintenance or restoration of economic growth. This is the dominant issue in all modern nations. The objective is taken for granted. The schools of thought, laissez-faire and interventionist, Keynesian and non-Keynesian, divide mainly only on the means to its achievement.

However, the fact of the matter is that a mature industrial economy is not apt to grow very much or very fast. The more reasonable prognosis for the foreseeable future is not a vibrant new age of expansive industrialism, but at best a stable economy, more likely, a gentle decline.

The best estimate must be that we are not apt to see a return to the golden age of expanding production and prosperity that the United States and Europe experienced in the 1950s and 1960s. The circumstances of that period were unique. Government had subsidized an enormous expansion of the industrial plant to provide for the wartime defense industries. This was available, and it proved to be quickly convertible, to meet pent-up consumer demand. The rapidly expanding consumer goods markets could be satisfied by relatively straightforward advances in design and production technology. But once each family has two refrigerators, bathrooms, cars and television sets, the going gets a little tougher. Productivity and growth, like everything else, seem subject to the laws of diminishing returns. Replacement and maintenance of existing stocks of goods is not the same as saturating the initial markets. Most of the ways of making production more efficient, of increasing productivity, for the basic goods, have already been discovered.

In fact, no one in the contemporary debate actually argues that we need to become richer, that we need ever more prosperity, a higher standard of living for its own sake. What is at stake now are not the direct, but the indirect, the "public" consequences of growth. We need jobs, and we need the public revenues to sustain a high level of public services and an elaborate defense force. To put the matter as bluntly as possible, it almost seems that in order to have full employment, quality education, the reconstruction of roads, bridges and sewers, protection in old age and for the poor, it is our civic duty to consume ever-increasing quantities of junk food, video games, obscure computer equipment, redundant kitchen appliances, and exotic camping gear.

This tends to focus the mind nicely. What we are after is not growth itself. For increasing abundance has become, at this point, simply a means to some other end. If we could discern that end more distinctly, the question of growth itself might come into clearer perspective.

Pragmatic Liberalism and Economic Growth

What distinguishes pragmatic liberalism from other contemporary patterns of thought is that it does not *rely* on growth as the fulcrum of its political economic strategy. Pragmatic liberalism is more concerned with what Veblen called "social provisioning" than with utilitarian "want satisfaction." It concentrates on production for its own sake, its "use value" rather than its "commodity value." It is interested in the actual things we produce rather than their secondary effects, their value in a strictly summing sense in relation to an abstract and impersonal notion of welfare.

For pragmatic liberalism, our fixation on the aggregate economy has blinded us to the performance of specific industries. The value of an industry is measured not only by its contribution to employment, growth, and trade. It is its *sustainability* that is fundamentally at issue, its ability to continue to perform well over time.

The sort of political economic counsel that pragmatic liberalism offers might not be appropriate for a society in the early stages of industrialization. It is intended more for a *constructed* society, one where the issues are of the persistence and perfection of productive process, rather than its initial creation. This is, of course, the economy of the stable state. And this seems to be the epoch we are likely to be entering.

Public Policy and the Productive Enterprise

This preoccupation with the composite, not the direct performance, or firms and industries, is in fact quite recent. Historically, our deliberations of economic policy were very much concerned with the aims and performance of specific industries. Thus we spoke of agricultural policy and railroad policy, coal, fishing, mining and timber policy, more recently of housing, mass transit, and energy policy. This highly specific level of analysis, oriented to the task at hand, was particularly characteristic of U.S. public debate in the great middle eras when we fashioned our characteristic institutions.

The rational enterprise, as we have noted, is always a collaborative undertaking, a mixture of public and private elements. The U.S. agricultural economy is particularly notable in this respect as the product of conscious, deliberate public design and the spontaneous unfolding of patterns of private initiative.

The settlement of the Western lands was carried out as a centrally planned, comprehensive agrarian reform. The rationalism of this effort is still apparent from the air. The grid of the square survey, marking off the continent west of the seventh range from the Ohio River, creates a landscape quite different from that sketched by the rambling property lines of more "capitalistic" patterns of settlement.

The object was to create a system of freeholdings, as a radical experiment in agrarian democracy. The smallholding was the alternative to the commercial plantation, the key institution of colonization in other parts of the world. The implication of this policy was that substitutes would have to be found for the functions of management, finance, risk, marketing, and the promotion of new techniques, functions normally vested in the owners and managers of large productive organizations.

Agricultural policy emerged from conscious plan and policy as well as from spontaneous discovery and entrepreneurial innovation. The result was a complex array of interdependent patterns of public and private effort.

It was necessary to constitute the pioneer farmers as communities of good practice, to reexamine traditional European peasant usages, rationalize cultivation, find techniques adapted to new conditions, soils, and climates. In this endeavor of creating and disseminating knowledge, the public university, the extension agent, the farm machinery, seed and fertilizer manufacturers and merchants, each played a role and worked hand in hand.

Finance, like marketing, required new institutions of management. Certain institutions of capitalization, for stabilizing markets and controlling risks, emerged directly from private initiatives taken to fill the apparent gaps in the system. Local banking, futures markets, crop insurance, and storage facilities emerged, and these, in time, were complemented and systematized through public action, in the interest of sustaining the reliable performance of the system as a whole.

Transportation and marketing policies were closely coordinated with agricultural policy. The railroads were to bind the nation together, but more immediately, they were understood as an essential link in the emerging system of settlement, and the commercialization of agriculture. A publicly subsidized system of private railroads, later closely regulated to protect agrarian interests, emerged as an essential component of the agricultural system.

An elaborate skein of processing industries and distributional and marketing services develops over time, largely as private undertakings responding to the logic of the emerging markets for agricultural products, although their standards of practice are regularized and maintained both by a system of trade associations (linked to universities and research institutes) and through close regulation by governments at each level.

The agricultural system we have developed is a complex and constantly evolving system of governance, a subtle and remarkably successful response to the problem of coordinating a system of production made intentionally as decentralized as possible. To critique and improve upon established methods, one has to understand the history and the nature of these peculiar arrangements of governance. Analysis must become fully political as well as economic. We have to think of the "constitution" of a sector, as well as to calculate its returns. And in such analysis we should keep in mind that, within a sector, there exists a great diversity of political economic arrangements, institutions, and cultures. The government of milk is not at all like that of wheat, or wood, or soybeans.

We continue to debate the rationality and sustainability of the complex purposive enterprise so developed over the years. It is clear that some of its elements may now represent an orthodoxy grown rigid. We seek ways to revitalize and reform the enterprise and its component systems. Yet, in present context, the important point is simply that we do have a tradition of political economic discourse that leads us to think of the specific systems of social provision comprehensively, critically, and imaginatively, and as an object of public policy and planning.

We can learn to think this way again. In recent years, we have thoroughly reexamined and reconstituted our medical system. We have put new emphasis on preventive medicine, on "wellness" and public health, as against the traditional interest of medical science in treating disease. We have changed our image of the mission of the hospital and the doctor. Medical care has been critiqued and reconstituted as a comprehensive "delivery system." New professions emerge, and though the system seems more impersonal in some respects, it has led to a systematization of effective compassion in others. Much of this reform came as the result of the recognition of a public interest in the economics of health care, as costs soared and public or semipublic insurers played an increasingly prominent role in medical finance. The reform involved a sustained dialectic between the state and the professions.

No one would claim that our present medical system is perfect.

Of course the critical deliberation of its practices stays open. And note, in this case especially, that this has been a public, a political deliberation, not at all restricted to the practitioners alone.

These are realistic examples of pragmatic planning, of political economic analysis with the focus on the particular. The problem now is to apply this mode of reasoning to transportation and energy, education and culture, housing and the press, to all the live and vital systems of everyday life.

Industrial Policy

The critics of market orthodoxy now often speak of "industrial policy" as the primary alternative to conventional political economic doctrine. Industrial policy connotes selective intervention by the state to improve the performance or competitiveness of specific industries or sectors. This would seem an approach to policy compatible with pragmatic liberalism, and indeed it is. However, there are important differences between the currently prominent doctrines of industrial policy and those that might best be associated with pragmatic liberal thought. Today, industrial policy is advocated primarily as an alternative strategy for achieving conventional macroeconomic objectives. In pragmatic liberalism, the direct aim would be that of enhancing the rational performance of an enterprise. The significance of this distinction will become apparent in the discussion that follows.

It is true that current ideas of industrial policy have a strong resemblance to certain themes in traditional pragmatic liberal thought. Just as earlier pragmatic liberal ideas of social insurance and corporatist organization were based not on abstract theory but on the experience of other industrial nations, so today's advocates of industrial policy appeal to north European and Asian examples of constructive state action, excellent public services, and organized collaboration between government, business, and labor as an alternative both to free market and Keynesian orthodoxy.[10]

At various times in the postwar period, European methods of capitalist planning have been invoked as suggestive strategies for achieving sustained high levels of prosperity and employment while minimizing inflationary pressures.[11] Today, however, industrial policy is advocated primarily as a response to problems generated by the restructuring of the international economy.

Industrial Policy and the International Economy

The issues of economic management now seem rooted in the rapid diffusion of industry throughout the world, in the shifting terms of trade. Strong foreign competitors have emerged. American corporations have shifted production abroad. The result is that the United States now imports products once the staples of its economy. A nation once largely self-sufficient is now as dependent on trade as most European or Pacific nations. This has meant a loss of American industrial employment, the rapid decline of industries, cities and regions, a restructuring of economic foundations unanticipated in the main, unwanted and threatening.

Liberalism, classically, entails a doctrine of free trade, and it is difficult for any version of liberalism to break fundamentally with this tradition. The moral claims of liberalism are universal. The idea of free trade is that the universal market would, over time, bring about the highest possible level of well-being for humanity. Certainly no liberal could adopt the position, as a matter of policy, that present global divisions between the rich nations and the poor ought to be continued. However, when the movement of industrial production to lower-wage nations becomes the general trend, awkward issues of policy arise for the hitherto most prosperous nations.

Furthermore, for any version of liberalism to move toward extensive protectionism or autarchy, in the contemporary internationalized economy, would be equivalent to ending the market game itself. The open competition of diverse industries and technologies cannot be sustained within a single nation. Small countries, historically exposed to world trade, which could only support a single manufacturer in any basic industry, have long known this. Now it is apparent in the United States as well. To attempt to enclose an economy is a recipe for short-run stability and long-run decadence.

Of course, we also know that the international market is something of an abstraction. We do not have free trade in any classic capitalistic sense. What we have instead is a mercantilistic market, a competitive trade among organized commercial republics which seems more reminiscent of the era of the Hanseatic League or the Italian cities in full rivalry than Adam Smith's "propensity to truck and barter."

Each nation pursues policies which work explicitly or implicitly to secure national advantage, perhaps crudely, by suppressing trade unions, perhaps through sophisticated measures of research or marketing support, or selective investment. Many deplore such measures as "artificial" incentives which distort markets. Yet from a pragmatic liberal point of view, if each nation sought, as a matter of policy, to enhance those enterprises in which it had a potential comparative advantage, we would achieve a kind of mercantilism compatible with the liberal objectives of free trade.

Problems of Industrial Policy

There are many today who urge the adoption of some form of industrial policy—a conscious plan for the transformation of the national economy in response to the changing character of international trade. We want to pass through a period of radical restructuring of our institutions with as much security and stability, as little productive loss and human misery, as possible. The aims are to promote industries that can compete effectively in world markets while letting go of those that cannot. This implies that there be a deliberate process of directing the flow of investment, a plan for compensating, reeducating, and perhaps relocating workers whose jobs are lost, and re-creating and redeveloping the public infrastructure on which the new pattern of productive enterprise will depend.[12]

Proponents of industrial policy have little faith that management or the market can do this job. In the current climate, industrial leadership is preoccupied with the short-run, the "paper economy" of assets management rather than deliberate planning for social provision or new technologies to substitute for archaic methods. Furthermore, international corporations have a frame of reference quite different from that of national policymakers. They would just as soon move productive operations abroad if savings can thus be achieved.[13]

The problem with any form of industrial policy, of course, is knowing where to place the bets. Proponents speak easily of "sunrise" and "sunset" industries. There is a vision of a general drift of older manufacturing processes and technologies to the newer industrial lands, while the presently most advanced nations would pursue ever more sophisticated, but presently unspecified, technologies.

At this point, serious practical problems quite obviously arise about how any council of investment planners would distinguish rising from declining industries and, perhaps more importantly, how they would justify those choices in an arena where many forms of political pressure could be brought to bear. There is in fact no clear economic theory that can guide the choice of what to promote and what to abandon. The competitive viability of an enterprise depends not only on its specific technology, but its total "rationality," its culture of management and practice, its system of governance, its existing position in the web of public- and private-sector political economic relations. We are back to the level of the particular again.

For pragmatic liberalism, industrial policy logically starts the other way around. Instead of looking first to the most sophisticated technologies, we would begin by asking how we intend to sustain those industries most essential to human well-being in everyday life. Once we have decided how to provide the vital necessities, we can begin to organize our plans for employment and trade around this economic core. This is the logical consequence of thinking first about how we get things done, rather than simply in terms of an abstract, impersonal "utility."

Pragmatic Liberal Industrial Policy

There is a set of major industries that traditionally has been the subject of specific sectoral policy in the United States. These include transport, energy, communications, agriculture in all its forms, banking and finance, education, medicine, and the complex of housing, construction, and urban design. This is the heart of the regime of public interest industries. Here public and private collaboration in planning for the rational development of the enterprise is legitimate and expected. All of these, it is apparent, are sectors where current practice stands in need of reexamination. Depending on how one calculates, these industries account for from one-third to one-half of the national product and employment in the United States.

Energy, transport, and construction form an interdependent set of industries particularly significant as a starting point for contemporary planning and public argument. It is obvious that the petroleum-based energy system developed over the past half century is neither sustainable nor reliable. This system will have to be almost totally reconstructed in time.

For pragmatic liberalism, the development of a sustainable energy system is a central subject for intelligent adaptive action. The choice of alternative energy sources is a privileged problem for investment strategy. The price mechanism will not guide investment toward the requirements of system transformation, for the long-term investments that will have to be made will, for the prudent business manager, always compare unfavorably with short-term strategies of response to current consumer wants and fashions.

For pragmatic liberalism, conservation need not imply diminished current well-being, when it is combined with the intelligent redevelopment of existing technologies. The fuel-economic car, the better-constructed home, the more convenient system of public transport, are not necessarily inferior goods. They are simply less wasteful. The very *fragility* of the present system, its susceptibility to interruption, or manipulation by those who control the critical resource base, is a symptom of irrationality, of obsolescent orthodoxy. A reliable system has a certain degree of redundancy and diversity, back-up systems built in. The costs of present development of alternative energy sources have to be balanced against gains in reliability, consistency, and universality of the system as a whole.

The transport and construction industries are intimately related to the energy system. No one would argue that these enterprises as presently constituted are stable or reliable. The present mix of transport modes—the heavy reliance on car, truck, and air, the neglect of rail and other means of surface transport—is hardly a "climax" technology, an obviously desirable end-result of industrial evolution. It is rather an imperfect interim arrangement, the temporary outcome of policies of preferment among the dominant modes, and differences in the political cultures of the constituent enterprises—the aggressive entrepreneurship of the auto and airline industries contrasting with the stale orthodoxy of the cultures of rail and mass transit.

Our basic foundation systems are more plastic and flexible than we might suppose. We did totally redesign the American pattern of mobility and settlement around petroleum. The change from the densely settled city and town, related to rail transport, to the open, fluid pattern of habitation of suburb, decentralized commerce and industry, a sprawling fusion of urban and rural life, a more extravagant pattern of land use—all of these represent a total pattern of social transformation that actually came to fulfillment within a remarkably short period of time, in the post–World War II era. This period of fundamental reconstruction of basic systems is, of course, also the one we associate with our highest levels of economic growth, general prosperity, and full employment.

What we changed fundamentally once, we can change fundamentally again. To take the reconstruction of our energy and transport systems, our attendant patterns of habitation, as a basic aim of policy (as once we coordinated policy around the settlement of the Western lands) would be at least as efficient in securing the overall aims of macroeconomic management as either free market or Keynesian orthodoxy, and would, in addition, move us closer to the goal of creative rational enterprises sustainable for the long run.

Concentrating on the basics is also the indicated strategy for stimulating foreign trade. Most of the products in which the United States has been internationally competitive in the recent past—agricultural products, airframes and aerospace, heavy construction, armaments and higher education—were not intended as export goods. Trade is a spin-off from domestic policy efforts in which the state is conspicuously engaged. (Computer technology is the obvious and significant exception to this rule.)

Public Purpose and Political Economy

Of course, productive efficiency is not the only aim of political economic policy. The goal of any strategy of macroeconomic management is to link economic production to the achievement of broader public ends. Political economy is precisely the study of how economic production can be brought to serve the well-being of the community.

Since Keynes, full employment has been construed as a principal objective of policy. However, for pragmatic liberalism, full employment must signify something more than enough jobs at some minimum rate of pay. The actual goal is not simply to secure livelihood but to enhance participation in the regime of rational enterprise. This means that political economic policy, when it focuses on the development of particular forms of enterprise, must aim toward the upgrading of skill, the enhancement of work, along lines compatible with the ideal of the enterprise as a community of practice and a community of inquiry.

The practical problem is that we have no very clear idea of how to go about doing this. Models and examples do not readily come to mind. In discussing the development of enterprise, I seized on the settlement of the Western lands as an example, rather than on the growth of the business corporation, for U.S. land policy was by intent both a design for economic development and agrarian democracy. What comparable images could we evoke today to guide the further development of the medical or educational systems, our institutions of commerce, transport, or communication?

The issues of full employment become most difficult when the aim is to incorporate those who have hitherto been left out or left behind—cultural or ethnic minorities, the handicapped, the "underclass"—into the regime of rational, reflective good practice. We are aware by now that here the issue of employment is not only one of the availability of jobs but of assimilation into the way of life of liberal civilization. Those at the margin must learn the skills of reliable performance, of critical analysis, which are the price of membership, even of survival, in the Enlightenment order.

Let us not evade the implications of the issue. Liberals would tolerate, perhaps encourage, cultural diversity. But, in practice, they cannot support those forms of cultural differentiation that discourage self-support and good performance within the rational society. There are tragic dilemmas in this realm, and it is better that we face them directly. One cannot successfully encourage both the preservation of native American traditions, for example, and assimilation into the dominant culture. Something has to break. The understanding and the empathy for diverse ways that we would cultivate in the majority culture are probably, in the end, instrumental. It is a way of making gentler, and more endurable, what probably must be, in the end, a process of cultural transformation.

The Institutions of Planning

What kind of planning institutions would a pragmatic liberal approach to industrial policy imply?

The most comprehensive system for combining sectoral and

macroeconomic planning was developed in France in the post-war period. At its height, in the 1950s and 1960s, French indicative planning was often regarded as a model for modern capitalism. The French based a series of five-year plans on exhaustive consultations between the "governments" of enterprise and the planners of the state. The formal structure included a series of "vertical" commissions representing the major industrial sectors (transport, textiles, agriculture, etc.) and an intersecting system of "horizontal" bodies for the major macroeconomic policy elements (employment, finance, trade, productivity, regional development, etc.). The idea was to reconcile plans for the development of each sector with those stipulated for the economy as a whole. The plan linked priorities for state investment, infrastructure development, education, and the like to specific programs for the various industries.[14]

This was a well-articulated model for combining the general and the particular. However, it may reflect Gallic logic more than American practicality. I have no intention of advocating anything like it in the name of pragmatic liberalism. The American genius for planning is simply different from that of Europe, or Asia.

The American tradition runs more toward large visions and complex, diffuse arrangements for the governance of enterprise, with little in the way of overall bureaucratic machinery or coordinative planning institutions.

In thinking about the proper institutions of planning, then, we might well begin by reflecting on the planning of the settlement of the West, the development of integrated transport and communications system during the early decades of the twentieth century, the recent transformation of the health care system, and many other examples of the way we constitute large-scale collaborative effort to achieve important social ends. Many of these once visionary undertakings are now established institutions. Many now stand in need of critical reexamination and, in some cases, radical reconstitution. However, each is an instance of the historic American approach to planning.

The main point then is that we are probably best off thinking about institutions for the planning of enterprise without being too specific about coordinating techniques. Given a strong commitment to putting the basics in order, these will presumably evolve along our own idiosyncratic lines.

To reflect on planning institutions in this way, it is best to begin from an analysis of the system of governance of the existing enterprise in question, from reflection on the nature of its constitutional order. To model, and to criticize, this system requires both a political and an economic frame of mind. We have to look at the enterprise with fresh eyes, identifying its authority structures, its rules of due process, its political culture and system of rights, as well as its mechanisms of trade, contractual coordination, and economizing. Only when this is done can we begin the process of measuring practice against theory, asking how the enterprise can be made more rational in terms of its inherent purposes and in its fidelity to liberal values.

Liberalism is a philosophy of impartial principles, and classical liberalism stipulates that all industry must be treated alike. All productive processes should be subject to the common disciplines of the market and the same general rules of law.[15]

However, in the American tradition, the relationship of each enterprise to the state is unique. Each has a particular system of governance, reflecting a distinctive history of organization and development and a distinctive set of public concerns and interests.

The classic liberal, like the advocate of comprehensive planning, thinks such arrangements both illogical and illegitimate. They do not seem to follow from a master conception of the proper relation of state to economy. They can, then, only be explained as the product of political venality. However, this is to miss the point almost completely. The political economic systems of enterprise arise from the application of liberal principles to diverse problems of practice. There are good reasons why the government of agriculture is different from that of the automobile, why the relation of the state to petroleum is different from its relation to coal. Any helpful critique of such systems of planning begins from an appreciation of the rationale for present practice. It does not begin from a theoretical framework that defines it, axiomatically, as illicit or illogical. The U.S. planning system is diverse and differentiated. To try to impose uniformity on it, whether in the name of the market or bureaucratic structure, would be an act of theoretical arbitrariness.

Once again, form follows function. The institutions of planning should be designed to make good on practical intent. How do we intend to produce food and other raw materials for the long run?

How do we propose to reconstruct our transport and energy systems? How will we bring new vitality to our ossifying but still extraordinary educational establishment?

To approach the problem this way would be a sharp break from our present fixation on the conventional categories of macroeconomic thought. It would imply a departure from our stylized debates about aggregate aims and abstract measures. But all that is actually involved is a reaffirmation of a longer tradition of political economic argument and analysis, one into which we can incorporate what we can from the diverse experiences of other modern industrial nations, and from classical, Keynesian and, for that matter, Marxian theory.

7

Distributive Justice

Both the generation and the distribution of the social product raise contentious issues of governance, of the proper management of the public household. The role the state should play in the productive work of enterprise seems a perpetual issue of liberal politics. But how the fruits of collective effort should be divided is perhaps an even more perplexing question, for here liberal doctrine is particularly ambivalent and uncertain.

In this area, issues of theory and practice are very much intertwined. However, the basic quandaries would seem to have their source in the way the idea of equality is understood in liberal thought and how it is related to the entire scheme of liberal reason. We start, then, from this question of principle and move to the issues of practice. Once again, the object is to point up how pragmatic liberalism's focus on the collaborative nature of the enterprise, and the public interest in its performance, yields a distinctive approach to policies of distributive justice.

Equality and Liberal Justice

Social economy and efficiency are the standards by which we measure productive performance. But equality is the basing point for discussions of distributive justice. Equality is the presumptive case in liberal logic. It is the departures from equal treatment that have to be justified.[1] Thus do questions of justice arise, as a matter of making relevant distinctions between cases. The problem of justice is really that of finding reasons to override the presumption of equality, of giving grounds for treating individual cases *differently*. Equality itself is not perplexing.[2]

But justice is, for the practical question is how to reward and honor people differently, and how to decide when it is proper to endow them with different shares of the diverse products of enterprise.

Liberalism is the historic doctrine of individual freedom. But equality is a strong norm in liberal thought as well. All the basic arrangements of liberal order presume equality as a condition of their legitimacy. Thus, contract as a basic building block of liberal institutions implies parity of power and opportunity, information and access. Disparities of wealth, power, or competence make contractual relationships suspect.

Similarly, in classic liberalism, the market is presumed efficient not simply because it is expected to provide a greater abundance of goods and services than rival systems. More precisely, the classic case is that the market is efficient because it will produce that array of goods and services that individuals want and need in their own estimation. It is this stipulation that makes classical political economy a closed, logical, self-referential system. But this obviously presumes a relatively equal distribution of income. There is nothing in the elemental logic of liberalism to suggest that the choices of the rich are to count for more than those of the poor in determining the character of the social product.

Classical democratic theory, even more than the theory of the market, requires that each individual vote count for one and no more than one. It would seem, then, that the integrity of the democratic political process may only be assured under conditions of relative income equality, for money too often magnifies the force of interest and issues; it "distorts" the free play of political forces and leads to results quite different from those that would obtain with equality of voice and vote.

Equality, it seems, must be a strong value in any version of formal liberal thought. Yet all liberals resist a strict egalitarianism. Equality, pushed to an extreme, leads to results that may be both arbitrary and unfair. To secure for all the *same* education, or vocational or cultural opportunities, would be manifestly irrational. We are creatures of diverse needs, interests, and abilities. And whenever the state *enforces* equality, it diminishes the autonomy of the individual and the enterprise. Pursue this course beyond a never quite discernable point and you no longer have liberalism.

The problem then is to determine when to take exception to the rule of equality in the name of justice. This is always a practical question, a matter of establishing what counts as relevant distinctions between individuals in particular situations, engaged in specific activities. For as I have already noted, the relevant distinctions that suggest differential treatment often seem to arise from attributes of function and purpose.

In this chapter, I explore two specific problems of distributive justice. The first is income distribution. Liberalism normally assumes that all should not have the *same* income, for individual deserts and needs are different. But on what basis, then, should income differentials be decided? The second problem is welfare. Liberalism assumes the responsibility for self-support. On what basis do we make exceptions to this rule? When is a person properly exonerated from this duty: when is an individual *entitled* to receive a living from the state?

These are questions to which pragmatic liberalism can give a distinctive response. As we shall see, the pragmatic liberal ideal of the enterprise as community of inquiry and community of practice yields a particular philosophy of the just distribution of income, reward, and recognition. And the pragmatic liberal concern for the diffusion of the most useful and necessary fruits of collective enterprise leads to a particular conception of the aims of the welfare state.

Income Distribution

No liberal stands for absolute income equality. The issue is to determine which forms of reward, honor, status and authority are justified. And once again, as in all forms of liberal argument, the point of departure is the market.

The classic case is that no explicit principles of just distribution are required. We do not have to make authoritative determinations of what individuals deserve and need in relation one to another. Rather, in the market regime, individuals appraise the worth of every other individual's performance by the respect they give, their willingness to follow, to transact, and most importantly, to pay.

If millions are willing to spend their dollars on an expensive toy, or to watch an outstanding athlete perform, then the inventer of the toy, and the athlete, deserve to reap a rich reward. If no one is willing to pay to hear the new sonata, then the composer must find a different line of work.[3] The cumulative effect is to reward each according to his or her contribution to the common good, as that is appraised, in the indiivdual's own terms. And this, paradoxically, generates precisely the kind of income inequality that makes the logic of the scheme untenable. For there is no reason why those who merit the higher rewards should, as a result, receive a greater voice in the determination of the social product.

Historically, pragmatic liberalism has raised two particular objections to the orthodox free market position on income distribution. (The objections may not be unique to the pragmatic liberal tradition, but they are insistent, in the long line from Veblen to Galbraith.)

The first argument is that it is very hard to prove that existing income differentials are actually the product of market forces. They are equally likely to be traceable to market power or unexamined custom, to beliefs, rooted in an age of privilege, that those in charge of particular institutions deserve to live much better than the rest.

It is possible that large corporations must pay their top officers from thirty to three hundred times the average wage if they are to attract competent help. But pragmatic liberals are doubtful. It seems just as likely that executives—and certain professionals— decide how much to pay one another based on rules of practice of their own devising.[4]

It would be possible, of course, to demonstrate that executive compensation was based on market competition. All that is required is to make submission of sealed bids part of the selection process. This is a convention of many other forms of competitive contract. It is hard to believe that the efficient corporation, determined to be lean and spare in all its operations, could not find eager executive recruits willing to underbid their rivals. (As long as the specifications are tightly drawn, as they are in performance-based construction contracts, and the bidding limited to a shortlist established on the basis of merit, there is no reason to fear any decline in the quality of leadership. The approach could be applied to other professions, including, yes, the professorate. What is at stake is simply a public guarantee that the compensation paid for privileged positions is in fact the market rate. The crucial question then becomes whether the market is the test of income inequality that we want.)

The second long-standing pragmatic liberal objection to a market-based scheme of income distribution is that it is extremely difficult to specify precisely the contribution of any individual to a collective undertaking. How does one establish the proportionate contribution of the chief executive officer, the key engineers, the division managers, the workers, to the success of the enterprise? A going concern is a composite of many performances. What is more, it has a history. Current management are the beneficiaries—or the victims—of an ongoing institutional culture and system of practice. To distinguish the worth of separate performances, which is what the orthodox individualist scheme of income distribution requires, must in the end be arbitrary.

Veblen knew this. He wrote:

> Technological knowledge is of the nature of a common stock, held and carried forward collectively by the community, which in this relation is to be conceived as a going concern. The state of the industrial arts is a fact of group life, not of individual or private initiative or innovation . . . It is only as an outcome of this discipline that comes with the routine of group life, and by help of the commonplace knowledge diffused through the community, that any of its members are enabled to make any new move that in this way may be traceable to their individual initiative.[5]

The point is central to the heritage of U.S. institutional economics. It is also part of progressive management science. Chester Barnard wrote that "the statement that any person is more important to the system than any other can only be made on the assumption that all other elements in the cooperation remain the same. Except for this assumption there can be no significant statement regarding the contribution of any person relative to the general or total results."[6]

Compensation Systems

However, once all of this is said, the problem is to recommend an alternative. In theory and practice, we do try to establish rational criteria of income distribution. Most complex institutions have compensation systems that are not based directly on market considerations. And any such codified system of income differentials rests on some theory of justice.[7]

The compensation systems of most hierarchical institutions,

such as those of a classified civil service, invariably assume that the greater rewards should go to those who manage, those who "supervise" or "organize" the work of others, followed by those who must take the initiative for organizing their own work. Last come those who are assumed to simply follow orders. This is an idea of merit that flows from the very nature of hierarchic organization of course, but the notion that "management" should be valued more highly than "execution" is not obviously uncontestable. Management of a well-organized going concern is not a particularly demanding task, as anyone who has tried it knows perfectly well. It is possible to routinize and constrain, to "de-skill" managerial responsibility, just as it is any task that initially called for workmanship, initiative, and special care. One can think of many institutions where rewarding administration over direct performance seems, at best, questionable. Should the business manager of a clinic be paid more than the doctors? Should deans be paid more than professors? What *is* the underlying justification for such distinctions?

Leaving aside the point that managers create compensation systems, my feeling is that our unconscious acceptance of such hierarchic schemes rests on what Weber would have called "the routinization of charisma." We perhaps impute to the current managers the qualities of the vigorous entrepreneurial spirits who took risks, persevered, and created a project for others. Or, as I suggested earlier, our view that management automatically deserves greater reward may be simply an unexamined residue of the tradition of aristocratic privilege.

It may well be argued that risk or deferred gratification is an appropriate reason for income inequality. The oil wildcatter may deserve a large reward, for the chances of coming up dry are very great indeed. Perhaps physicians deserve high incomes, as compensation for the years spent outside the work force and the costs of medical education. But those costs can be readily calculated (as can the risks of premature loss of skill), and the result cannot readily justify or explain existing professional differentials.

Similarly, income differentials may be justified on considerations of compensatory justice. Social democrats have often proposed that "unpleasantness"—the difficulty, danger, or repugnancy of work—should be compensated by higher remuneration. The inference sometimes drawn is that garbage collectors warrant higher pay than intellectuals. I have discussed this matter with members of the trade in question and have found few who would trade their way of life for mine. For members of the learned professions, however, "unpleasantness" may justify superior reward for college presidents and deans. Someone has to do the dirty work, and in justice, there should be some compensation for the flak-catching, for all the evenings out, the pointless round of meetings.

Obviously, there is no simple *rational* basis for just income differentials that is a clear alternative to an ideal market allocation. Merit and unpleasantness, deserved compensation, difficulty and risk are often in the eye of the beholder. There is no apparent logic that would tell us how these factors are to be weighed against one another generally, or in the marginal case. A just compensation scheme is obviously a part of the constitution of an enterprise and arises ideally out of the political deliberations that are appropriate to the creation of any form of legitimate authority, any prescriptive system of rules. To this theme we shall return in due course.

Equality of Opportunity

In recent decades, the actual political debate about the justice of inequality has fastened on one very narrow point. The parties of the right have argued, in effect, that the logic of the market justifies *existing* inequalities. The parties of the left have responded that inequalities *would* be justified if the race were fair, if unequal outcomes could be shown to be the product of differences in performance, under conditions of equality of opportunity.

To secure justice, then, it is necessary to make sure that the market actually does reward nothing but achievement, productivity, and talent. Outstanding contribution deserves superior reward. But the appraisal of merit must be truly competitive. Discrimination on the basis of race, sex, handicap, ethnicity, on *any* ground that cannot be causally linked to performance, distorts the market's capacity to evaluate merit. The duty of the state is to assure the integrity of market justice, to guarantee that such factors do not affect the determination of individual reward.

The main dispute among "liberals" has been over the *extent* of the guarantees required to secure effective equality of opportunity. It becomes evident that simple equality of access to education, the historic American way of seeking to secure the equal competence of choosers, will not also secure the equality of all achievers. What additional measures are required, when so much of "success" can be shown to be the product of cultural background, family connections, social ties, or simple luck?[8] In the end, the more adamant reformers press the point that a rather high level of equality of condition—and thus, presumably, income—is necessary to justify inequalities of reward within the liberal regime.[9]

This view may seem compatible with pragmatic liberalism's generally reformist temper. But, in fact, it leaves the specifically pragmatic liberal concerns unanswered. It tells us nothing about how we are to appraise individual contributions to collective undertakings, how one can determine what any individual "deserves" as participant in an ongoing community of practice. And it still does not tell us how inequality of income is to be reconciled to equality of choice.

Furthermore, meritocracy, in itself, is not a particularly attractive social ideal. The "bitch goddess success" (significantly, the pragmatist William James coined the term) does not always bring out the best in people, particularly if the aim is to encourage public responsibility and the sense of workmanship.

Also, if the race is fair, then there are no excuses for failure. Given our ideas of what "success" implies, most people do not succeed. Meritocracy means that most people would have to conclude that their modest accomplishments in life, the fact that they had not won the top prizes in competitive struggle, meant that they were lacking in worth and merit. As Michael Young, the father of this thought, put it, if we *could* guarantee pure equality of opportunity, "For the first time in human history the inferior man has no ready buttress for his self-regard."[10] This is an abominable public ethic and a way of framing the problem which is totally at odds with the spirit of pragmatic liberalism.

Liberal Egalitarianism

In formal liberalism, John Rawls provides the main alternative to market justice. Rawls's doctrine, basically, is that once political equality (the right to vote and to participate; freedom of thought and conscience; the right to personal freedom, property, and due process of law) has been established, social and economic inequalities are only justified when they can be shown to benefit the least advantaged, and that they "attach to offices and positions open to all under conditions of fair equality of opportunity." [11]

There have been a thousand interpretations of Rawls. His argument is labyrinthine, puzzling, often obscure, and hedged about in various ways. Nonetheless, the implications in present context seem clear. If one were actually to apply Rawls' theory to practice, the result would be an increasingly egalitarian distribution of income over time.

Some have argued that it might not work out this way. A very loose construction of the "difference principle" might suggest that those who did a little bit for the poor might claim a very large reward, and the result would be considerable continuing inequality. This is ingenious, but clearly not Rawls's intent. Not just any "trickle down" effect will do. The arrangements that justify inequality must be technically efficient. They must be the best possible way of aiding the least well-off. [12] And besides, the closer one comes to equality, the fewer justifications there will be for unequal rewards.

To be sure, the principle of "basic liberties" is prior to the principle of preference for the least well-off in Rawls' scheme. This is what makes the theory liberal. One cannot create equality through totalitarian regimentation, by *forcing* the most capable to work for the betterment of the poor. All people are free to pursue their own life plans. If you prefer to be the patron of the elegant, or to sit idly and watch wheat grow, so be it. But if you *want* unusual reward, you must earn it by working for egalitarian ends.

This is a theory of incentives. It is to say, the only legitimate reason to give *inducements* to performance is when the goal is equality. Here the contrast with orthodox market liberalism is stark. Orthodox liberalism would justify income inequalities on the ground that differences in reward arise from the free choices of individuals in the market. But orthodox liberalism then must assume an unequal overall distribution of income. In that case, the incentives of special reward go to those who serve the interests of the well-enough-off, perhaps even the rich and powerful, but certainly not those with the least resources. The result is a maxim of justice which liberalism cannot logically endorse.

Rawls has gone to the heart of the paradox of the market. Rawls's principles of justice are in fact a plan for liberalism to legitimate itself, to become consistent with its foundational premises. Only if the choosers are equal can social institutions be defended as the product of individual will, as liberalism requires.

Rawls has relentlessly pursued the ultimate implications of formal liberalism, the requirements of a pure logic of individualism. And as we have seen, the implications are very radical indeed. This is a project for liberal societies that would become, over time, more consistent with their governing philosophy. But is the point of the venture, in fact, simply that liberalism should become more logically consistent?

The Enterprise and Distributive Justice

None of these approaches to the subject of distributive justice comes to terms with pragmatic liberalism's specific question: How do we fairly evaluate differences in individual contribution given the collaborative nature of human effort?

Pragmatic liberalism is suspicious of the claim that income inequalities that arise from market relations accurately reflect differences in individual social contribution. It is the *composite* product that the customer rewards with patronage. But how that reward is distributed among the contributors depends on the constitutional order of the enterprise. Within the various enterprises, diverse conceptions of justice, and injustice, may prevail.

There is an idea of just distribution that is compatible with the ideal of the rational enterprise, understood both as a community of inquiry and as a community of practice. Where there is a normative community, where there are standards of good practice and a clear end in view, it is possible to distinguish levels of individual performance and contribution.

The egalitarian morality that arises from such considerations is more an equality of respect than an equality of opportunity or outcome. It is the kind of mutual respect that arises among those who depend on one another for the success of a common venture.

This is a strong egalitarianism. It emerges from the recognition of good workmanship, responsibility, and creativity in any craft or calling. It is the kind of respect one sees in the recognition that the skilled doctor, scientist, craftsman, and cook have for one another. This has nothing to do with conventional distinctions of social rank or status. It is esteem founded, purely, on performance. It is an ideal of equality reminiscent of the ancient Christian doctrine of the equal worth of all vocations in the eyes of God. This is no raw belief that all are equally deserving. There are good reasons here for differences in honor, recognition, and reward. Nor is this a wretched meritocratic ideal, an idea that the cause of equality is served if all can be shown to have equal opportunity to scramble for the top positions.

The normative basing point for such a scheme of income distribution would be that all vocations are entitled to equal *average* earnings. Differences in contribution, performance, responsibility, difficulty, and sacrifice would have to be justified *in relation to the ends of the particular enterprise*. Appropriate differentials could not be assumed on the basis of traditional occupational status. In principle, it would be assumed that the mediocre manager would earn less than the competent craftsman. There would be no reason to expect that the distinguished professor, tool and die maker, journalist, and corporation executive should not make, roughly, the same. I have in mind a distributional ideal in which the highest net earnings in any field would be between two and four times the average income.

This is not a particularly radical proposal. *Within* most professions and crafts today the ratio between the top and average incomes is roughly two or three to one. The scandal is not with our system of income distribution as a whole, but with the apparent arbitrariness and irrationality of particular differentials in *interprofessional* incomes. How do we justify the differences in compensation between top executives, engineers, and skilled workers? Trial judges and lawyers? Firefighters and police? Doctors and nurses? Scientists, social scientists, and teachers of the humanities? Pilots and air traffic controllers? None of these differences can plausibly be explained by a coherent theory of relative contribution to the enterprise in question any more than they can be shown to result from the "free play of market forces." It is more likely that these "traditional differentials" are simply the result of unexamined usage, or one-time differences in power relations that, embedded in practice, seem in the end natural, and go unchallenged and unquestioned.

Compensation differentials then are properly defined by the constitutional order of each enterprise. They are the product of political deliberation and conscious choice. They are appropriately determined by the practitioners concerned on the basis of clear, impersonal criteria of workmanship, contribution, and performance. This is a most important function of democracy within the enterprise. The closest approximation to such a system in contemporary practice is probably the merit income systems of the great universities. But this is an ideal that could be applied, with appropriate adaptation, to a wide range of productive enterprise.

Karol Soltan has proposed a conception of general criteria for differential compensation which is in some ways compatible with this pragmatic liberal ideal of reward based on workmanship. He suggests that one can measure the importance and difficulty of work, as constituents of responsibility, by examining the costs of error in various tasks. The importance of a job is indicated by the maximum or average cost of errors in its performance. Difficulty involves the probability of error in performing a task. We can then distinguish between satisfactory and exceptional performance. In assigning wages to jobs, we need take into account only the requirements for satisfactory performance. However, when we are allocating wages to individuals, the requirements of exceptional performance become relevant. As Soltan says, "In ordinary use . . . a task may be considered difficult when effort and ability are required to do it *well*, rather than just satisfactorily." [13]

Soltan's scheme is suggestive but far from complete. In the end, it reduces workmanship to economizing. "Error reduction" is not the form that recognition of excellence should take on all occasions, or in all enterprise. Such a scheme would be virtually meaningless in a university, or in many forms of creative or artistic endeavor. Nonetheless, it shows us how to begin thinking about the subject, and, remarkably, it does so along lines that have not been tried before.

At this point, it may well be objected that compensation in an enterprise will, in the end, inevitably reflect market forces. Each enterprise must bid for the scarce resources of talent, energy, and intelligence. This is, no doubt, a fact of life. But let us not confuse the economic issue with the issue of justice. As Rawls has argued, it is hard to claim that we actually *deserve* reward for innate talents and capabilities.[14] Granted, it is difficult to distinguish between the "gift" of intelligence or creative ability and the individual effort that goes into nurturing and applying such talents. Nonetheless, the notion that those who have superior ability can *withhold* their services until they are rewarded according to their own estimate of their worth, that they can hold out for the highest bidder, smacks distinctly of blackmail. We may in fact have to pay more for the services of those who possess rare talent or skill, but we do not have to like it, and we do not have to dignify it with the name of justice. The members of a community of practice know the difference between recognition and reward freely given and that which is a product of market coercion. (This is not to deny that the market is often a good check on the judgment of the community of peers.)

If it is so difficult to distinguish individual contribution to collective effort, why endorse any inequalities at all? Perhaps Rawls is right to think that the only rationally tenable inequalities of reward are those that work to the promotion of equality itself.

However, I think we will find, even after full reflection on what it means to *deserve* differential reward, that recognition of differences in performance within the enterprise is a requirement of justice, that to endorse a strict egalitarianism in this realm would be in fact unfair. In part, this is a matter of compensation. Outstanding commitment to the common effort entails difficulty, unpleasantness, and sacrifice of other opportunities and interests. All of this may be only in the eyes of the beholders. The dedicated practitioner may experience no sense of loss. However, the judgment that a burden has been borne in the interest of a common end is best made not by oneself, but by one's peers. Sacrifice is best understood and acknowledged by those who understand the work at hand, one's fellows in the common endeavor.

Honor, respect, and reward for outstanding performance, for excellence in a craft or calling, may simply be a consideration of natural justice. And it would seem that in a community founded on an ethic of workmanship, honor would be as important as reward, and it seems far easier to justify inequalities of honor, recognition, and respect than inequalities of income.

The justification for inequalities of reward is normally incentive. Pragmatic liberalism, while deploring the view that rationality is merely calculated interest, cheerfully admits that we *are* creatures who respond to reward and recognition. But what kind of incentives do we intend to establish? Each version of liberalism is consistent with its own premise. Market liberalism would reward those who produce the greatest "want satisfaction." Rawlsian liberalism would give incentives to those who would best serve the least well-off, who would promote the cause of equality itself.

Pragmatic liberalism would honor and reward those who promote the ends of rational enterprise, those who innovate and create, those who demonstrate excellence in any craft or skill.

Differences in workmanship, in that broad sense of craft that embraces both creative innovation and painstaking performance, justify inequalities of recognition and reward, inequalities that must be particular to the nature of the enterprise in question. These inequalities presumably would not be as great as those generated by a market system of justice. There would be fewer grand prizes, although these are obviously possible. Recognizing differences in craftsmanship as an *inherent* question of justice, pragmatic liberalism cannot provide as neat a solution to the problem of liberal logic as that of John Rawls. Obviously, we have not solved the mystery of how, with any degree of inequality, liberalism can be true to its root postulate, that social institutions emerge from the free and equal choices of individuals. But liberalism can stand a little rough justice, and an ethic of income distribution that presumed the equal worth of vocations and rewarded excellence according to the standards of good practice appropriate to each would certainly seem fairer than the liberalism we experience today.

Why Do People Seek Extreme Rewards?

Several elements in a pragmatic liberal scheme of distributive justice still require specification. If the redistribution of rewards is particular to the enterprise, and if individuals are to choose freely among the alternative enterprises, as liberalism requires, then the rewards of practitioners doing similar work in different undertakings could vary greatly. This jeopardizes both the principle of *relative* equality of reward, required by the collaborative nature of productive endeavor, and the "rough justice" of *approximate* equality, required by the principle of liberal legitimacy itself.

To be sure, differences in return among enterprises, reflecting consumer demand, are necessary to establish the appropriate relative diffusion of various opportunities in the pluralist order. Pragmatic liberalism cannot do without this marketlike effect and remain faithful to its notion of the open regime. Let us admit that some incentives may be necessary to draw people toward the occupations most in demand, though with relative equality, places as much as prospective income can do much of the job. However, none of this justifies disproportionate differences in individual reward for comparable performance and work *between* enterprises. Again, to do so would be to compromise the principle that the appropriate basis for reward is workmanship.

In the end, then, a progressive income tax is a requirement to secure proportionate equality between those exercising comparable skills in different sectors and industries. While the principle of progressive taxation is easily justified to anyone who accepts the assumptions of pragmatic liberalism, its specific incidence is not. Neither the utilitarian idea that progressivity reflects the declining marginal utility of income nor the view that progressivity reflects the increasing value of public goods, such as protection of property, for those with high incomes, can quite tell us how to set the rates.[15] How define the ratio that ought to prevail among all incomes in a society on the basis of clear and nonarbitrary principle? There is no way of doing this. All schemes of progressivity are approximations and compromises, rough justice in the end, though all are more defensible, on pragmatic liberal premises, than any proportionate or flat-rate system of taxation.

I cannot satisfactorily answer the question. But I can pose another in its stead. What is the source of the demand for excessive income? In any mature industrial society, an income two to four times greater than the norm would be sufficient to provide a most comfortable and secure life, with all the material and other satisfactions that this civilization can afford. Why would anyone crave more? Social commentators, of course, have mused on this for a long, long time.

There are some who come by large incomes almost by accident. I have met more than one millionaire who seemed more astonished than justified by the fact of excessive good fortune. They were not quite ready to give it all back, to be sure, but they had not actually sought extraordinary wealth. This is not the case that interests us at this point.

Income, of course, is intimately related to the prestige system of any commercial society. As Fred Hirsch reminds us, there are "positional goods."[16] Yet, the status that excess wealth brings is very specific to occupation and enterprise. The symbols of truly conspicuous consumption are not common currency, but vary greatly from calling to calling. That which brings prestige in one guild is disdained in another. Automakers know this. The Cadillac,

Mercedes, Volvo, Cherokee, and Bronco represent fine gradations of invidious distinction. They are badges not so much of status as of honorable membership and estate.

In much of business, excessive income has no intrinsic value. It is not meant to be consumed. It is token of achievement, of reputation. There is no perversity in this. The hope for recognition by peers is part of the instinct of workmanship. Academics, scientists, and artists can be driven to obsession by the lure of much paltrier rewards. Perhaps were we to establish a system of prizes for outstanding entrepreneurship, we could do with a much narrower range of income differentials.

However, the quest for excessive wealth may also represent a human pathology, one closely related to the lust for power. One historic argument for capitalism was that commercial competition, money-making, was a desirable substitute for the more dangerous human tendencies toward combat and domination. The "interests" as Albert Hirschman puts it, were enlisted to tame the "passions." [17]

All of this is well known. However, in contemporary America, the search for income well beyond the norm may have another source. The drive, often desperate, for unequal reward, seems rooted as well in an intense need for *separation* and a dreaded fear of falling into the common way of life.

Income buys the ability to live apart, educate one's children apart, to be cured and recuperate apart, enjoy leisure, companionship, and solitude apart, in exclusive domains.

It has been observed that the demand for income inequality is less pronounced in the prosperous, homogeneous, small societies of northern Europe. This is not a triumph of socialist consciousness. The bourgeois spirit is very much alive in Scandinavia and the Low Countries. It is rather that the norm is comfortable, familiar, safe, and quite good enough. There is no reason to escape or differentiate oneself by much from the lot of one's fellow citizens.

There are elements of racism and a fear of the "others" in the American reaction. We do not necessarily celebrate diversity. Not in our backyard.

This quest for separation is not necessarily ignoble. For many who seek more than sufficient wealth, the aim is not ostentation. It is rather to protect themselves and their families from a social order that they regard as brutal and broken, from quite identifiable evils and addictions.

There is also an unspoken aristocratic impulse in all of this, a desire to sustain outposts of excellence and civility, of taste and gentleness. This is not necessarily a matter of mass against class. It may as well be one of noise against quiet.

Thus, in an important respect, the demand for inequality is rooted in the failure of social enterprise. It is the inadequacy, the decay, and the irrationality of the normal services of everyday life that leads to the quest for wealth beyond sufficiency. It is the pursuit of good schools, good housing, good health, good police that motivates the escape from the norm.

Where high-quality standard services are generally available, the rationality of this demand for excess wealth breaks down. Where high quality public schools and universities exist, private schooling *does* become an ostentation, or a matter of particular conviction. Where public parks and forests are superior goods to private recreational facilities, to spend more for less is extravagant. Where average health care is excellent, additional investments cannot yield appreciably better care. And, for that matter, the technology that produces the excellent average car, appliance, or boat diminishes the rationality of investment in its luxury counterpart.

The steady rationalization of basic enterprise, public and private, its increasing perfection, diffusion, and reliability, diminishes the only rational basis of demand for excessive income. What is left is ostentation and greed, and these are not concerns of justice. At the same time, a reduced income inequality in itself enhances the *political* demand for excellent general services, for the most competent, articulate, and quality conscious cannot as readily escape the common lot.

Each of these effects is congenial to the spirit of pragmatic liberalism.

Welfare Policy and the Problem of Poverty

Distributive justice is a pivotal issue of liberal political thought. However, few liberal governments have actually tried to bring about a fundamental change in the distribution of income as an object of policy. Rather, the practical problem that has perplexed liberal politics throughout its history is welfare policy: what to do about the condition of the poor. And here too contention centers on certain basic dilemmas inherent in the nature of liberal political thought.

Given liberalism's presumption that each individual will earn his or her own sustenance, and thus contribute to the common good, the crucial issue becomes: *When is an individual legitimately exonerated from the responsibility of self-support?* Far more than we consciously realize, for almost two centuries our deliberations on social justice and social policy have been a perplexed effort to answer this question.

There have been certain categories of the "deserving poor," where there has been little doubt about the community's duty of support. These include children, the seriously handicapped or disabled, and the mentally incompetent. Our attitudes toward age are a little more complex: while we recognize this as a legitimate condition of dependence, our social security system, as I have noted, is designed to ensure that the individual does not come to depend on the community for support in later life. There is little dispute today that such groups are *entitled* to some provision of community support.

Only in the early twentieth century did unemployment itself become a condition of legitimate dependency, and this marked a notable, and still contentious, reversal of liberal thought. The classic assumption was that there was work for all at some price, that unemployment was the fault of the individual, the product of bad habits or excessive demands. At least from the time of Charles Booth,[18] at the turn of the last century, this view was seriously contested. It was not that the poor lacked the will to work. Sufficient jobs were simply not available. However, only with the reception of Keynesianism did it become an assumption of liberalism that it was the state, and not the individual workers, which bore the primary responsibility for full employment.

In the United States, and uniquely there, in the 1960s low income itself came to be understood as a condition of legitimate dependency. Such progressive liberals as Michael Harrington and John Kenneth Galbraith, thought poverty itself inexcusable, given the conditions of prosperity in a mature industrial society. Orthodox liberals, like Milton Friedman, thought income support more congenial than categorical assistance to classical liberal values. Better simply to provide a minimum living, without question, than to create an elaborate, regulatory, and paternalistic welfare state. Better to let the poor spend cash as they saw fit in the market, rather than instituting a degrading and officiously administered set of prescriptive entitlements: food stamps, rent subsidies, health programs, and the like.[19]

Income, as a criterion of legitimate dependency, remains a contentious ideal. At this point, the liberal mind has become irresolute in its commitment to welfare. And, in fact, it is far from clear that the idea of a "minimum guaranteed income" is a sufficient or appropriate response to the problem of legitimate dependency, or that it is a more effective method of policy than the historic conception of the welfare state, as it was formulated in progressive and pragmatic liberal thought.

A commitment to a minimum guaranteed income is one thing. A commitment to relative income equality is quite another. The first may protect against destitution. It may even, by establishing an income floor, raise the general level of wages throughout society. But it does not thereby legitimate the market as the privileged institution of distribution.

To stand for the right of the poor to spend their poverty-level incomes freely in the marketplace does not obviously represent a full solution to the problem of distributive justice. By what logic do we assume that those who are *legitimately* exonerated from the duty of self-support deserve no more than subsistence income? Why is not an *average* income a more appropriate level of compensation for those who have been denied full opportunity to support themselves?

The idea of a minimum guaranteed income is probably a historic residue of the principle of "less eligibility," that welfare should not be as attractive an opportunity as the most unattractive employment, else the incentive to work would diminish. To assure that some do not take advantage of entitlements intended for others is a legitimate concern of liberal justice, but penury for the least fortunate, as official policy, has never been a very satisfactory response.

The persistent question of "Who are the deserving poor?" despite its vaguely archaic sound, is probably still the right one, and the response, "Those of low income," may very well be an inadequate answer. The first obligation of liberalism is to secure the responsibility and the opportunity for self-support and social contribution. To say this, of course, is easier than to make good on it.

That implies, at least in this time and country, a massive, sustained social commitment to education, social change, employment creation, and precious little sensitivity to certain forms of "cultural diversity." It implies an answer to the question of whether impoverished children deserve a mother or day care, or which proportion of each. Beyond this, the question of what those of us who can't quite cope *deserve* will continue to perplex us, as well it should.

Pragmatic Liberalism and Welfare Policy

Within the deliberations of liberalism on the questions of social justice, the special concern of pragmatic liberalism has always been for universal access to and participation in the fundamental enterprises of the society. The practical policy problem has been this: how to reach the most remote, impoverished, and unassimilated citizens with adequate education, medical care, housing, cultural and recreational facilities, transport, and social insurance? These have been the means to secure equality of opportunity, decency, and self-respect to all citizens.

The U.S. welfare state, with its differentiated and categoric services, bears the mark of this pragmatic liberal theory of state responsibility. And it was precisely this idea of the welfare state that both egalitarian and free market liberals called into question in the great debates on welfare reform of the past generation. Again, in the 1970s and 1980s, categoric services were thought bureaucratic, expensive, and demeaning. Better a guaranteed income that the poor could spend in the market as they wished.

In fact, it was always apparent, even to its strongest advocates, that this approach to welfare was a second-best solution, an approximation of justice. However, at the end of the day, it is also clear that this way of thinking about the problem of welfare has not been discredited.

The pragmatic liberal approach to welfare policy cannot readily be reduced to a tight, formal theory. To base welfare on the universalization of essential services entails a constantly open estimate of the engagements and opportunities that are crucial to the good life. Thus, the problem of welfare is never settled. It is open to continuing debate. All depends on changing understandings of the nature of the public interest in particular undertakings, on specific perceptions of arbitrariness and irrationality in the evolving pattern of purposive enterprises and in the enterprise of liberalism itself. At one period, differential access to the legal system will loom large as a cause of distributive justice. At another point, it will be access for the handicapped. This is, as always, a matter of piecemeal reform.

The range and scope, and the discrete composition, of the regime of universal services is a matter for the continuing exercise of discretion. We can constantly reappraise the several technical questions of justice which are part of any such policy: Which services are to be available as a matter of right to all citizens? Which are to be means-tested? What is our rationale for the distinctions we make?

This approach to welfare cannot be reduced to a single maxim. Consequently, formal liberals, both free market and egalitarian, think it corrupt. The array of public services offered at any time reflects no clear criterion of justice, it is charged, but the relative power and intensity of specific interest demands. Furthermore, any such conception of welfare is implicitly paternalistic. The state prescribes, particularly for the poor, which goods and services they shall have. The pattern of consumption and engagement does not emerge from free individual choice. That is only possible when welfare takes the form of income.

Pragmatic liberals will readily concede that a market distribution, under conditions of relative income equality, is fairer and freer than any authoritative allocation of goods and services. However, the practical problem is that no liberal government has been able to put into effect a distribution of income that would make a market outcome roughly legitimate. It is not even clear that the people of long-established liberal regimes would think a more egalitarian income distribution fair.[20]

This, then, is the enduring problem of pragmatic liberalism. Liberalism has failed to secure the more fundamental just distributions that would make a regime of greater individual freedom possible. It must then persist, as best it can, realistically, as occasion and opportunity permit, in its effort to secure the benefits of liberal civilization to all citizens, and particularly to those who have been systematically disadvantaged by accident and fate. This it must do, stealthily and strategically, against persisting resistance.

Sustainable Systems

Despite the very great, perhaps decisive, importance of the subject, my treatment of environmental policy can be relatively brief. The argument has been foreshadowed. It follows inevitably from what has been said so far.

Reliability, again, is a defining characteristic of rational order, as it is of scientific statement. "Best practice" connotes the dependability and repeatability of a skilled performance, or of organized human effort. Such considerations, we have observed, are linked to liberal politics as conditions of freedom, of the capability of individuals to lay intelligent plans for projects in company with their fellows. It is, then, a rational criticism of any established usage that it is not sustainable over time. The tendency of any significant enterprise on which people depend to self-exhaustion begs the obvious question of what will replace it when it is gone.

Pragmatic Liberalism and Environmentalist Thought

Consciousness of the interdependence of human endeavor and the natural order is peculiarly associated with the pragmatic version of liberalism. Historically, liberalism is not notable for its sensitivity to the natural limitations of human enterprise. Classic liberalism encouraged the transformation of earth for human purposes. It taught, and in this it simply underscored a dominant theme of the classic and Christian traditions, the rightful domination of man over nature.

Contemporary environmental writers often seem to suggest that a sound "land ethic" requires the repudiation of liberal politics and political economy.[1] Some think the entire Western rationalist worldview at odds with a proper respect for the habitability of earth. In this chapter I try to show why this view is mistaken.

Present day environmentalism did not appear full blown, without antecedents. Rather, it represents a clear political and intellectual continuation of the conservation movement of the early decades of the twentieth century, a movement that was conspicuously associated with pragmatic liberalism from its inception. The prophets and poets of latter-day environmentalism—John Muir and Aldo Leopold being only the most prominent—wrote in close proximity to the pragmatic liberal tradition. The dominant themes and concerns of the two movements are very much intertwined.[2]

Like pragmatic liberalism, the environmental ethic is born in philosophic reflection on the implications of recent scientific discovery. Classic liberalism was inspired by the mechanics of Newton. But this latter-day liberalism was struck less by the symmetry of the natural order and more by the mystery of the long stretches of evolutionary and geologic time. The sacred sense of nature of the progressive environmentalists was rooted in a new understanding of the antiquity and continuity of the earth. It was in this spirit that Leopold, for example, thought meditation on the age of an oak significant for the formulation of a land ethic. This sensitivity is only possible in twentieth-century thought. It could not have informed the earlier legacy of liberalism and Western rationalism which did not know these things.

Like historic pragmatic liberalism, environmentalism is close, perhaps too close, in time to Darwin. Its radical vision is to see man primarily *of* nature, as essentially a biological phenomenon. The larger Western tradition saw man as *in* nature, but apart from it as well. Of course, to see man totally as a natural phenomenon enhances the sanctity, and the finality, of the natural order. From this, the worldview of "total ecology," and its politics, logically follows.

Which fundamental image of man we endorse will, in the end, frame our substantive view on practical matters of environmental policy. Our peculiar age, still too close to evolutionary and geologic science for proper perspective, still reeling from the implications of the "discovery of time," is not a good one in which to come to terms with such foundation issues. We live in a time in which the clear light of scientific reason has made the world not more familiar and comprehensible, but actually a good deal more mysterious and enchanted than it was before.

It is true that the founders of pragmatic liberalism taught a basically naturalistic ethic. But they were far from certain, and they wrestled conscientiously with the problem of "the ghost in the machine." They never settled for a simple materialism or naturalism.

Suffice it to say that this reconstruction of pragmatic liberalism presumes that a purely naturalistic ethic is not good enough. There is more to it than that. A final answer to the question of the nature and destiny of man is not yet in.

A Perspective on Environmental Policy

As usual, as a doctrine of practical reason, pragmatic liberalism provides an alternative to certain extreme positions which might otherwise define and structure the debate.

The extreme market liberal position would be that the environment is not a distinctive policy concern. The market will automatically adjust human productive systems in relation to resource scarcities. The market will provide precisely that level of conservation which is consistent with optimum human well-being. Any conscious intervention in this process will either conserve too much or too little. It will either deny present generations the standard of living they might otherwise have or deplete resources prematurely and wastefully. Markets provide mechanisms for gradual transition from one mode of production to another. They give ample warning of impending scarcities through rising marginal prices for short resources, and they provide incentives for adaptive action which shifts production from scarce to abundant resources at just the right rate. Markets are efficient and economic in reconciling productive processes with the capabilities of the earth.[3]

The strong environmentalist view, in contrast, sees liberal political economy itself as logically untenable and self-exhausting, given its assumption that unlimited growth is desirable and warranted. Liberalism places man outside the natural order. The remedy is to understand man as part of the ecosystem, dependent on its delicate relationships, its life-chains and balances. The admonition is to "live according to nature," but this is meant, now, in a strictly biological sense, not, as it was in classical philosophy, to live according to the larger rationality of universal law. The problem is to design productive systems that are harmonious with nature, that do not intrude on ecological relationships, and that are not self-exhausting. In the more extreme versions, this implies a renunciation of most modern technologies and rational organizations. Most of all, it means to disavow the assertive, competitive, Western rationalist worldview, in favor of an ethic of gentleness, acceptance, and proportion.[4]

Sustainable Systems

The approach to environmental policy that one might best associate with a reconstructed pragmatic liberalism is different. It follows naturally from the dominant presuppositions of this discipline of thought. It is inherent in the idea of rational enterprise and intelligent collective action. It is congruent with the conservation ethic which is part of its intellectual history.

Again, the rational enterprise represents forethought, organization, and planning. It is not simply a response to market forces. The aim is continuity and stability over time, not constant fluidity and flux. Markets, and natural processes, give essential clues to needed adaptations. But the object of rationalism is not constant adaptation. It is rather to create orders that will remain stable in the face of shifting human conditions or raw natural processes.[5]

The idea of rational enterprise entails an ethic of stewardship and husbandry. Good practice means taking pains and taking care. It requires conscientious forethought to preserve the *equipment* of an undertaking. This means maintenance in relation to technology, integrity in the conduct of institutions, and conservation where human effort touches the earth.

Theory and Practice

Once again, the significance of a pragmatic liberal conservation ethic, its place in the criticism of the rationality of enterprise, depends on the characteristics of the practice in question. Three very different cases illustrate the *range* of application of the criterion of sustainability to the development of rational enterprise and the critique of established systems. Two cases are in effect exemplary tales taken from the legacy of pragmatic liberalism itself. The third is a case of abject failure.

Agriculture

We have already discussed the settlement of the American West as a paradigm case of the creation of a rational enterprise. Critical scrutiny of European customs, the adaptation of existing methods to fit new soils and climates, led to the formation of a community of good practice, a "professionalization" of agriculture, that unified the otherwise independent and market-oriented farmers. But the first generations of prescribed technique were imperfect. Soil erosion and resource depletion were too often the result, as the Dust Bowl of the 1920s dramatically illustrated a failure of technique. The highly coordinated system of inquiry that lay behind the agricultural enterprise reassessed its doctrine. Conservation became a first principle of good practice in American scientific agriculture in the 1930s.

In recent years, production and technology seem to have overshadowed this commitment. American agricultural practice, in many areas, has become once more environmentally perilous and potentially self-exhausting. The fault lies not simply with market economics but with the *guidance* given the enterprise by its system of governance and its community of inquiry. It seems time, again, for critique and self-correction within this undertaking. It has become imperative to reexamine orthodox assumptions and to draw on the larger intellectual traditions of the enterprise, as a basis for reform and renewal. We have to assure that this most basic of our productive systems remains reliable, for the long run.[6]

Wilderness

The environmental ethic has informed the characteristic rational enterprises of American life in different ways. The preservation of wilderness was a distinctive part of the Progressive conservation ethic and of the emerging public plan for the settlement and development of the land.

To distinguish certain areas of outstanding natural grandeur and beauty from the general plan for development, to create a system of quiet places, was to constitute a new form of rational enterprise, one grounded in the land ethic itself.

Wilderness preservation took the form of a normative culture. It led to the formation of a program of inquiry, from which were derived canons of good practice that constituted a profession, and systematic standardized forms of organization, management, and control.

The object, in this instance, was not, of course, that of making a productive process sustainable. The point was rather the protection and preservation of sacred places. The rational enterprise of wilderness preservation, as constituted in such organizations as the National Parks Service and its counterparts, has more in common with a "practice" of religion than a productive technology. Americans do not formally articulate the matter in quite this way, of course. But "the heartbreaking beauty of the land," as Gary Snider put it, seems to have sacramental significance for this people.

Oil

The petroleum industry is a prime example of an enterprise that has failed to find a way to correct the conditions of standard practice in the interest of the long-run sustainability of the industry.

The peculiarity of oil, in comparison with other fuels, is that it is both remarkably efficient and remarkably cheap. Oil is abundant; unlike coal, it is not particularly labor intensive to produce. Once wells are in place, there is every reason to produce at full capacity, to recover high initial exploration and drilling costs. No producer, of those sharing a major new discovery, has any incentive to hold back on production in anticipation of higher prices later. What one does not pump out of a shared pool, others will. This form of market failure is distinctive to oil and led to early attempts to regulate and order the industry, to limit production so as to maintain prices. However, this economic incentive was never strong enough to create a true conservation ethic, nor, given oil's evident advantages over other fuels, did governments have strong reason to limit or control its use.[7]

The dynamic of the industry was to produce as quickly as possible and then discover more. And for a brief period, this strategy worked. Only once the Middle Eastern fields were in full production did it begin to become evident that further sources would come at a higher price.

Only in the 1970s did the OPEC cartel attempt to reconstitute the industry, to condition low prices and rapid depletion with price and production controls. While this brief period of higher prices and limited supply did yield rapid gains in conservation, the system of governance was unstable, the efforts to preserve the more intelligent use of the resource short-lived.

The failure to incorporate a conservation ethic into the governance of oil means that the period when world technology was transformed by this energy resource will be relatively brief and intense.

A Question of Proportion

Again, the moral is the same. Theory must be related to the particular characteristics of practice. There is not one conservation ethic, there are many. The principle of sustainability, inherent in the very idea of the rational enterprise, has very different implications when applied to agriculture, wilderness preservation, and energy. As a constituent principle of public health (waste disposal and population policy) or genetic engineering, it means different things again. It would be well if we adopted a general political economic orientation as sensitive to environmental as developmental concerns. But the significance of environmental considerations is still relative to the point and purpose of the particular rational enterprise.

The issue of "development" or "environment" is often posed in categoric terms. However, the actual question for practical political reason is one of extent. It is a matter of weighing environmental concerns against other liberal principles and values. "Sustainability" is in itself a many-dimensional concept. It is the total value of a human project that we are called upon to preserve. We do not "conserve" by trading suitability to use for simple environmental purity. Sustainability is a challenge to intelligence. Renunciation, as mindless developmentalism, is merely an act of will.

The ideal of the steady state is a prototype, a pure standard of sustainability, that can be placed alongside the liberal images of mutuality of contract and democratic consent as an ideal of rightful order. Herman Daly defines a steady-state system as one with a "constant stock of people and artifacts," maintained at some desired level by the "lowest feasible flows of matter and energy from the first stages of production (depletion of low-entropy materials from the environment) to the last stage of consumption (pollution of the environment with high-entropy wastes and exotic materials)."[8]

The steady-state ideal implies both a "limit to growth"—a goal of constant population and goods (though not of technology, organization, or culture)—and an economizing motif, that present technologies aim to minimize the use of scarce or exhaustible resources.

Again, the purpose of such a prototype is to stipulate a model for the appraisal of practice. The actual policy problem is to determine which approximations of the ideal "will do" in consideration of other liberal values and the inherent purposes of the enterprise.

Formal liberalism suggests that we simply assimilate this problem of proportion to the relentless logic of utilitarian calculation. Thus, we can count environmental consequences as "externalities," costs of production not fully accounted for in the price of a product. If we can monetize and internalize these costs, we can weigh social "goods" against "bads" and determine which undertakings are, on the whole, worthwhile.[9]

Sustainability can be understood as a problem of "justice between generations." We thus assimilate the interests of the unborn to the utilitarian calculation. The problem is now one of fair distributions across time.

All of this, of course, is sounder in theory than it is in practice. It presumes that we can put an appropriate economic value on the sacred places and fairly discount the long-run habitability of earth.[10] In some straightforward situations, such estimates may be helpful. But in the hard cases, the calculations quickly become remote and conjectural, as we try to establish the money value of a historic church, or compare the costs and benefits of an airport runway and a quiet neighborhood.

The Enterprise and the Dilemmas of Environmental Policy

When, then, is environmental damage sufficiently compelling to require the reconstitution, perhaps the abandonment, of a vital human enterprise? These judgments are difficult, often tragic. And in fact, it is the very nature of the rational enterprise that makes them so.

Again, the rational enterprise is understood as an evolving, ongoing, experimental way of accomplishing a social purpose. Its defects are seldom apparent in the incipient stages of development. They are *discovered* over time. The irrationalities that provoke criticism and compel reform change with the evolving scale, structure, and technique of the enterprise.

The enterprise normally begins small, as innovation, option, or deviant technique. Only in time does it become dominant practice. But by then, a people have come to depend on it. It is part of that intricate frame of order that makes life possible. Furthermore, it is taken for granted. It is hard to imagine alternatives.

The environmental implications of an enterprise are seldom apparent at the outset. Normally, the environmental impact, and the sustainability of a system, is a function of scale. The automobile poses no threat to the habitat when its use is restricted to an elite. The tranquillity of wild places is not endangered when only a few can get to them. It is universal access that poses the problem of sustainability of an enterprise. Yet universal access to the most significant products and institutions of civilization is precisely the goal of the liberal project.

For all of these reasons, the environmentalist case is difficult. To argue that the rational enterprise endangers the life process itself is a perilous venture in liberal discourse. It may be profoundly threatening. In liberalism, the presumptive case is for the autonomy of enterprise. It is the environmental critic who bears the burden of proof, who must give reasons. Yet such criticism is absolutely essential to the sustenance and completeness of the project of liberal rationalism. And it is, in fact, a tribute to our capacity for civic deliberation that such testimony has been heard and has been weighed, and has in the end had a profound impact on our thought and on our policies.

The problem is to determine when environmental considerations are compelling, when they require the reconstitution of enterprise. Surely not any disturbance of nature is sufficient warrant to terminate or divert a human project. Since our first excursions into settled agriculture, man has always been in the process of transforming the environment.

The ecosystem is complex and interdependent. Any unusual intervention may bring unexpected, distant, and potentially disastrous effects. Given the magnitude of the risks, it might seem that prudence would dictate that any human activity that could possibly cause irreversible damage to some fundamental natural process should not be pursued. But many prophecies of environmental catastrophe are remote or conjectural. Just what level of evidence do we require as a condition of calling off a significant social effort?

Of course, some environmental problems admit of purely practical solutions. Where the enterprise is relatively insignificant and the environmental costs significant (fluorocarbon destruction of the ozone layer) or where the project insignificant and the ecological consequences insignificant (highway construction that implies relocating but not destroying wildlife habitat), the appropriate solutions are relatively clear. But the hard cases, where both the human endeavor and the potential, long-run environmental effects are large and significant (commercial agriculture in the tropical rain forests), are increasingly frequent. They have come to constitute a characteristic dilemma of our age.

We need more precise and reliable knowledge of life chains and ecological relationships if we are to judge accurately the potential consequences of various forms of human intervention. Only a more fully developed environmental science will enable us to fairly weigh environmental concerns against other values. It is here, more than at any other point, that we simply need more information if our judgments are to be intelligent at all.

Some may see the rational enterprise as the end product of a Western compulsion to technique and organization, now gone out of control, ending in a doomed assault on the natural order. But it is also possible to define liberal rationalism as a sustained struggle to create an order that *is* in harmony with nature. The excesses of our technology call for correction, not disavowal. The very object of rational critique is to construct forms of practice that are both universal and sustainable. This may be the essence of the long project of liberal rationalism. And it may be the peculiar challenge of practical reason in our era.

A Discipline of Political Judgment

9

The Discovery of Principles

At the outset, I described pragmatic liberalism as a discipline of political judgment. It is a method of decision making, one that applies not only to large scale policy and the more exalted affairs of state, but equally to the everyday acts of governance of the association, the firm, and the other more immediate communities of inquiry and practice.

The task of these concluding chapters is, in effect, to give instruction in the use of this method. I describe its implications and show how it differs from—and relates to—other forms of liberal reason and other methods of policy analysis. My purpose is not to set out a series of steps for effective decision making. I do not write in the style of the handbook. The discussion takes the form, rather, of a quest, of an exploration of mind. My initial object is to show why the prescriptions of formal liberal philosophy, as well as certain exercises prescribed by writers concerned to make policy analysis more principled, seem equally unsatisfactory as a basis for practical political reason. I try to show why something like pragmatic liberalism seems necessary if we are to relate liberal theory to practice.

I begin with what might be called an *individual* theory of decision. The matter of thinking through a problem to a reasonable conclusion is to some extent a solitary process, one that begins in a single mind. However, this activity depends upon a supporting social process. Thus, in the next chapter, I must provide a *collaborative* method of political judgment. I try to show how political deliberation depends upon a specific structure of argument, an awareness of certain vital considerations. The next step, in chapter 11, is to return to the primary concern of liberal political theory, which is the place of liberal principles

in constituting the political regime. I consider the relation between the specific rational enterprise which is our focus of
attention and the larger, ongoing rational enterprise that is liberalism itself. I conclude with a discussion of the aims of political education. Any theory of decision intimates a set of ideas of
good practice for teaching politics and political economy. What,
then, are the skills of civic competence? What should a citizen
be expected to know how to do?

Starting from Principle

At first glance, it seems unexceptionable to say that decisions
should be made on principle. We naturally oppose principled
judgments to those of expediency and interest. As I have noted, in
liberal thought, acting on principle is a necessary restraint on the
vagaries of human thought and the diverse temptations of human
impulse and passion. To the extent that we act consistently, binding ourselves to treat all similar cases by the same general rules,
our decisions are at least not whimsical or random. Again, to act
on principle is to participate in the development of rational order,
to take part in the fashioning of a stable frame of reference of laws
and institutions within which people can design life plans with
some degree of confidence in their outcome.

Nonetheless, the idea that decisions should be based on principle is not as obvious as it may seem. This is actually a distinctive
peculiarity of liberal political thought. Neither Marxists nor conservatives think in quite this way. Acting on principle is not the
same as acting out of compassion or pity, respect for tradition or
authority, or on the basis of an understanding of the dynamic
forces of history. Furthermore, acting on principle may connote a
certain self-righteousness and rigidity, an ideological approach
to politics that may be oblivious to cries for help, hard facts, or
subtle opportunities.

In fact, it is not at all clear what acting on principle means.
The view that one infers from formal liberal philosophy is that
we should *have* our principles at the outset of action. The process
of political judgment is one of *applying* principles to cases. The
order of reason is deductive. We move from a universal rule (as
major premise) to a description of the situation (as minor premise) and derive an imperative as the conclusion of the syllogism.[1]

It is not surprising that such a view of practical political reason should emerge from formal liberal philosophy. The very object of such philosophy is to create universal rules, principles that would, when applied to public problems, invariably result in good decisions. Political theory is written to recommend that, at the moment of choice, one apply the utilitarian maxim, or Rawls's two principles, of Ackerman's rule of neutral discourse, or a principle of individual rights, or majority rule, or undistorted communication.

From this point of view, the task of political philosophy, as community of inquiry, is to manufacture rational principles. The entire process of philosophical criticism, discussion, and argument is to certify the worth, the rational reliability, of these principles. The task of the practitioner, then, is to be guided by these rules of good practice much as the doctor is guided by the certified results of medical research, or the farmer those of the experiment station.

The more one thinks about it, the more audacious this all seems. The effort is nothing less than that of reducing the great imponderables of politics to rules of standard practice, as though we were discussing the rationalization of an industry or the principles of range management. But this is precisely what is intended, and it is not an indefensible project, once the implications are fully appreciated. This is but another element in the general project of Western rationalism, which holds that human purposes are best served if founded on reliable system.

The difficulty, from the practitioner's point of view, is not with the nature of the effort itself, but that the effort is inconclusive. There are a variety of systems of liberal principles and no sure metatheoretical standards for deciding among them.[2] The difficulty is that the method of liberal philosophy does not result in a unique set of principles. It is possible to order the guiding values of liberalism in a number of ways, and the meaning of such fundamental liberal concerns as right, freedom, equality, and the like seems always contestable. It is possible to create systems of liberalism, but liberalism has never been reduced to a system. Choice from among the various versions of liberal theory then becomes a matter of belief, or commitment, or persuasion, or tradition, but it is not a matter of rational demonstration.

If we cannot start from principle, then we must discover principle in the process of deliberation itself. Perhaps the search for policy and principle is simultaneous. This sounds promising.

However, here we must proceed carefully. There are turnings we can take that will lead us back into unwelcoming thickets. In place of the demand that we *adopt* a formal theory, we may be asked to *create* one as the price of political plausibility. Let me describe, briefly, how this can come about.

Searching for Principle

The fact of the matter is that we are seldom aware of our principles at the outset of inquiry. Today there is wide agreement that the classic deductive (and inductive) models of reason do not adequately represent human problem-solving capabilities.[3] It is now generally supposed that the activity of reason is one of testing the worth of conjecture and supposition, of hunches and hypotheses that have come rather spontaneously to mind. This parallels our contemporary understanding of the nature of scientific exploration, as described by Kuhn, Popper, Lakatos, and others.

It is likely then that, rather than starting from principle, we will *find* our principles as a product of our effort to give reasons for our first intuitive appraisal of a situation. This process of argument, of justification, is not a mere effort to "rationalize" what we intend to do anyway. Rather, the formulation of argument is a heuristic, a method of criticism, that is key to the rational correction and control of the initial impulses of mind. Thus, if the grounds we are about to give in support of our proposals seem inadequate, we must revise either our reasons or our policies.

This process is *similar* to John Rawls's idea of "reflective equilibrium," though Rawls regards this as a test of the worth of formal philosophy rather than a method of practical reason. We begin with our "considered moral judgments," our *strong* convictions about various states of affairs (the wrongness of slavery, the rightness of universal education). We then see whether proposed principles express these intuitive sentiments and whether we are satisfied when they are extended to other situations. (If differences in reward are wrong when based on accidental attributes like race, are differences in reward based on innate talent or intelligence wrong also? If education is an enterprise that should be universally available, should fine art be also?) We then "go back and forth," revising our convictions, or our philosophy.[4]

But how far should this process go? Philosophical reflection is one thing and practical political reason quite another. Our public decisions are made under pressure, in the face of controversy and conflicting counsel. We have to know when we have reached a *satisfactory* reconciliation of thought and action, incomplete and provisional though it may be. By what standard do we know when our deliberations have gone far enough?

Writers on normative policy analysis differ widely in their views of what is required. Some hold to Max Weber's basic prescription that we must be explicit about our values. The most important concern is not to conceal value judgments, to treat them as givens, or hide them behind a veil of scientific competence or impartiality. Others should be able to judge "where we stand" as protagonists in the public debate.[5] For some this might be enough. But as David Braybrooke and Charles Lindblom long ago reminded us, a simple statement of "naive preferences"—saying, for example, merely that one favors increased equality—does not take us very far. Some effort, it seems, must be made to justify the principles we invoke, to show why they should be regarded as definitive in resolving an issue of public concern.

Thus we find that many writers on practical political reason prescribe that those who would take part in public affairs engage in an effort at value clarification. Often this implies a kind of rough-and-ready Kantianism, an exercise in ethical generalization. One is asked to examine the implications of adhering to a certain maxim of choice in a wide variety of situations. "Lying is wrong," but there are times when lying seems a moral imperative. Would one uphold the ideal of free market choice even in the face of irreversible environmental damage? Would one pursue equality to the point where there was no incentive for anyone to lift a plow again? By seeking out "hard cases" where a general rule becomes doubtful, we qualify a universal principle. By defining those circumstances that require an exception to the rule, we *bound* a principle in relation to others, and thus establish an order of priority among them. The goal of this procedure is nothing less than the formulation of a coherent schema of principles, one that could be upheld consistently as a formula for public choice.[6]

Thus, Duncan MacRae, and Brian Barry and Douglas Rae,[7] among others, would have policymakers test their value commitments against certain "metaethical" norms, to the end that their principles are general, consistent, and clear. Similarly, Frank Fischer argues that we are logically required to *vindicate* the principles we invoke in policy analysis, to show how they are related to a "valued way of life."[8] David Paris and James Reynolds see policy inquiry culminating in the statement of "rational ideologies," coherent systems of principles that can guide, inform, and justify public choice.[9]

We seem to be back where we started. If we do not *begin* from a formal political philosophy, then it appears that we are expected to end there. Our search for principles must culminate in consistent system, it would seem, before we are fit for public responsibility, perhaps before we are entitled to act as citizens. After all, the alternative to acting on deliberately chosen, reasonably defensible principle is to act out of passion, or interest, or simple "naive preference."

It is interesting that these methods are not expected to yield a *unique* set of principles. Nor is this the aim of Rawls's idea of reflective equilibrium. The object is not to show that one's actions conform to some universal scheme of values that all rational beings would endorse. The analysis does not end in Cartesian proof. Rather, it culminates in a *stand*. The purpose seems to be to generate a broad sustainable statement of what one takes to be the ideal ends of the liberal order.

It would seem then that political judgments are to be justified by showing their relation to some overall partisan effort to steer society toward a particular conception of the liberal project. Perhaps the issue before us is no more than a request for a zoning variance in a small town. But in justifying on principle one's response to such an issue, one is saying in effect either that one is for a political order in which persons have the right to use their own property largely as they please, or that one favors a regime in which property is progressively regulated in the name of community interests.

This can't be right. Of course it is important that we be self-conscious about the sense in which everyday decisions are part of the larger fabric of liberal politics: that we see a land-use plan as an assignment of rights, and that to manage a factory is an exercise in distributive and commutative justice. But this cannot mean that the condition of justifiable argument is to show that each everyday decision is part of an overall plan for the reconstruction of the liberal order. Nor can it be the case that we are required to develop a fully articulated liberal philosophy before our acts of governance are regarded as sound and responsible.

There must be a way of distinguishing our commitments to the overall liberal order from those that apply to the specific functional undertakings for which we are responsible. There must be a way of *applying* liberal principles to concrete problems without being required to show that they are part of a comprehensive theory of the regime. We are citizens of two realms, the polity and the enterprise. It must be possible to distinguish our duties to each of these communities.

We need a more proximate goal for reason. There must be a way of establishing a justification for an action before we are led back through layer after layer of higher-order principles, in what seems to be an infinite regression.

Historic pragmatism taught that values would emerge from context, from an appreciation of the problematic situation.[10] However, historic pragmatism was quite vague about how this could be accomplished without falling into sheer expediency. Specifying a workable relation between theory and practice requires a relation of philosophical argument and contextual interpretation in which each serves to reduce the degree of ambiguity in the other. It is a matter of not expecting either the method of logic or that of experience to carry the entire burden of reason.

Theory and Practice Once More

Let us look again at what it might mean to derive theory from practice. Philosophical pragmatists have long suggested that principles "emerge" out of contemplation of a particular problem of action. (So have Aristotelians, Marxists, some Kantians, and phenomenologists, but there is no need for an elaborate philosophical disquisition at this point.) But how does this come about? What process of thought can lead us from the "facts of the matter" to the controlling criterion of liberal value? That is what we must now attempt to determine. Once again, by practice we mean simply an established way of doing things. And again, the task of critical reason, in the tradition from the Enlightenment, is to scrutinize prevailing practice, looking for means to its improvement, which is to say, greater fittedness to purpose and greater congruity with certain ideals of right order.

Thinking in this way, we invoke principles, in the first instance, to distinguish "problems" from "states of affairs." Inflation is not by definition a problem. A rise in the price level is simply a condition. Inflation becomes a problem if we think it redistributes income in socially undesirable ways or hampers the productive process. Similarly, differential treatment of persons is only a problem if we think it unfair. Otherwise, it is simply the "way things are." And by the same token, a technique can only be defined as "inefficient" if we can propose a better way.

To thus invoke principle is not only to identify a problem. It is also to make a claim. The improvement of practice is to be regarded not only as expedient but rightful. As we have seen, such principled judgments identify the public character of an enterprise, and the public interest in it, which, again, is not to say that it thereby becomes subject to state authority.

As I have said, this process of applying theory to practice is similar to subsumption in scientific reason. To explain a phenomenon scientifically is to relate it to a general category or law. This, we say, reasoning scientifically, is a reptile, or an example of late glaciation, or of the dispersion of gas. By a similar logic, this, we say, reasoning politically, is a problem of rights, or of distributive justice, or of social economy.

But how do we know that we have invoked the right principle? How do we distinguish a compelling case from a mistake in judgment? Obviously, the whole problem of liberal reason is that we can associate the same pattern of events with different standards and thus come to radically different conclusions about appropriate action.

How do we support the contention that a particular state of affairs is properly subsumed under a particular principle? This is a different problem from scientific or even legal reason, where the fittedness of a general category to the case at hand is established by the presence or absence of stipulated elements. (Thus, "reptile" requires cold bloodedness, as "murder" requires intent. But what does "freedom" or "nonarbitrariness" require?)

A practice develops over time, and every pattern of practice represents the successful refinement of technique in relation to some configuration of principles. The criticism of practice then normally depends on the identification of some *imbalance* in performance. The claim is that some set of principles has been pursued at the expense of others. To invoke principle to identify problem then is to point to some presumably vital consideration that has been neglected in the calculus of action.

It is not conventional to do so, but it is apparent that, in this view, liberalism can be treated as a theory of just proportion. Like the "golden mean" of Aristotle's *Nichomachean Ethics,* virtue is identified as a course between recognizable evils. As Aristotle thought that we could know courage by its opposites, the extreme states of timidity and recklessness, so in liberal reason we may invoke freedom to identify an excess of equality, and unfairness as arbitrariness may be recognized as the pursuit of rational order carried to an illegitimate extreme.

Formal liberal philosophy would have us seek a rule we could apply consistently. But any basic liberal principle, pursued relentlessly, leads to excess. Extreme freedom is license, and extreme equality, injustice. Each liberal principle signals a potential excess in another. This is precisely how the dilemmas of liberal political theory arise, and it leads some to think that liberalism is incoherent.

However, if we regard liberalism as a logic of just proportion, then our reasoning takes another form. We see liberal principles as defining and bounding one another. The relation *among* liberal principles is that each defines an unacceptable extreme of the pursuit of any other.

Thus, to assert that excessive standardization is a problem in medical practice, we are in effect saying that the pursuit of reliability and universality in technique may be pursued at the price of responsiveness to individual need. Or to say that a form of work is degrading and demeaning may be to imply that efficiency has been pursued beyond the limits set by considerations of individual freedom and respect for persons. This is not the language of trade-offs. Rather, we are responding to a more ancient resonance in our heritage of political thought. To invoke principle to identify problem is to suggest a sense in which the enterprise is *aidikia,* out of harmony with its essential aims and purposes. This is a notion that originates with Plato.

From the identification of such imbalance, or excess, we derive a conception of improvement or reform. Practice now becomes the test of theory. The justification for the principles we invoke is not their conformity to higher-order metanorms, or their coherence in a philosophic sense, but their *pertinence* to the issue at hand. We may be committed to strong participatory democracy. Does this mean that all production decisions, all questions of good practice, should be submitted to vote? The burden is on the protagonist to show that the realization of a liberal ideal is compatible with the improvement of some specific idea of practice. It is this, rather than the case that a principle conforms to some idea of the human good, or that it is a maxim that any rational being would endorse, that constitutes the effective *test* of principle in this scheme of reason.

Kantian consistency—the test of ethical generalization that would have us measure the worth of principles by our willingness to endorse them as a general rule—now has a specific referent. We delimit the application of abstract principles, specify the cases to which they do and do not apply, by appealing to the purpose of particular forms of practice. We are for freedom of speech, yes, but that does not imply that all should have unrestricted access to the forums of the university. For the function of the university is disciplined inquiry. It is not just another arena of public argument.

Not only the formal ideal of logical consistency but the order of priority among liberal principles can be understood as a matter for situational analysis. We do not debate the primacy of freedom and equality in the abstract. Each of these values, we suggest, signals an extreme of the other. The actual issue of liberal reason is not the priority of these values, but their reconciliation.

Too much freedom may be signaled by a claim to equal treatment. A private club should be free to select its own members, yes. But when that club is understood as a forum for business and civic discussion, the situation changes, and discrimination on grounds of race or sex becomes a public concern. Equality trumps liberty, *because* of the purpose of the enterprise concerned.

Interpretation and Deliberation

The approach to political analysis that I have sketched so far is hardly complete. I have described a totally solitary process of thought. This is a way in which personal deliberation and the process of formulating argument can guide and correct judgment. However, this process can yield but an *interpretation* of an issue. The adequacy of that interpretation as a basis for public action is not yet known.

The *force* of an argument, in this scheme of reason, depends on the relation between three elements. First is the liberal principle invoked. Second is the depiction of the state of affairs, the evidence adduced to characterize a practice as problematic. Third is the idea of remedy, the plausibility of the reform that will improve practice in the direction of principle.

The fit between the elements may be more or less tight and compelling. But it is clear any such interpretation is contestable. Others may perceive the essential elements, and the relationship among them, quite differently. To have created such an interpretation, as a product of systematic practical reason, is nonetheless an act of conjecture. It is to introduce an argument into the process of public decision. This may be the starting point for political deliberation, but it is not the end.

Political judgment, in the final analysis, is a collaborative and not a solitary affair. In historic pragmatic thought, it was the concurrence of a community of inquiry, following procedures that could be shown sufficient to affirm or deny the reliability of a proposal, that was the effective test of a conception of practice. Throughout, I have taken pains to underscore this essentially collaborative nature of human rational effort.

We test and correct our initial judgments, not through introspection alone, but by taking into account the judgments of others. Appraising the judgments of others, and reflecting on their judgment of our own statements, is the core of the collective process of rationality. The scientific community asks of each newly articulated proposition whether following its implications will yield more reliable knowledge. The political community asks of each new contention whether adopting it as authoritative will yield better practice.

Some versions of utilitarian liberalism, and public choice theory, teach that politics is a game played out among persons of fixed preferences, that all political interaction is a matter of compromise, bargaining, and exchange. However, what makes political deliberation possible is that we might change our minds. In deliberation, we may modify or abandon our initial conjectures, in recognition of a better way of understanding.

Our first-order political judgments culminate in an argument, in a provisional stand. Our second-order judgments are adjudicational: they are judgments among judgments, of which our own is one. (For we do not start from a position of impartiality. This is a myth, even for judges. We start from some predisposition, some hypothetical interpretation of the matter at hand.) In a situation of controversy, we are asked to determine which of a variety of rival views will become authoritative for the polity. We often associate such adjudicational reason with the law and the work of judges. However, the appraisal of, and decision among, competing claims and cases is in fact the basic task of citizenship.

We may say that in such reasoning, theory emerges from a consideration of the "facts of the matter." We do not mean this literally. This is no raw empiricism. We do not mean that decision can turn on evidence adduced about the nature of the state of affairs alone. Rather, the "facts" that define the "situation," which is the starting point for practical political judgment, are a construct of argument. The "facts" that must be adjudicated are the rival interpretations that constitute the controversy.

To reason from "situation" thus defined to controlling principle is a collaborative act, and it requires a certain setting for argument. Certain conditions must be met, certain considerations entertained, if the judgment of the community is to be regarded as soundly based, if we can justify our collective will to one another. It is, thus, to the constitution of this process of deliberation that we must now turn.

10

Political Deliberation

To deliberate literally means to weigh. But one cannot balance rival views simply against one another. One must weigh them against *something*.

The collaborative process of arriving at a single authoritative policy for a community cannot arise from simple discussion, merely from an airing of all points of view. In political deliberation, as in scientific inquiry, each remark must be assessed as a *contribution*, appraised for its bearing on the object at hand. Political deliberation requires a specific underlying structure. It is not mere conversation. What then are the requirements that must be met if political judgment is to be taken as sound and well considered?

Contemporary democratic theory is particularly concerned to secure the conditions of neutral discourse. The object is that the process of deliberation and decision not be biased toward any particular outcome or set of interests. This is, of course, the intent of Jurgen Habermas's universal pragmatic, in which common commitment properly arises from a situation of ideal speech, where every participant has the same ability to make arguments, and to criticize and question the arguments of others, where no point of view goes unrepresented because its exponents are dominated, inhibited by authority relationships, or lack assertiveness. As we saw above, in chapter 2, these conditions of equal individual competence to participate in deliberation may also be taken to be the ideal requirements of democracy.

However, this is not actually quite enough. These procedural guarantees are but another way of trying to assure liberal impartiality. The aim is that all individual *opinions* will be equally

well expressed. This is no more than another version of utilitarianism, one supposes, the object being that policy should
reflect an aggregation of individual "expressed preferences."
But the assumption seems to be that every argument, every
statement, has equivalent worth. We still do not know how
these equally expressed opinions are to be appraised, or on
what basis we should determine which should prevail. We are
left with no more than the single rule that one should not prefigure argument. This is, indeed, good advice, but it is not
enough.

I discuss four themes for reason—themes that must arise and
be taken into account if a community is to contrive a course of
action that will at once enhance the realization of liberal values
and perfect the performance of a substantive enterprise. These
are requisites of deliberation that actually show how theory is to
be applied to practice.

I call these four: reasons of trusteeship, critical reason, entrepreneurial reason, and meliorative reason. Normally, we think of
these four modes of reason as incompatible rivals. We presume
that, to be rational, we must identify with one to the exclusion of
the rest. We view the adherents of these methods as philosophical
and political opponents. Each is normally associated with a complete method of political thought. Each is usually presented in-
dependently as a unique path of right judgment, as the *correct*
approach to reaching conclusions on desirable public policy.
Each is identified with a particular political philosophy and each
with a specific mode of policy analysis. Each presupposes a particular cognitive focus, a unique idea of rationality, and a distinctive justificatory logic.

I try to show that these approaches to practical reason are in
fact interdependent. None alone is sufficient as a guide to public
decision, and each has a part to play in the process of intelligent
collaborative political reason. Rationality is better understood as
a matter of learning from each and being conscious of the factors
that lead us to assert, in the end, that one should prevail in the
decision at hand.

Reasons of Trusteeship

When reasoning in the mode of trusteeship, we are asked to
focus attention on organizational norms and rules and the col-

lective purposes of an enterprise. Rationality is a matter of satisfying the requirements of authority and function. A policy is justified by showing that it follows from a conception of "my station and its duties" or from established norms of good practice. The ground of judgment is formally conservative, in the classical Burkean sense. Tradition is prescriptive. The approach is in accord with the counsel of such contemporary writers as Roberto Unger, Alasdair MacIntyre, Michael Oakeshott, and Michael Walzer, who all argue, in various ways, that normative judgment must be anchored ultimately in custom, precedent, and usage. In policy analysis, the "saticficing rationality" of Herbert Simon, in which the object is to find a course of action that "will do" in furthering the objectives of an undertaking, is consistent with the ideal of trusteeship.

Liberal rationalism is uneasy with this style of thinking for it seems uncritical and unreflective. Yet this is in fact how most of the world's work gets done. Most everyday decisions are based on a tradition of practice. This is the mode of judgment that brings meaning and legitimacy to most undertakings. Furthermore, as a style of decision making and ethical judgment, trusteeship evokes strong norms and moral virtues. One speaks of duty and obligation, prudence and responsibility, a mature understanding of what is entailed in guiding a human concern.

For pragmatic liberalism, trusteeship is the indicated starting point for argument. The rational enterprise evolves through a process of trial and error, persistent reconsideration and adaptation. Existing practice has survived repeated iterations of close scrutiny. It has prima facie validity.

Thus, the case for prevailing practice must be heard. Especially when criticism of dominant institutions is widespread, it is important that the rationale for the going concern be fully appreciated before reform is attempted. If the natural advocates of orthodoxy are halting or inarticulate in their defense, it may be the task of the detached citizen to redress the imbalance of argument by *reconstructing* the case for existing practice, for the fuller rationale of technique is often lost in time. What is needed then is that the deliberations of an earlier age be retrieved, that the cases and contentions that led to this road being taken rather than another be reintroduced into argument. Only by such historical retrieval can the rationality of that which is now accepted as commonplace be made manifest. The task of critical reason is to find ways of doing things that are identifiably better than the status quo. But the status quo is always an option, and given the inherent legitimacy of established practice, it is wise to treat it as a basing point for reform.

However, trusteeship is not a sufficient basis for judgment. Those who think only in this way will miss the whole point of liberalism's ideal of critical detachment.

One of the most distinctive features of classic liberal thought was the idea of the state of nature and the social contract. Liberalism pictured solitary individuals contemplating the advantages and disadvantages of entering into civil society, accepting obligations to political authority. The object of this thought experiment, the foundation of the political theory of Hobbes, Locke, and Rousseau, was to establish the kinds of political authority that totally free individuals might rationally accept as binding and thus establish a criterion for judging when any form of political authority was rightful and when it was not. Social contract theory seemed to suggest that we were free to start all over again, to found society on entirely new foundations.

However, the allegory of the solitary, natural individual and the social contract also suggests a vantage point for the appraisal of *established* institutions, practice, and belief. The point now is that we are capable of stepping back from inherited custom and usage, and reexamining how well suited existing practice is to our purposes. Such liberalism teaches that the perspective of the detached individual, who can contemplate fundamental questions of aim and purpose without preconception, is better than that of the experienced but unreflective master of an inherited body of technique.

The trustee's perspective, the argument for the going concern, then, is a necessary part of considered deliberation. But it is not the whole of it.

Critical Reason

Critical reason focuses on principles. A policy is rational to the extent that it meets a standard that can be expressed as a general rule. One justifies decisions by pointing to a coherent set of values that are served by policy. This is, of course, the method of formal liberalism, and we are by now well acquainted with its implications.

We may think of a politics of principle as a high-minded kind
of politics. We may associate it with civility and order, legalism
and propriety. Yet the function of principles in ordinary political
argument is normally critical. Argument from principle is more
convincing as protest than as justification; it is more potent as the
tool of the outsider than the insider. The reason for this, of course,
is that liberal ideals are inherently radical. No undertaking ever
quite lives up to the highest standards.

To invoke principles, again, is to point to some disparity between theory and practice. The idea of freedom, or justice as relevant distinction, is the basis for taking issue with intrusive,
pointless, or overbearing regulation. Economy and efficiency are
standards used to raise questions about the reassurances of trustees as well as the initiatives of entrepreneurs. If a way can be
shown to perform a function more economically, prevailing practice is properly regarded as socially wasteful. The economic analyst stands in constant judgment of all practices and projects. No
human undertaking is ever quite optimal. Similarly, the determined democrat can always find fault with the enterprise, for rational hierarchy or strong leadership is part of most collective
activities. The advocate of individual choice and free markets can
always discern a way to replace organization with bargained collaboration. Those whose concern is for reliable performance can
always show that existing practice does not quite hang together,
that greater system is needed.

To invoke principle against practice is automatically to trigger
an alarm. Such claims constitute a standing case in liberal political
discourse. They *activate* the process of political deliberation. By
the rules of liberal political argument such charges cannot be ignored or dismissed. The protagonist of the going concern cannot
say that the "wastefulness" of prevailing technique is "irrelevant"
or that "procedural arbitrariness" is "beside the point."

Such claims based on principle require assessment and response. But they are not definitive or compelling. They create
a tension in political argument, but they do not decide it. In the
end we must weigh theory against practice, evaluate the case of
the critic who, looking always for a better way of doing things,
protests that the existing order of things fails to meet its own
standards against the counsel of trustees and the plans of entrepreneurs.

It might be thought that the critic is under some obligation to propose a workable remedy. Once one has learned the trick of it, it is too easy to find fault, to rejoice in revealing the many ways in which the whole rationalist civilization "contradicts itself." To be sure, in the hands of nihilist philosophy, this sort of thing can get out of hand and become wearying.

However, in the normal case, the critic who invokes principle against practice is not actually required to propose an alternative to be taken seriously. I know that at several points so far I have suggested that pragmatic liberal argument is distinctive precisely because it is grounded in argument among workable alternatives. However, it also seems inherent in the very idea of liberal discourse that one cannot dismiss a charge of serious injustice by saying only that the claimant has suggested no remedy. Public decision making is a collaborative process. It implies a division of labor. We are all in this together. Particularly when those who speak are the awkward or afraid, it is up to the rest of us to provide the missing elements in argument. However, the crucial point here is simply that the function of the critic can be distinguished from that of other roles in the deliberative process.

Principled criticism is an essential part of reasoned political deliberation. Without it, the claims of trusteeship go uncontested, and prevailing usage, tradition, and technique are not questioned. Liberal rationalism, again, *requires* that detachment from existing practice which it is the function of the critic to provide.

Those who speak for principles take the measure of established practice. Their claims must be taken seriously, but they do not automatically enjoin us to action. Someone must speak for the rationale of the going concern, and someone must propose alternatives to it if we are to create more serviceable designs for action.

Entrepreneurial Reason

The work of the entrepreneur is to propose a new undertaking, a project or policy, a better way of doing things.

In entrepreneurial reason, we focus on projects and the means to their realization. Rationality is instrumental, argument a matter of showing how means match with ends. The economic entrepreneur must fashion a new relationship of capital and labor, supply and demand. The political entrepreneur must win the support of voters and power brokers, fashion a coalition, develop the mechanisms to implement policy.

Entrepreneurial initiative is assumed to be the source of that ever-tentative, ever-changing pattern of institutions and enterprise that is the hallmark of pluralist politics. The modes of production and exchange, the forms of religion, the disciplines of the arts and sciences are all to arise from the competitive efforts of innovators. Entrepreneurship, understood in this fuller, richer sense, is an act of political leadership. Bertrand de Jouvenal defined politics as the effort to "enlist the support of other wills" in an endeavor.[1] The essence of entrepreneurship lies not in the buying and selling but in the design of the enterprise—its technique, its norms, its system of governance.

Entrepreneurial reason starts in the perception of a new pattern of relationships among the elements of an ongoing activity. To invoke examples both banal and exalted, it is Ray Kroc seeing a significant relationship between systems analysis and the hamburger stand, Martin Luther King a connection between the American commitment to civil rights and the strategy of civil disobedience, and John Dewey a link between the experimental method of science and the function of the schools.

Entrepreneurial argument turns on a question of improvement. The burden is to propose a better way—an improved technology, a new form of worship, a theoretical approach that resolves puzzles and quandaries within a science. Entrepreneurial thought is always grounded in a tradition of practice. The *suggestiveness* of the entrepreneurial insight is that it resolves a problem of recognized purpose and function for an ongoing enterprise. The entrepreneur never starts at the beginning. All human activities have somehow been carried on before.

In formal liberalism, the justification for an entrepreneurial initiative lies in the willingness of others to associate themselves with it. The new product, the new firm, must win the support of investors, workers, and customers; the new religion must win adherents. Presumably, the entrepreneurial visions that become institutionalized, part of the standard practice of a free society, are those that meet the utilitarian test. They reflect the calculated preferences of those who throw in their lot with the project.

But this view is too simple. We test entrepreneurial initiative not only through choice but argument. We deliberate the merits of innovation in comparison with prevailing practice and in the light of the principled objections and concerns that arise as a community examines the implications of a new undertaking. We judge initiatives not for ourselves alone, but in relation to the purposes and values of a community also.

Thus, the entrepreneurial initiative is important to practical liberal reason, but it is not the whole of it. The instrumental rationality, the advocatory mode of argument, that is associated with entrepreneurship is essential to liberal politics, but it cannot be taught as the essence of liberal politics. This is but one of the modes of reason and judgment that is pertinent to political deliberation.

Meliorative Reason

The cognitive focus of the trustee is on practice, that of the rational critic principles, and that of the entrepreneur, projects. Those who practice meliorative reason concentrate on "problems," and a problem arises, in Dewey's definition, precisely when there is conflict over how a pattern of activity should be performed.

Thus, the aim of meliorative reason is to contrive agreement. Justification is a matter of showing why a particular proposal might satisfy diverse aims and values.

The standard prescription for doing this, as described by David Braybrooke and Charles E. Lindblom, is to proceed "incrementally," proposing marginal adjustments in the going concern which might make things "better" in the eyes of the diverse protagonists, moving by successive approximations, reopening the argument on which aspects of practice are to be regarded as problematic after each iteration of reform. The process is serial and remedial. (Braybrooke and Lindblom introduced the term "meliorative reason," and I use it here to suggest a particular affinity with their ideas. However, I use the term to suggest a somewhat broader mode of reason than the specific decision-making strategy of incrementalism.)[2]

In theory, the pragmatic analyst is an impartial mediator, merely the contriver of consent. However, the claim that the method is both realistic and impartial rests on some rather tenuous and not altogether innocuous assumptions.

First, one has to assume that all values have the same weight and merit. If a reform is good when it "works in the direction of desired values," the idea that minorities should be kept firmly in their place would have to have equal standing with an appeal to equal rights. The basis of classic incrementalism is manifestly utilitarian. The idea is to adjudicate not the simple hedonistic interests of the participants, but their values.

Second, one must assume that all parties hold their values subject to trade-offs. They will gladly accept a policy that is "a little unjust" if it at least leads to concurrence on a positive course of action and seems more equitable than existing arrangements.

Third, one must expect that, over time, all relevant values will be accounted for. If the method is to be truly neutral in the liberal sense, it must accommodate the concerns of the silent, the awkward, and the oppressed as well as those of the vocal, the active, and the intense. This would seem to require conditions approaching perfect democratic pluralism—something like Habermas's state of ideal communicative competence.

Obviously, we are going to have to rework the idea of incrementalism somewhat if this conception of method is to find a place in our scheme. This is not merely a neutral technique for contriving compromise.

In fact, when the problem is to decide what should be done when entrepreneurial visions, principled objections, and the prudent counsels of trustees are in contention, the implications of incrementalism appear in an entirely different light. It becomes apparent that the stance of the analyst is not neutral. The justification for any incremental remedy will now have to turn on the point that it works toward the realization of some liberal principles, that an entrepreneurial initiative should be supported despite objections, or that some form of established practice should prevail, despite the force of rational criticism or the appeal of alternatives.

One cannot have it all three ways at once. Any act of meliorative reason, any incremental reform, will necessarily work in some direction, and some set of protagonists will be asked to accommodate to what the analyst as adjudicator adduces as an overriding claim or consideration.

I think this formulation is closer to the historic spirit of pragmatism. For Dewey, reform was always understood as change that worked in the direction of the greater realization of liberal values. Yet such reform was always context-dependent. It had to be measured against the values of institutionalized experience, and those of a course of action acknowledged to be workable. In the end, meliorative reason is a form of pragmatic analysis. It is, again, the search for means to accommodate principle to practice, for advancing the course of liberal democracy without impairing the integrity or efficiency of vital institutions. The search, as always, is for a suggestive fit between theory and practice.

In any event, in the end, meliorative reason yields an *argument*, not a self-evident "solution" to a problem. This form of analysis does not actually adjudicate among the other types of reason: it does not resolve the tension among them. Rather, meliorative analysis simply contributes a *fourth* line of argument to deliberation. It attempts to achieve agreement. It reasons that there should be concurrence on a particular fit between theory and practice, one that should seem, to all, a workable course of reform. It is sane, accommodating, and practical. *But there is no particular reason why such counsel should prevail.* Depending on the particular circumstances, perhaps it is better to stick to established practice. Or to stand firm on principle. Or to press on with a vision of a larger project.

The meliorative mode of reason is not in a privileged position. There is no good reason for the parties to a controversy to acquiesce in any particular formula for accommodation simply because it is a formula for accommodation. The principle that everything can be negotiated is a position too, and sometimes the stakes are too great for this entreaty to ready agreement to prevail. The very method of pragmatic liberalism requires strong advocates of carefully considered positions if it is to have point and purpose. Sometimes, the interest of pragmatic discovery of a good fit between principle and practice is best served if the protagonists hold out for a good deal more than "reasonable" accommodation would seem to require. Sometimes it is better to give the "problem solver" a more difficult problem to solve.

The essential question of judgment, of deciding, in the face of conflicting counsel, which policy should prevail, is yet unanswered. And this is the essential task of citizenship.

The Interdependence of the Modes of Reason

None of the basic methods of political reason prescribed by political philosophy or taught in the schools of policy analysis can stand by itself as a basis for public choice. Rather, there is an organic relationship among them. All are required if political judgment is to be wise and practical. Trusteeship is tradition-bound and unreflective unless tested against principle and schemes for improvement. The maxims of formal liberalism are empty and sterile unless applied to particular human activities and projects. The merit of innovative projects is properly judged not by assent alone but only in relation to the values realized in established practice and the norms of rightful order. And incrementalism is merely expediency unless its aim is to reconcile principle and practice. Unless there is strong, carefully thought-out advocacy, there are no differences to adjudicate, there is no "problem" to resolve.

However, when we are actually called upon to play a part in the political process, each of us is apt to seize on one or another of these modes of analysis as the starting point for reason. We become the defender of established ways, the promoter of a project, the proponent of standards, or we seek to bring the rest together, to play the peacemaker. Once inside such a frame of mind, the opinions of others appear, initially, merely as forces to be reckoned with. The trustees, concerned to protect the "integrity" of the enterprise, may compromise with those who bring claims based on principle, but they see this only as a way of "meeting demands," a matter of restoring tranquillity to the ongoing operation. Those who stand on principle, in turn, may moderate their claims in the face of what they take to be "political realities." Half a loaf is better than none. The positions of others appear as "facts" to be taken into account, not as arguments worthy of consideration.

But the object of deliberation is that each shall broaden his or her sense of the considerations that bear on policy. The aim is that each *assimilate* the point of view of the others and in this way come to a more complete understanding of the desiderata of public action. And ultimately, the goal is that each might be moved, potentially, to a change of mind, that the protagonists might come to adopt a different orientation than that from which they started. The trustee may come to appreciate that existing practice is unfair and become the champion of reform on principle. The incrementalist mediator may turn into the enthusiastic promotor of a novel initiative.

In closed, axiomatic systems of thought, the solution to a

problem is always inherent in the premises. In open systems of thought, it should always be possible to end up elsewhere than where one began. It is this possibility of "changing one's mind"— that mysterious capacity of people speculating in the company of others, our ability to end up in a position we could not have anticipated before we explored the views of others—that makes reasoned deliberation so different from any system of formal logic consciously insulated from other modes of thought.

The Place of Policy Analysis

What is the role of the specialist, the professional, in such an idea of political deliberation? The social sciences have long tried to cultivate an approach to public problems that would be detached, impartial, analytic. However, the techniques taught as methods of policy analysis provide no specialized claim to knowledge. Rather, they are based on quite ordinary forms of political argument. In effect, the policy analyst may be trustee, critic, entrepreneur, or pragmatic mediator.

However, there may be a special place for the "intellectual" in all of this. At any time, on any subject, the roles we have specified as essential to reasoned deliberation tend toward a natural disequilibrium. Momentum flows with the spirit of novelty, or defense of established ways, or outrage at the failings of the existing order, or hard-headed immediate practicality. Such collective moods may represent the spirit or an age, or the more transient "common sense" of a group seized with a particular problem.

Scholars, on the whole, have a propensity to think otherwise. Thus, their special function in deliberation may be to speak for neglected perspective. In an atmosphere of criticism and contempt for tradition, the rationale for prevailing practice should be clearly restated. When everything seems most sure and settled, the inquiring mind seeks novelty and innovation. Where everything is chaotic and up in the air, it may be time for the academic to be merely practical. As the partisan of neglected perspective, the vital function of the intellectual is to bring balance to deliberation. Perhaps this is where the analytic interest in "objectivity" and "neutrality" actually lies. The function of the policy analyst, thus understood, is to keep the argument open, not to presume to settle it. This important work of reason, of complicating matters when everything seems most obvious to others, is never much appreciated, and it often requires great courage.

The Reason of Citizens

What is the lesson in all of this for the protagonists, for the citizens, who must in the end adjudicate among rival views? There is no technique of reason that is sufficient to bring closure to political argument. Do not expect some transcendent synthesis. On the whole, we end as we began. Our judgment will be grounded in one of the four modes of reason. Every decision needs a turning point, and we can only find that in the possibilities already available to the mind. We cannot simply "consider everything."

I realize that in saying this, I am taking sides in an ancient controversy. Many might say that they base judgment on a complex of reasons. But if asked to defend such a judgment, I think we would find that we could identify a crucial and central consideration. Again, we cannot just "weigh" everything against everything else. We must weigh the diverse considerations in argument against something.

My position than is very much like that taken by John Stuart Mill:

There must be some standard by which to determine the goodness or badness, absolute or comparative, of ends of objects of desire. And whatever that standard is, there can be but one: for if there are several ultimate principles of conduct, the same conduct might be approved by one of those principles and condemned by another; and there would be needed some more general principles as umpires between them.[3]

Brian Barry has objected to this view that judgment needs a turning point. He suggests that we can very well entertain diverse standards and define indifference curves, or trade-offs between them. That may be so, but we have to weight the diverse standards in that case. And once again, we will find, in the marginal case, that judgment turns on a single point.[4]

Thus, in the end, we decide on a specific course of action *because* of the importance of preserving some feature of practice;

or *because* of inefficiency or injustice, or responsiveness to individual need, or on the basis of some other neglected value; or *because* of the improvement promised by a proposed scheme; or *because* of the workability of a particular reform, its ability to satisfy divergent considerations and interests. However, when we *arrive* at such a position through the process of deliberation, rather than *start* from it, our justification lies not in an appeal to considerations of first philosophy, to abstract norms of thought, but rather to factors in the situation, to the specific nature of the problem at hand. Our reasons take into account the reasons of others and the substance of the case. In this sense, we show that we have done our best as parties to a community of inquiry, that we have been responsible in seeking the best fit between theory and practice. Again, political deliberation must inevitably end, not in unassailable proof but in an act of commitment. But that commitment may be more or less thoughtful and serviceable in helping us to pursue the liberal vision while getting on with the work at hand.

CHAPTER

11

The Liberal Enterprise

I have tried to chart a course for practical political judgment that would simultaneously satisfy the requirements of liberal politics and advance the aims of a particular enterprise. So far I have been concerned primarily with the ways in which judgments based on liberal principles can guide the development of various forms of practical endeavor. Over time, one assumes, this piecemeal and decentralized process leads to a greater congruence between the norms of the liberal order and those of the various forms of enterprise. However, I have not yet directly considered how this approach to political reason applies when the aim is the development of the liberal enterprise itself.

The appeal to principle arises in different ways. Liberal principles can be invoked to identify problems in a particular endeavor. However, it is equally, or perhaps more likely, that the issue that prompts political deliberation will be the effort to generalize a liberal rule for its own sake. As we have seen, there is a strain toward consistency in liberal logic. If due process of law is essential to public justice, why should not the basic requirements of fair procedure apply to the tribunals of the firm? If discrimination is wrong in public facilities, how far can it be justified in private ones? Throughout, I have been concerned that the claim to consistency not be carried so far as to undermine the rationality of practice. All undertakings are not essentially political in form, and they should not be subordinated to the purposes of the state. However, one must be concerned as well that the "autonomy" or "privacy" of the enterprise not be invoked to frustrate a legitimate public purpose. The test, again, is that the application of liberal principle be consistent with rational performance. The aim, as always, is the increasing correspondence of theory and practice.

All of this implies that political judgments have to be appraised not only in relation to their impact on the project immediately at hand, but for their larger implications for the rational development of liberalism itself.

Liberalism as a Rational Enterprise

Liberalism, of course, is more than a philosophy. It is also a specific historic political project, one that started in the West but has become global in scope. It emerged in criticism of established ways of law and statecraft. In some nations, it has become the orthodox conception of political practice, taken for granted and seldom questioned. Elsewhere, it contests with other notions of the political enterprise. Often, its adherents are thought subversive of legitimate order.

All of this is well known. What is less apparent is that liberalism, like any other enterprise, is itself subject to rational development through a process of critical, reflective deliberation and self-conscious innovation and reform. This is not as unexceptionable a statement as it may at first seem, and it is not a view that is particularly congenial to certain main currents in contemporary political philosophy. The aim of much political theory written today is to argue either that liberal principles are immutable and timeless or that they are merely contingent and conventional. One group thinks that we can do no more than abide by the eternal verities, while the other thinks liberalism simply another historic usage. The idea that liberalism, like a technology or science, is subject to *improvement* through disciplined analysis is quite another matter.

Precisely what I mean by this will only become clear when we understand the relationship between pragmatic liberalism and liberal idealism.

Pragmatic Liberalism and Liberal Idealism

Many may think liberalism no more than systematic skepticism. If we conclude that the most essential questions—the nature of things, God's will, and human purpose—can be discussed but not decided, we may endorse liberalism simply as an entailment of our doubt.[1]

However, there is a stronger version of liberalism that we must come to terms with. Classically, liberalism presumed that its principles were dictates of natural reason and that they reflected the God-created rational order of the universe—and of the mind.

This idealist liberalism would affirm rights of choice, of expression and conscience, not merely on the skeptical ground that these are the conditions for the neutral aggregation of preference, but because individuals are to be understood, fundamentally, as moral agents. Take away such freedoms and you take away the meaning of choice between right and wrong, good and evil.[2]

By the same token, from this point of view, there *are* ideas of justice which are inherently reasonable—conceptions of nonarbitrariness, proportion, relevant distinction, and compensation which would be recognized, ultimately, in any cultural setting, no matter how much local interpretations and applications might diverge. Such ideas of reason simply exist. They are part of the architecture of mind.

Liberalism, in this classic version, presumed to base its case on an ideal of rational order, on principles that were taken to be universal and enduring, somehow written into the order of the universe and in human understanding. And all of this, to the twentieth-century mind with its great uneasiness about idealist notions, is disturbing doctrine indeed.

This sort of idealist liberalism might seem particularly incompatible with philosophic pragmatism. After all, it was precisely the point of pragmatism to argue that the quest for certainty was misplaced, that the search for truth culminated not with transcendental insight but, simply, in human purpose. There is a tough-minded version of philosophic pragmatism whose quarrel was specifically with idealism. There is, they argued, no dualism between appearance and reality, mind and body. There is the life process of humanity and nothing else. This is at once mental and material, a matter ultimately of human inquiry and action, which creates and alters the actual scheme of things and the human understanding of the world.[3]

However, there is a sense in which pragmatism shares the deeper faith in reason which we associate with classic science and classic liberalism. The aim was not to deny rationalism but to give

it clear, sounder foundations by grounding it in the more commonplace processes of practical thought.

In this respect, the version of pragmatism taught by Charles
Sanders Peirce is most important. Peirce tried to explain how
practical understanding and human purpose, scientific procedure
and the logic of inquiry, all related one to another and to the
larger questions of human knowledge and actual reality.

Peirce's idea of inquiry was a direct response to the Cartesian
conception of rationality.[4] For Peirce, inquiry did not begin by
"questioning everything." Rather, "we begin where we are," with
theories and preconceptions. The problem of practical reason is
the "fixation of belief." We try to find ideas that will provide dependable guides to action. Doubt is a sign of some irresolution in
belief. We waver and vacillate, uncertain of the outcome. The purpose of inquiry is to remove doubt. We "fix" a belief as we become confident of its results. It is in this sense that the meaning
of our ideas is known by their consequences for action.[5]

The end, then, was reliable knowledge, thought that would
stand up over time and provide a secure, intelligent guide to conduct. The "truth" of propositions did not depend on their conformity to unassailable philosophical maxims, but on their utility for
practice. The only way to establish the reliability of ideas was
through experience. For Peirce, this meant experimental method.
We become sure of our beliefs only when they hold up under
stipulated conditions. To speak for a belief is to show, specifically,
that it acts as it is expected to. To confirm a belief is for others to
test it in their own experience. Only in this way could we come
to count on ideas as reliable guides to action. Systematic inquiry
was a process of overcoming doubt and irresolution as to how
best to proceed.[6]

There is something more here than immediately meets the eye.
This is no sheer experimentalist empiricism or instrumentalism.
Classic rationalism had always assumed that human thought could
represent the order of nature, not with perfect truth perhaps, but
certainly not in error. God was no deceiver. Peirce had a lingering
debt to Hegel, and there is much more than a hint in his thought
that scientific inquiry progressively uncovers ultimate reality. The
end of inquiry was a *singular* answer to problems of doubt, one
that would be agreed to by all qualified observers. This sense that
the object of thought is predictable knowledge and "ideas inde-

pendent of observation itself," the notion of an order that is becoming better known to the human mind, is very much in the classic spirit of objective idealism,[7] the tradition, in effect, of Plato as well as Kant.

Pragmatism starts with intimations that reason can reflect the transcendental realm. Perhaps it is a "leap in faith" to suppose that in the process of acquiring practical knowledge we are also uncovering principles of natural order. Still, this is what Peircean pragmatism implies. For Peirce, the fact that we could discern coherent order was a strong indication that the human mind was attuned to the "nature of things," and it was also an argument for the reality of God.[8]

However, Peirce's idealism is always balanced by his strong sense for the limits of reason. Reason is fallible. We can never "close the door to further inquiry." We can never assume that we finally have it right. Peirce's fallibilism is not far from the Christian conception of the flawed power of reason to know final things.

Thus, our capacity to formulate propositions that predict, and even to subsume them under general laws, is no guarantee that we have understood the "thing in itself." For Peirce, the real is "that whose characters are independent of what anyone may think of them,"[9] which is precisely to say that truth is not merely consensus among qualified observers on what is useful for human concerns.

It is possible to find in Dewey, but more particularly in Peirce, a strong suggestion that what was actually taking place in the self-correcting, experimental process of inquiry was a gradually unfolding relationship between human reason and natural order. From this perspective, what was essential in pragmatism's critique of the dominant versions of nineteenth-century liberalism was their supreme self-assurance that the essential character of the rational order of the universe, and the laws of human conduct that followed therefrom, had already been discovered, and that the matter needed no further investigation. It was the arrogance of supposing that Newton confirmed Locke and Smith, or Darwin, Spencer, that most dismayed those who would defend liberalism by pragmatic means.

There are idealist elements both in pragmatic and liberal thought, and in this sense, pragmatic liberalism becomes compatible with the longer continuities of Western thought, with the

Platonic, Stoic, and Christian conceptions of natural reason. The purpose of human inquiry, for most of Western history, was, after all, to discover what human reason could about the underlying pattern of natural order and thus the intentions of God.

From this point of view, pragmatic liberalism presupposes a progressively evolving social and political order, in which constant and universal values, of human freedom and the larger significance of the enterprise of reason, provide a consistent reference point for evaluation, interpretation, and action. They define what is anomalous about the existing order, what is perplexing, out of balance, disharmonious, unjust. They define the problematic situation which sets the stage for inquiry.

I think some such understanding is essential to complete the analogy between science and politics. Each science requires a certain act of commitment: in physics, to the notion that natural order can be expressed as mathematical law; in biology, that natural order can be expressed as a matter of organic development. So liberalism, in any form, requires a commitment to an order that progressively refines a certain notion of human worth and excellence.[10]

However, all of this is more by way of confession than argument. It is a way of making my own presuppositions clear. The case for pragmatic liberalism does not hinge on acceptance of these idealistic foundations. One can, if one prefers, regard the relation of liberal values and pragmatic method in a purely contingent sense, as though to say, *if* one wants to maximize social arrangements based on free choice among equal parties, then this method is appropriate to settling issues of specific interpretation. Or one could regard the relationship of liberal principles and the pragmatic notion of science as a self-confirming system of argument that serves to reinforce an ideal of democratic process. You can ground pragmatic liberalism, as you wish, in any number of strategies of skeptical reason. You will be missing only the essential point of the venture.

Historical Experience and Liberalism

The important point here, for a discipline of practical political reason, is that we think and act not in terms of a never-quite-tangible ideal form of liberal theory but in relation to a specific historical version of liberal thought. And the only way in which our liberalism can come more closely to approximate the ideal is through continuing conscious analysis and reflective practice.

Our everyday acts of political judgment occur at a specific time both in the development of a particular practical enterprise and of liberalism. Our judgments *reflect* the puzzles and anomalies characteristic of a certain stage in the development of a particular practice and in the practice of liberalism, and they *bear upon* both the improvement of the practical technique at hand and the doctrine of liberalism itself.

The liberalism we use in practice is never quite a neutral or impartial system of principles. At any time and place, certain liberal principles are given greater emphasis than others. In one nation, at one moment, legalism, the rule of law, may be the paramount concern. A decade later it may be personal freedom, or equal treatment, or the vindication of the democratic "will of the people."

So to highlight one liberal principle, and relegate the rest to background for a time, is of course characteristic of the transient enthusiasms of politics. It is an indication of the workings of power and interest. However, such emphases among principles may also have their source in an inherent quality of liberal logic, in the idea that a principle established in one area of public life should be generalized to all similar cases. However they arise, these natural imbalances in liberal doctrine at any moment will greatly affect our practical judgment. At one point, the treatment of minorities will seem the most problematic aspect of the prevailing pattern of practice. At another, it will be economy. At a third, quality and craftsmanship, reliable performance.

As I say, there is more at work here than political power or passion, or the natural changes in the momentum of argument, its ebbs and flows. When a principle is accepted as prescriptive in regulating the development of one enterprise, there are strong pressures, in the name of rational consistency, to apply it to others. If market competition is good in transport, why not in the postal system or the schools? If discrimination on grounds of race is unlawful, should not discrimination based on gender or physical handicap be similarly treated? The strain toward consistency, inherent in liberalism, will privilege certain principles in relation to others at any particular time. This will seem the unfinished business of the liberal enterprise, and it is apt to dominate the agenda. And once again, the crucial question for judgment is when to accept this force of argument, in the name of the further development of the liberal order, and when to resist it, in the name of particular attributes of practice.

Every nation has its own unique historical experience with liberalism. Americans have pursued neither the egalitarian and solidaristic strains of Scandinavian social democratic thought nor the more organic, corporatist, and paternalistic version reflected in German Christian Democracy. In Latin nations, liberalism is still associated with anticlericalism. American liberalism was born in a classic ideal of minimal, balanced, and decentralized government. Later, laissez-faire was embraced as a touchstone for economic policy. The national crisis grounded in the incompatibility of liberal principles and the practice of slavery led to a particular concern for equal protection of the law and equal opportunities. None of these particular patterns of American liberalism quite has its counterpart in other lands. Americans are as instantly recognizable by their arguments as by their accents. All liberals have a distinctive national identity.

At any time, in any nation, the liberal project will focus on some liberal commitments to the neglect of others. And unless interrupted by events, or a conscious process of critical reexamination of first principles, there is a tendency for the rational development of the liberal polity to unfold as a continuing elaboration upon established themes. Thus, in the United States, the imagery of corporate capitalism becomes a dominant metaphor, influencing institutional development in all areas of organized collective endeavor.[11] Or as in the Scandinavian nations—at the height of social democracy—politics becomes a steady process of further extending and refining universal services, as a matter of individual right.[12]

At any time, then, an ongoing liberal project is asymmetric. And thus, at any time, a liberal project is subject to criticism in the light of neglected values. Again, it is the faith of Western rationalism that the individual can stand back from established usage and tradition, and reexamine custom dispassionately, in terms of fundamental aims and purposes. It is the work of rational criticism, then, to point up the disparity between the liberal enthusiasms of any period and the never quite realizable ideal of liberal theory, as an idea of universal human right and reason.

No liberal system is ever quite in balance. None is ever fully "impartial," and impartiality is the tangible second-order norm against which liberal projects are rightly tested. It is the proper work of critical theory to "reveal" these "distortions" in liberalism. It is in order that Marx propose that capitalism is not quite liberal, for, in his view, the appropriation of surplus value by the capitalist violates the right of the individual worker to that with which "he has mixed his labor." It is similarly in order for neoconservatives such as James Buchanan to propose that "excessive" democracy may undermine its own legitimacy, as self-interested individuals are led to make demands on the state in excess of its capabilities.

Unchecked and unchallenged by such criticism, a liberal society will simply proceed by momentum to the further elaboration of its dominant principles. It will become more "coherent" over time, and more complacent. Liberalism can thus become a form of prescriptive tradition, authoritative and reverenced but unexamined, and it was precisely that form of prescriptive traditionalism that liberal rationalism came into the world to contest. Thus it is incumbent on the liberal polity to take stock continually, to reappraise its convictions and commitments, its ideals of good practice, in the light of the intrinsic aims of the enterprise itself. This is the work generally expected of competitive politics, and of its handmaiden, political theory.

Partisan Politics and the Liberal Enterprise

It is our custom to carry out this reflective reexamination of the conditions of political practice through competitive elections among parties advocating different versions of liberalism. At least, that is the ideal expectation. In effect, an electoral campaign is, or ought to be, a periodic deliberation on the course of the going concern, an opportunity to make changes in emphasis within the overall liberal project.

The election establishes the principles to be emphasized in the subsequent period. The key constitutional assumption of liberal democracy is that the direction of the enterprise *will* be reassessed at intervals. There can be no last election. In this, liberals have differed absolutely from those parties which assume that one election is sufficient to establish the definitive course of the regime.

Political theory plays a part in these collective reflections, these periodic reappraisals of the liberal program. By this account, the task of political theory is to add to this partisan contention, not to find an incontrovertible proof of some version of liberalism. The purpose of political theory is to explore the larger implications of the various forms of liberal theory in contention at the moment.

John Rawls is the most recent formal liberal theorist to express his intentions along these lines. While the structure of Rawls' *A Theory of Justice* seems ahistorical, abstracted from specific circumstances, his later reflections—in an essay where, incidentally, he links his intentions explicitly to Dewey and the pragmatic tradition—give a different impression. Now his intent seems to be to pull together and give philosophic expression to the scattered intuitions of the citizens of a specific historic version of the liberal enterprise, to provide an alternative to a presumably dominant utilitarian form of liberalism, one specifically tailored to the conditions of a mature industrial society. As Rawls writes:

> The aim of political philosophy, when it presents itself in the public culture of a democratic society, is to articulate and to make explicit those shared notions and principles thought to be already latent in common sense or, as is often the case, if common sense is hesitant and uncertain, and doesn't know what to think, to propose to it certain conceptions and principles congenial to its most essential convictions and historical traditions.[13]

It is precisely in this spirit that this book is written. My intention has been to recommend pragmatic liberalism as a conception of public philosophy for a nation at a specific point in the historic evolution of its version of the liberal enterprise. Pragmatic liberalism is the product of a specific tradition of practice. I evoke this tradition to suggest a different distribution of emphasis among core principles than that which prevails at present and to advance certain projects and policies.

The society to which pragmatic liberalism seems most pertinent is a mature liberal order. It is an order in which fundamental institutions have been created and are well established. It takes the problem at hand to be sustained rational scrutiny of these institutions, to the end of achieving a higher degree of performance from them, of securing their reliability and serviceability, their internal justice, and their responsiveness to the diverse interests of citizens.

Everyday Decisions and the Liberal Enterprise

Our participation in the larger politics of the liberal regime is not limited to the simple act of voting, or to involvement, usually sporadic and peripheral, in partisan politics. If that were the extent of it, citizenship would be a shallow and ephemeral part of our lives indeed. For many if not most citizens of a mature liberal democracy, the more substantive acts of political participation come through engagement in the government of the enterprises of work and service. As Elaine Spitz wrote:

> Because the critics of liberalism have failed to come to grips with many features of liberal democracy their portraits of modern citizens lack verisimilitude. In the United States people devote astonishing amounts of time and energy to public service—coaching sandlot ball clubs, serving as docents in museums, planting bulbs in public parks, raising money for community projects. A society that starts its children out selling Girl Scout cookies and graduates them to *pro bono* work as lawyers may be the most participatory the world has ever known.[14]

We may think of decisions taken on behalf of a particular enterprise to be parochial and local, no more than an indicated response to the situation at hand. But such everyday decisions contain intimations not just of our aims with regard to the immediate community of practice, but for the larger society as well. In the marginal case, at least, we will try to move the enterprise for which we are responsible toward a greater reliance on marketlike arrangements, or democratic process, or equal treatment, or the ideals of the community of inquiry and the community of good practice. Our decisions will betray an inclination toward either greater interdependence with the state, or greater independence, an intent to sharpen the distinction between the public and the private realms.

Again, the classic liberal will say that if we invoke a liberal principle we must be prepared to uphold it consistently. This is construed as an essential check on arbitrariness. In present context, this test of political justification has curious implications. In effect, when we base a decision on a liberal principle, and we do not defend our use of that value by pointing to some characteristic of the enterprise at hand, we seem to be saying that we intend to apply the principle generally, whenever circumstances permit, that our aim is to move the regime, insofar as it is in our power, in the direction of the cited principle. Thus, if we base a decision on the ground that it will make the organization more responsive to the will of the members (and if we do not specify how this is required to enhance performance), we are in effect saying that it is our intent to make society as democratic as possible, starting with the situation at hand. If our practical decision turns on the point that it will "help the least well-off," we are, by the discipline of consistency, implying that our aim is to achieve, generally, a more egalitarian pattern of distribution.

The implication seems to be that everyday political judgments, if they are to be regarded as rational, must be shown to be part of a larger scheme to move the liberal enterprise toward a conception of liberalism as a final state. This is, I think, what the formalist counsel that judgment be grounded in a "coherent philosophy" entails. And this certainly seems to be what those who write on behalf of pure free market individualism, liberal egalitarianism, or participatory, "strong" democracy want as our commitment.

We have traveled this path before. This is where *starting* from principle or *ending* with principle seems to lead us. And it is precisely to avoid such outcomes that the discipline of pragmatic liberalism suggests a different conception of reason and reasoned political judgment. Once again, with Peirce, we "start from where we are" rather than in absolute skepticism or absolute certainty.

For pragmatic liberalism, when we advocate greater democracy, or decisions that favor the least advantaged, or that secure greater individual freedom, we are in effect recommending a different distribution of emphasis within the liberal regime as it is constituted in our particular society. Our case may be that certain elements of the liberal project have been pressed to excess. Thus, our dominant institutions may be *unnecessarily* undemocratic or inegalitarian. We may have created hierarchic structures, or incentive systems, considerably in excess of what efficiency and economy require. Presumably, we could move some distance in the direction of democracy or equality without jeopardizing the realization of other crucial values.[15]

In such an analysis, we make no commitment to pursue democracy or equality "consistently"—if that means indefinitely. The problem is construed as one of balance within a set of standards, each of which is defined by an extreme, or unwarranted, case of every other. The question of the appropriate realization of any value is one of extent. We expect to reassess our commitments to principle in the light of changing circumstance, in consideration of the ongoing development of the liberal enterprise. And we expect that the polity of which we are a member will continuously reappraise its dominant commitments as well, changing emphasis among the components of the liberal project while maintaining the strong continuities of expectation that are the condition of the rule of law.

In the end, then, detachment from prevailing practice is the essential condition of reasoned political judgment. Rationality, in our tradition, is understood precisely as the capacity for dispassionate examination of established usage, custom, and tradition. Arbitrariness and interest, the cardinal political vices which liberal thought contrives to control or overcome, may be the product of venality, but they are just as likely the consequence of following the dictates of practice without perspective. Political justification, the process of defending judgment with good reasons, is largely a matter of showing *why* prevailing practice should be followed in a particular case, or *how* an innovation would constitute an improvement in practice.

To relate theory to practice, as I suggested at the outset, is to see our everyday political actions in larger perspective. In the first instance, this implies subsuming the particular under the universal, identifying the political quality of a specific problem with a general principle. However, it also means understanding that we are parties to a particular episode in the history of liberal politics, and that the norms we apply in taking the measure of performance and policy are neither final nor inevitable. All of this may sound grandiose as a counsel of practical reason. Our influence on the larger course of history is very, very small. But that is not the point exactly. The object of such theoretical self-consciousness is rather merely that we become competent to leave the conditions of political practice, in our own immediate vicinity, a little better than we found them.

12

The Competent Citizen

It seems fitting to close with an essay on political education. The teaching of politics, and political economy, is an enterprise of great importance to liberal democracy. In the United States, particularly, it has always been assumed that the preparation of citizens was a central task of the schools.

One might think then that political science, as an academic calling, would regard political education as its special province and that its aim would be to develop a body of knowledge and technique particularly pertinent to preparation for public life.

However, it does not seem that contemporary political science has such a specific sense of mission. Its manifest purpose seems rather to be the explanation and interpretation of political phenomena, according to rules and methods generic to science, whatever the field. It is distinguished not by a particular problem of reason but by a range of phenomena which it takes as its specialized field of study. It would instruct students to approach politics with those questions and concerns in mind common to scientific investigation. But the disciplines of scientific inquiry, understood in this sense, are not at all the same as the disciplines of political judgment.

It was not always so. In its formative years, American political science seemed to endorse a conception of purpose that was designed to link theory and practice, research and teaching, with the purposes of a specific rational enterprise explicitly in mind.

When the American university was being "professionalized" after the German model, at the turn of the last century, the basic departments were organized around established traditions of inquiry. Physics, chemistry, and mathematics were ancient dis-

ciplines. Economics could build on the legacy of classical political economy. The new American university was mainly an
exercise in the rational organization of research programs that
had been developing gradually for centuries.

But political science was different. Political science became
an organized discipline in the United States not because it was
supposed that there *was* a science of politics but that there
ought to be one. The rational and systematic, the "scientific"
scrutiny of the practice of government, was thought important
to the maintenance and improvement of the liberal democratic
experiment.

The spirit of the times was progressive and pragmatic. If the
practices of medicine, agriculture, "home economics," and engineering could be made more efficient, reliable, and responsive
through scientific analysis, then the same could be done for the
practice of politics as well.[1]

This vision of the purposes of the discipline has been virtually
forgotten. Astonishingly, today it is not assumed that political
theory frames the research program of the field, or even that the
concerns of political theory have much to do with the aims of
political research, a situation that must be unique in the learned
professions. Most political scientists, I suspect, would be embar-
rassed—or think it a violation of their positivist creed of "value
neutrality"—to have it suggested that the test of the significance
of their research might be its contribution to the rational improvement of liberal democratic government. Liberal democracy
is regarded as an *ideology*, to be taught, alongside other systems
of political belief, not as the paradigmatic foundation of the field.

It is true, of course, that mainstream political science research
still has its foundation in these earlier aspirations. Students of political institutions and practices continue to base their studies
on problems of democratic responsiveness; comparativists keep
looking for the conditions of stable democracy. But the source
and the rationale for the conventional problems that orient research have pretty much been lost. The rituals of scholarly investigation go on, carried out by priests who have only a dim notion
of the meaning of the mass.

To be sure, the earlier pragmatic liberal conception of the aims
of the discipline now seems quaint and out of date. I have no
intention of trying to recover it in detail. Nonetheless, my task
herein has been to try to reconstruct the theory of pragmatic lib-

eralism, to adapt it to the contingencies and temper of the times, and the theory of political education is part of it. So, against this background, let us ask again: What are the capabilities of the competent citizen? What is it that a contributing member of a liberal democracy should know how to do?

The Skills of Civic Competence

What follows is a very tentative sketch of the goals of a system of political education that would be compatible with the basic presuppositions of pragmatic liberalism. I am under no illusions that political scientists will rush to embrace a program for integrating theory, research, and teaching which follows directly from the field's distinctive mission as educator of citizens. My hope at this point is at most merely to provoke a discussion. I certainly do not expect in this brief sketch to settle all the issues involved.

What I have in mind is a scheme something like Lawrence Kohlberg's theory of the stages of moral development.[2] But this would be a hierarchy, not of levels of moral reasoning but of skills that seem essential to the ideal of citizenship in the liberal democratic regime. This is what those who would be parties to public life should be able to do if they are going to engage responsibly and constructively in the ongoing public deliberations of the society.

My thought is that these skills are logically sequential. Each builds on the last. As with Kohlberg's scheme, each appears more "adequate" than the last, both in the sense that it resolves issues left unresolved at lower stages and that the mind will move to reflect at subsequently higher levels as each is mastered in turn. The scheme represents a movement from a passive "consumer" orientation to public life to an active "participatory" engagement with public issues, a movement from the view that the best one can do is to understand the political forces that act on one's life to the view that one can assume responsibility for deliberating and trying to resolve public issues.

I think we will be able to recognize these various levels of civic consciousness in everyday political life and that we would appraise the potential competence of others—as leaders, as candidates—in terms of their demonstrated abilities along these lines. Finally, I think these skills can be identified with specific *performances* that can be taught and evaluated, perfected and nurtured.

I think they evoke specific expectations for the achievement of those we educate and grounds for certifying the capacity for political analysis of students.

Underpinnings

Analyzing the Rationale of Complex Practices

The foundation of civic competence is the ability to understand how institutions work, how they perform their functions. This means that one can re-create the logic of the separation of powers and the monetary system, the conventions of mortgage finance and land-use planning. However, this is not a mere matter of extensive descriptive knowledge of the rational arrangements of one's society. The skill involved is the ability to size up the rationale and dynamics of any complex system, as a competent mechanic can infer the function and operation of a piece of machinery by studying the pattern of intention inherent in its design.

In the first instance, the purpose of cultivating this skill is simply that the citizen feel competent to deal with the institutions of the society, precisely for the same reasons that the educated individual should understand the principle of the internal combustion engine and the larger inscrutibilities of the domestic water heater. The initial object is that the individual not feel helpless or estranged from the rational order of the society, nor be led to believe that such matters are beyond one's ken, questions that should be left to the experts.

However, as I have emphasized throughout, thorough understanding of the rationale of prevailing practice is a precondition for critical analysis. Granted, the fashionable pedagogy today is to encourage criticism before students have mastered the case for existing institutions and techniques, ideas and procedures. But this is putting the cart before the horse. For pragmatic liberalism, prevailing practice is the basing point for critical analysis. It is essential to understand why something was put there in the first place before one tries to change it or tear it down.

At this first level of civic competence, all that we hope to cultivate is a passive understanding, a "consumer's skill." All that is essential is that the citizen be able to construct a relatively accurate portrait of how the basic institutions of society work in practice. Clearly, even this level of mastery would not be characteristic of the population of any extant liberal democracy (though one does find a surprisingly widespread working knowledge of the ways of banks and local authorities, for example, diffused throughout the population, with little relation to class or educational level). Clearly also, this skill is not sufficient as a basis for competent citizenship.

It is interesting to note that the conventional social sciences, which take the point of rational analysis to be only that of understanding, or interpreting, social institutions and practices, can provide a discipline only at this level of civic competence. Eschewing normative analysis, they cannot go beyond it.

Analyzing the Rationale for the Liberal Democratic Regime

As it is with institutions, so it is with ideas. Understanding precedes critical analysis. Thus, the second foundation of citizenship is the ability to reconstruct the rationale for liberal democracy, to show why liberalism was thought a more adequate philosophy of governance than its historic rivals. Again, to stipulate this as an educational objective is to take issue with the dominant view that, in the interest of neutrality, liberalism is to be construed only as an ideology, that the student, in the marketplace of ideas, once fully informed of the options—this is the main function of the teacher—should be free to choose to be liberal, Marxist, Fascist, or whatever. Here, instead, we take liberalism to be the foundation of our system of political understanding. Again, against the view that the first function of political education is to cultivate critical reason, it is here understood that a thorough, constructive appreciation of the logic of liberalism should be demonstrated prior to induction into the systematic critique of it.

I suppose one can teach theory either as logical system (as economists tend to do) or historically (as is more common in political science), as a sustained and unfolding exploration and deliberation over time. My view is that the approach of reducing theory to system makes it appear contextless and finished, a predetermined matter, whereas the historical approach more characteristic of political science preserves the image of theory-making as an enterprise, reveals its contingency, all of which is more congenial to the spirit of pragmatic liberalism.

It also seems to me that one tends to *explain* an institution, a machine, or a philosophy systematically, showing the relation of the parts, how they work together to some purpose, but I think *justification* more often tends to be historical. To show why an institution, a machine, or a philosophy might be thought to be a good idea, one must go back, it seems to me, and recapture the terms of the debate that led to one pattern of practice being regarded as better than the rest, in pursuit of a particular purpose.

Skills of Analysis and Argument

Reasoned Argument

The fundamental *active* skill of political analysis is the ability to support judgment with reasons, to show why a personal interpretation should be thought also to be the most adequate *public* orientation toward a problem. Even this much is frequently neglected in our current pedagogy of political education, focused as it is on the acquisition of knowledge, or on the interpretation of phenomena according to the conventional protocols of "scientific" analysis.

However, if we taught no more than rigor of argument, we will have taught but rhetoric, a "lawyerly" skill.

To move beyond this is to cultivate the broader facility for relating theory to practice in such a way as to check the adequacy of initial assumptions and claims, interpretations and proposals. It is to invoke principle in criticism of practice, to show clearly why a "state of affairs" should be construed as a "public problem," to delineate a repertoire of options for public action, and to argue for a specific recommendation for policy, based on explicit criteria of good practice and government. These are the fundamental skills of instrumental reason.

It is at this level of analysis that the citizen becomes competent to participate in that process of reasoned deliberation which is the hallmark of liberal politics. It is here that the process of critical review of prevailing practice begins. But this is only the beginning, not the culmination, of the craft of civic competence. For taken by itself, the skill of reasoned argument is but an exercise. The formulation of argument can be carried out in isolation, apart from the perspectives and expectations of others, remote from conflict and controversy. This is, then, not yet fully *political* reason.

The Deliberation of Diverse Perspectives

Reasoned argument, by itself, is a solitary skill, and it encourages resolution more than perspective. It is the art of differentiation and distinction, of clarity and definition: its aim is the reduction of uncertainty. It is not a skill, practiced by itself, that is necessarily congenial to tolerance, ambiguity, or breadth of vision.

To have worked out a reasoned case is not the end of analysis. It is also necessary to interpret public issues from diverse points of view, from the perspectives of different representative persons. The point now is to cultivate a sympathetic understanding of the way general practices and policies will affect persons situated differently in relation to them. This is a fundamental source of one's understanding of the "problematic," and it leads to principled criticism, to entrepreneurial initiative, and more refined conceptions of trusteeship.

For pragmatic liberalism, judgment arises from deliberation. The serviceability of a practice is a product of diverse performances, and it affects, and serves, diverse individuals in different ways. Pragmatic liberalism insists on the primacy of the particular. It will do no good to speak only of the hypothetical interests of abstract individuals. Hence, deliberation must be both balanced and specific. And this means, particularly, that the analyst must become protagonist of neglected perspective.

It is at this level that understanding of the enterprise, and of the configuration of enterprise that constitutes the regime, becomes more explicitly critical. We can now ask, beyond the rationale of practice, *whose* purposes are served by practice and whose are not. We look at the enterprise not only from the point of view of those who endorse it, but those who feel themselves ill-used by it as well. (But again, in some circumstances, it will be the point of view of the trustees of prevailing practice that will be the neglected perspective.)

In the currently fashionable pedagogy, a sympathetic understanding of diverse points of view—particularly those of certain specified minorities—is sufficient to cultivate that gentle relativism and tolerance for diversity that is deemed the crucial element in liberal sensitivity. But here we must ask for something more. The political point of view requires not just sympathetic understanding but an appreciation of the implications of diverse perspectives for public orientation. Hence the case for each must be made, as potential definitions of the aims of public policy, and this done, the question must be put, as clearly as possible, of which view should prevail.

The Skills of Adjudication

The actual test of performance in political judgment, in civic competence, is that one can represent the dilemmas of public choice by developing alternative compelling cases, grounded in principles and other relevant considerations, and *then* decide among them, offering good reasons for what is in essence a tragic choice. This is what Ronald Dworkin calls the logic of "hard cases." This adjudicatory skill, which lies beyond simple reasoned argument and case making, which is more than incremental melioration, is what pragmatic liberalism would want to teach, and what it would regard as the crucial test of civic competence, of "good practice" in the arts of liberal democratic politics.

Here the search for the principle that fits the case, the perspective that can be shown to advance the goals of liberalism as it advances the project at hand, becomes most demanding. The final test of political reason is that a particular course of action will indeed appear reasonable to persons with different claims and perspectives of their own, different stakes in the outcome. Failing this, power, compromise, or authoritative decree are the only solutions to political controversy. In many cases, reasons will fail and such means will be the only recourse. But each of these means is fundamentally "irrational" in the sense that we have been using the term, and it must remain the faith of the liberal that reasoned deliberation, the search for a *common* basis for collaborative action, is to be pursued until it is evident that intelligence, in this case, is not going to prevail.

Theoretical Criticism

The Critique of the Practice of Liberalism

The final step, one supposes, is the cultivation of a kind of "theoretical self-consciousness," a sense of purposive detachment from foundations, presuppositions, the epistemology and the conventions of discourse and practice, of the liberal democratic heritage itself.

The object of this is not relativism or neutrality. Nor is it "demystification" or "authentic subjectivity," or any of the other esoteric ideals of those brands of critical theory which think the goal of political education to be to estrange students from all traditions of rationality, rendering them fit only, it would seem, for fastidious cynicism.

The object of theoretical self-consciousness is not this at all. Rather, the simple fact is that there is no particularly good reason to believe that our existing political and political economic ideas are a finished product. Liberalism is obviously a rugged and versatile heritage of thought. Many moves are possible within it, and its implications are far from exhausted. Nonetheless, the largest task of citizenship is to carry on the argument of the civilization. Our liberalism is undoubtedly an interim ethic. To move further implies getting some perspective on our conventions of thought, even as we sustain them, and work within them, as the source of meaning, order, and fairness in our public life.

Of course, political education is not the exclusive concern of political science. All the disciplines have a part to play in the development of the skills of citizens. Conversely, political education is but one part of that program of preparation of the human mind and spirit that we call, significantly, *liberal* education.

There is much more that could be said about this matter, but that is a tale for another time, and another place.

NOTES

Chapter One

1. William Y. Elliott, *The Pragmatic Revolt in Politics* (New York: Macmillan, 1928). Thanks to the efforts of Richard Rorty, it is now fashionable to associate pragmatism with the general assault on rationalism associated with much of postmodern philosophy. My view is that Rorty distorts the pragmatic tradition, with its strong affinity to Western rationalism, particularly scientific rationalism, and its idealist elements. I stress these in this analysis, rather than "anti-foundationalism," See Richard Rorty, *Philosophy and the Mirror of Nature* (Princeton: Princeton University Press, 1979); idem., *The Consequences of Pragmatism* (Minneapolis: University of Minnesota Press, 1982); but on this point, see particularly his *Contingency, Irony and Solidarity* (New York: Cambridge University Press, 1989).

2. Louis Hartz, *The Liberal Tradition in America* (New York: Harcourt, 1955), 19.

3. Some speak of political judgment as a matter of experience, which cannot be articulated, as, perhaps, in cooking or art criticism. See Michael Oakeshott, *Rationalism in Politics* (London: Methuen, 1962), 7–13, and T. D. Welden, *The Vocabulary of Politics* (Baltimore: Pelican, 1953), 15. In a similar vein, Michael Polanyi speaks of the "tacit knowledge" that is part of scientific discovery. Michael Polanyi, *Personal Knowledge* (Chicago: University of Chicago Press, 1958), 86–102.

4. Philip B. Selznick, *Law, Society and Industrial Justice* (New York: Russell Sage, 1969).

5. The reason this is so is well explained in the writing of James Fishkin. See particularly his discussion in *Beyond Subjective Morality* (New Haven: Yale University Press, 1984), 82–157.

6. The exemplary works, of course, are Friedrich A. Hayek, *The Constitution of Liberty* (Chicago: University of Chicago Press, 1960), and Milton Friedman, *Capitalism and Freedom* (Chicago: University of Chicago Press, 1962).

7. John Rawls, *A Theory of Justice* (Cambridge: Harvard University Press, 1971). Perhaps the egalitarian liberalism of Rawls is not the most radical position in the liberal spectrum. Marxism of course holds that the proletariat will recognize, once scarcity is overcome, that the appropriation of surplus value by the capitalist is no longer functional and will demand their "natural right" to "that with which they have mixed their labor." Perhaps Marxism is no more than the consequence of taking the axiomatic conditions of Lockean liberalism very seriously indeed.

8. Interesting, if different, examples of this approach include Benjamin Barber, *Strong Democracy* (Berkeley: University of California Press, 1984), and Robert A. Dahl, "Procedural Democracy," in Peter Laslett and James Fishkin, eds., *Philosophy Politics and Society*, 5th Series (New Haven: Yale University Press, 1979), 97–133.

9. For a full discussion of this problem, see Thomas A. Spragens, Jr., *The Irony of Liberal Reason* (Chicago: University of Chicago Press, 1981).

10. Relentless reliance on market processes will generate inequalities of wealth and power that undermine the conditions of equality of choice that liberalism presupposes. A thoroughgoing utilitarianism could lead one to assent to the impoverishment, perhaps the enslavement, of some part of the population if it would lead to the greatest overall aggregate utility. Pure procedural democracy might require that some be "forced to be free," as Rousseau put it. And Rawls, taken to the extreme, might require consistently favored treatment for the least well off in ways that would eventually be perceived as irrational and unfair.

11. In different ways, representative samples of this case might include Roberto Unger, *Knowledge and Politics* (New York: Free Press, 1975), Michael Walzer, *Spheres of Justice* (New York: Basic Books, 1983), and Alasdair MacIntyre, *After Virtue* (Notre Dame: Notre Dame University Press, 1981).

12. Many theorists of decision making have argued that a good decision is one that represents a "satisfactory" response to a problem, one that "will do," given the requirements of a specific role and the aims of a particular organization. See Herbert A. Simon, *Administrative Behavior* (New York: Free Press, 1976). Or it is an action that returns an organization or system to equilibrium after some disruption of the parameters that define its optimum level of performance. See Geoffrey Vickers, *The Art of Judgment* (New York: Basic Books, 1965). Or it is the contrivance of consensus among diverse factions and interests. See David Braybrooke and Charles E. Lindblom, *A Strategy of Decision* (New York: Free Press, 1963).

13. Jeffrey Lustig, *Corporate Liberalism* (Berkeley: University of California Press, 1982), 19–21, 109–49. This is the right place to note that my conception of communities of practice and inquiry is quite compatible with Alasdair MacIntyre's idea of an intellectual "tradition." In fact, some

may want to take this as a broadening of MacIntyre's theory, to cover all forms of practical endeavor, thus constituting a political economy as well as a philosophical critique. In any event, Aristotelian *phronesis* is an idea of practical reason congenial to my version of pragmatic liberalism, as is MacIntyre's analysis of the development of traditions. See Alasdair MacIntyre, *Whose Justice? Which Rationality?* (Notre Dame: Notre Dame University Press, 1988), 88–145, 349–404.

Chapter Two

1. Many of the classic essays on private government are conveniently summarized in Sanford Lakoff, ed., *Private Government* (Glenview, Ill.: Scott, Foresman, 1973).

2. Selznick, *Law, Society and Industrial Justice*.

3. For a vivid example, see Gary Becker, *The Economic Approach to Human Behavior* (Chicago: University of Chicago Press, 1976).

4. On the idea that liberalism would organize on the basis of market-like arrangements all human endeavors, and not simply economic ones, see Michael Walzer, "Liberalism and the Art of Separation," *Political Theory* 12 (August 1984), 315–30.

5. Wolfgang Friedmann, *Law in a Changing Society*, 2d ed. (New York: Penguin, 1978), 130–32.

6. Charles E. Lindblom, *Politics and Markets* (New York: Basic Books, 1977), 356.

7. The conditions defining the perfect market will be found in most introductory economics textbooks. On the conditions of perfect democracy, see Dahl, "Procedural Democracy," 97–133.

8. This is the position of Hayek, who I have followed closely on this point. See *Constitution of Liberty*, 156–59.

9. Which is, of course, as Kant intended. See Onora Nell, *Acting on Principle* (New York: Columbia University Press, 1975), and Marcus Singer, *Generalization in Ethics* (New York: Knopf, 1961).

10. All of which is most fully developed in Thorstein Veblen, *The Instinct of Workmanship* (New York: Norton, 1964).

11. For pertinent criticisms of the adequacy of cost-benefit analysis as a standard of political and political economic judgment, see Lawrence H. Tribe, "Ways Not to Think about Plastic Trees," *Yale Law Journal* 83 (June 1974): 1315–33, and Peter Self, *Econocrats and the Policy Process* (Boulder, Colo.: Westview, 1975).

12. Exemplary arguments are those of Robert A. Dahl, *A Preface to Economic Democracy* (Berkeley: University of California Press, 1985), and Carol Pateman, *Participation and Democratic Theory* (New York: Cambridge University Press, 1970).

13. Friedman, *Capitalism and Freedom*, 85–107.

14. *Wisconsin v. Yoder,* 406 U.S. 205 (1972).

15. Marshall Cohen, ed., *Equality and Preferential Treatment* (Princeton: Princeton University Press, 1977); Robert Fullinwider, *The Reverse Discrimination Controversy* (Totawa, N.J.: Rowman and Littlefield, 1980).

16. This is the familiar position of Friedman, *Capitalism and Freedom,* and Robert Nozick, *Anarchy, State and Utopia* (New York: Basic Books, 1974).

17. This position is more restrictive than that of J. S. Mill, who seems to argue that antiliberal and antireligious ideas should flourish so as to demonstrate the worth of true belief. John Stuart Mill, *On Liberty* (New York: Norton, 1975), chap. 2.

18. Paul K. Feyerabend, *Against Method* (London: Verso, 1975), and idem., *Science in a Free Society* (London: Verso, 1978). See also C. Fred Alford, "Epistemological Relativism and Political Theory: The Case of Paul K. Feyerabend," *Polity* 18 (Winter 1985): 204–23.

19. Donald McClosky, in his perceptive study of the rhetoric of economics, quotes approvingly Einstein's remark that "whoever undertakes to set himself up as a judge in the field of truth and knowledge is shipwrecked by the laughter of the gods," and goes on to say that "the methodologist fancies himself the judge of the practitioner. His proper business, though, is an anarchistic one, resisting the rigidity and pretension of rules." See Donald N. McClosky, "The Rhetoric of Economics," *Journal of Economic Literature* 21 (June 1983): 490.

20. This is as good a place as any to note that the entire case I am making can be regarded as a large extension of the argument put forward by Albert O. Hirschman, *Exit, Voice and Loyalty* (Cambridge: Harvard University Press, 1970). Hirschman sees "exit" through markets and "voice" through protest or deliberative processes as complementary mechanisms of liberal political economy for reducing and checking the deterioration of the performance of an enterprise.

Chapter Three

1. Perhaps for our purposes the best general treatment of Habermas is that of Thomas McCarthy, *The Critical Theory of Jurgen Habermas* (Cambridge: MIT Press, 1978).

2. John Gray, *Hayek on Liberty* (New York: Blackwell, 1984), 1–55.

3. Braybrooke and Lindblom, *Strategy of Decision.*

4. Spragens, *Irony of Liberal Reason,* chap. 9.

5. Stephen Toulmin, *Human Understanding: I* (Princeton: Princeton University Press, 1972); Imre Lakatos, "Falsification in the Methodology of Scientific Research Programmes," in Imre Lakatos and Alan Musgrave, eds., *Criticism and the Growth of Knowledge* (Cambridge: Cambridge University Press, 1970); Spragens, *Irony of Liberal Reason,* 357–95.

6. Michael Polanyi, *The Logic of Liberty* (Chicago: University of Chicago Press, 1951), 39–49.

7. A. Bartlett Giametti, *A Free and Ordered Space: The Real World of the University* (New York: Norton, 1988), 28.

8. The exemplary statement along these lines is, of course, Herbert Marcuse, *One Dimensional Man* (Boston: Beacon, 1964).

9. The classic statement of this position is found in Harold Laski, *A Grammar of Politics* (London: George Allen and Unwin, 1973), 251.

10. Robert A. Dahl, *Dilemmas of Pluralist Democracy* (New Haven: Yale University Press, 1982), 1.

Chapter Four

1. Lustig, *Corporate Liberalism*, 6–7.

2. John Locke, "The Second Treatise of Government," in *Two Treatises of Government*, ed. Peter Laslett (New York: Cambridge University Press, 1960), 187–95.

3. Mill, *On Liberty.* A good recent commentary on this ambiguity in Mill is Amy Guttman, *Liberal Equality* (New York: Cambridge University Press, 1980), chap. 2.

4. Hirschman, *Exit, Voice and Loyalty.*

5. "Economic history reveals that the emergence of national markets was in no way the result of the gradual and spontaneous emancipation of the economic sphere from governmental control. On the contrary, the market has been the outcome of a conscious and often violent intervention on the part of government which imposed the market organization on a society for noneconomic ends." Karl Polanyi, *The Great Transformation* (Boston: Beacon, 1944), 250.

6. This is a central thesis of James Willard Hurst, *Law and Markets in U.S. History* (Madison: University of Wisconsin Press, 1982), whose argument has very much shaped the following discussion.

7. Adam Smith, *An Inquiry into the Nature and Causes of the Wealth of Nations* (New York: Modern Library, 1937), bk. 1, 128.

8. Again, the exemplars of this position are Friedman, *Capitalism and Freedom*, and Hayek, *Constitution of Liberty.*

9. John R. Commons, *The Legal Foundations of Capitalism* (Madison: University of Wisconsin Press, 1968), 47–64.

10. 94 U.S. 113, 131–2 (1876).

11. Hurst, *Law and Markets in U.S. History*, 69–72.

12. Gabriel Kolko, *Railroads and Regulation* (Princeton: Princeton University Press, 1965). See also, Alfred D. Chandler, Jr., *The Visible Hand* (Cambridge: Harvard University Press, 1977).

13. Murray Benedict, *Farm Policies of the United States: 1790–1950* (New York: Twentieth Century Fund, 1953).

14. The dominant temper of recent thought on the matter may perhaps be represented by the following works: in economics, George Stigler, *The Citizen and the State* (Chicago: University of Chicago Press, 1975); in law, Richard Posner, *The Economics of Justice* (Cambridge: Harvard University Press, 1981); and in political science, James Q. Wilson, ed., *The Politics of Regulation* (New York: Basic Books, 1979), and Theodore Lowi, *The End of Liberalism* (New York: Norton, 1969). Throughout the early 1980s, the American Enterprise Institute's *Regulation* and the neoconservative *Public Interest* reflected the dominant terms of this critique of regulatory policy.

15. George J. Stigler, "The Theory of Economic Regulation," *Bell Journal of Economics and Management Science* 2 (Spring 1971), 3–21.

16. On the general logic of this position, see Paul W. MacAvoy, *The Regulated Industries in the Economy* (New York: Norton, 1979), and Timothy Clark, Martin Kosters, and James C. Miller III, eds., *Reforming Regulation* (Washington, D.C.: American Enterprise Institute, 1980). On risk reduction specifically see Yair Aharoni, *The No-Risk Society* (Chatham, N.J.: Chatham House, 1981).

17. Walter Gellhorn, "The Abuse of Occupational Licensing," *University of Chicago Law Review* 44 (August 1976): 12–13.

18. Jethro K. Lieberman, *The Litigious Society* (New York: Basic Books, 1981), 21.

19. John Stuart Mill, addressing the question of how such preference for new options is justified in the putatively neutral liberal state, writes that "a thing of which the public are bad judges may require to be shown to them and pressed upon their attention for a long time, and to prove its advantages by long experience, before they learn to appreciate it, yet they may learn at last, which they might never have done, if the thing had not been thus obtruded on them in act, but only recommended in theory." John Stuart Mill, *Principles of Political Economy* (Toronto: University of Toronto Press, 1965), 947–48.

20. On the history of social insurance, see Gaston Rimlinger, *Welfare Policy and Industrialization in Europe, America and Russia* (New York: Wiley, 1971). On the logic of liberal welfare policy see Polanyi, *Great Transformation*, 33–100.

21. Gifford Pinchot, *Breaking New Ground* (New York: Harcourt, 1948).

22. Eugene Lewis, *Public Entrepreneurship* (Bloomington: Indiana University Press, 1984).

23. James M. Buchanan, *The Demand and Supply of Public Goods* (Chicago: Rand McNally, 1964), esp. chap. 9.

24. Smith, *An Inquiry into the Nature and Causes of the Wealth of Nations*, bk. 3, 244.

25. Such a reading is consistent with the spirit of other great classical political economists. See Mill, *Principles of Political Economy*, 975ff.

26. Walzer, *Spheres of Justice.*
27. Arthur Okun, *Equality and Efficiency: The Big Tradeoff* (Washington, D.C.: Brookings, 1975).
28. On the historic relationship between science and religion, see particularly David C. Lindberg and Ronald Numbers, eds., *God and Nature* (Berkeley: University of California Press, 1986).

Chapter Five

1. W. B. Gallie, "Essentially Contested Concepts," *Proceedings of the Aristotelian Society* 56 (1955–56): 167–98.
2. Walzer, "Liberalism and the Art of Separation," 315–30.
3. Leicester C. Webb, ed., *Legal Personality and Political Pluralism* (Melbourne: Melbourne University Press, 1958); Anthony Black, *Guilds and Civil Society in European Political Thought from the Twelfth Century to the Present* (London: Methuen, 1984).
4. James Willard Hurst, *Law and the Conditions of Freedom in the Nineteenth Century United States* (Madison: University of Wisconsin Press, 1967), 15–18.
5. Stephen L. Elkin, *City and Regime in the American Republic* (Chicago: University of Chicago Press, 1987), 19–21.
6. Hurst, *Law and the Conditions of Freedom in the Nineteenth Century United States*, 15–16.
7. Friedmann, *Law in a Changing Society*, 120.
8. *Kedroff v. St. Nicholas Cathedral of Russian Orthodox Church in North America*, 344 U.S. 94, 122 (1952).
9. Selznick, *Law, Society and Industrial Justice*, 51.
10. Leon D. Epstein, *Political Parties in the American Mold* (Madison: University of Wisconsin Press, 1986).
11. Hirschman, *Exit, Voice and Loyalty.*
12. James Willard Hurst, *The Legitimacy of the Business Corporation in the Law of the United States, 1780–1970* (Charlottesville: University of Virginia Press, 1970), 15–16.
13. Stephen B. Smith, "Hegel's Critique of Liberalism," *American Political Science Review* 80 (March 1986): 121–40.
14. Wolfgang Streeck and Philippe Schmitter, "Community, Market, State—and Associations? The Prospective Contribution of Interest Governance to Social Order," in *Private Interest Government* (Beverly Hills, Calif.: Sage, 1987), 1–29.
15. Emile Durkheim, *The Division of Labor in Society* (New York: Free Press, 1933).
16. A splendid discussion of the corporatist ideal is to be found in Black, *Guilds and Civil Society in European Political Thought.*
17. John Dewey, *The Public and Its Problems* (New York: Holt, 1927), 71.

18. John Meynard Keynes, "The End of Laissez-Faire," in *Essays in Persuasion* (London: Macmillan, 1931), 41.

19. Mary Parker Follett, *The New State* (New York: Longmans, 1923).

20. On the pluralist effect on Progressive policy, see Ellis Hawley, *Herbert Hoover and the Crisis of American Capitalism* (Cambridge, Mass.: Schenkman, 1973); Robert F. Himmelfarb, *The Origins of the National Recovery Administration* (New York: Fordham University Press, 1976); Morton Keller, "The Pluralist State: American Economic Regulation in Comparative Perspective, 1900–1930," in Thomas K. McCraw, ed., *Regulation in Perspective* (Cambridge: Harvard University Press, 1981), 56–94.

21. Robert A. Dahl, *A Preface to Democratic Theory* (Chicago: University of Chicago Press, 1956).

22. See, among others, William E. Connolly, ed., *The Bias in Pluralism* (New York: Atherton, 1969), and Peter Bachrach, *The Theory of Democratic Elitism* (Boston: Little, Brown, 1967).

23. Philippe C. Schmitter, "Still the Century of Corporatism?" in Frederick Pike and Thomas Stritch, eds., *The New Corporatism* (Notre Dame: Notre Dame University Press, 1974), 85–131.

Chapter Six

1. The most important contemporary expressions of this theme include: Bruce A. Ackerman, *Social Justice in the Liberal State* (New Haven: Yale University Press, 1980); Ronald Dworkin, *Taking Rights Seriously* (Cambridge: Harvard University Press, 1978); Nozick, *Anarchy, State and Utopia*; and Rawls, *Theory of Justice*.

2. Some may feel that these four objectives do not fully define the political economic goals of the modern industrial state. For a more comprehensive typology of the instruments and ends of modern capitalist planning, see E. S. Kirschen, et al., *Economic Policy in Our Time* (Chicago: Rand McNally, 1964), 1:148.

3. H. W. Arndt, *The Rise and Fall of Economic Growth* (Chicago: University of Chicago Press, 1978).

4. Lester C. Thurow, *The Zero-Sum Society* (New York: Basic Books, 1980), 11–15.

5. Buchanan, *Demand and Supply of Public Goods,* and James O'Connor, *Fiscal Crisis of the State* (New York: St. Martin's, 1973).

6. Some economists, including R. F. Harrod and E. D. Domar, who did much to develop the technical theory, thought growth essential if the ultimate welfare goal of full employment was to be achieved. R. F. Harrod, *Toward a Dynamic Economics* (London: Macmillan, 1949), v; E. D. Domar, *Essays in the Theory of Economic Growth* (New York: Oxford University Press, 1957), 5.

7. Michael B. Levy, "Mill's Stationary State and the Transcendence of Liberalism," *Polity* 14 (Winter 1981): 273–93.

8. John Meynard Keynes, *The General Theory of Employment, Interest and Money* (New York: Harcourt, Brace, 1964), 221.

9. Donella Meadows and Dennis Meadows, *The Limits to Growth* (London: Earth Island, 1972).

10. The most explicit recent example of this approach is Robert Kuttner, *The Economic Illusion* (Boston: Houghton Mifflin, 1984).

11. Andrew Shonfield, *Modern Capitalism* (New York: Oxford University Press, 1965).

12. One of the fullest statements of this position is Ira A. Magaziner and Robert B. Reich, *Minding America's Business* (New York: Random House, 1983).

13. Robert B. Reich, *The Next American Frontier* (New York: Times Books, 1983).

14. See Shonfield, *Modern Capitalism*, 121–75; Pierre Bauchet, *Economic Planning: The French Experience* (London: Heineman, 1964).

15. Again, this is the central theme in Lowi, *End of Liberalism.*

Chapter Seven

1. However, some would argue that equality itself has to be justified as a standard for distributions. See Joel Feinberg, *Social Philosophy* (Englewood Cliffs, N.J.: Prentice-Hall, 1973), 109–11.

2. In this, I am making a different point than Douglas Raw and associates, who find equality perplexing. My view is that these authors only are concerned about the seeming ambiguity of equality because they are in fact dealing with justice. See Douglas A. Rae, Douglas Yates, Jennifer Hochschild, Joseph Morone, and Carol Fessler, *Equality/Equalities* (Cambridge: Harvard University Press, 1981).

3. This is, of course, the famous Wilt Chamberlain example from Nozick, *Anarchy, State and Utopia*, 160–62.

4. As John Kenneth Galbraith has pointed out, "The notion of an impersonally determined salary scale is extremely important to its beneficiaries." The president of Amoco or General Motors is unlikely to argue that he deserved compensation so much greater than that of his collaborators or co-workers. Rather, it is extremely convenient to believe that all of this is determined by outside forces. "But as one accepts the succession of the seasons, the acts of God and the onset of old age, one accepts the dictates of competition." John Kenneth Galbraith, *Economics and the Public Purpose* (New York: Houghton Mifflin, 1975).

5. Veblen, *Instinct for Workmanship*, 103–4.

6. Chester Barnard, *The Functions of the Executive* (Cambridge: Harvard University Press, 1966), 250.

7. The best discussion of this problem of distributive justice is Karol Soltan, *The Causal Theory of Justice* (Berkeley: University of California Press, 1987).

8. Christopher Jencks, *Inequality: The Reassessment of the Effects of Family and Schooling in America* (New York: Basic Books, 1972).

9. On this point, see the several discussions in Norman Bowie, ed., *Equal Opportunity* (Boulder, Colo.: Westview, 1988).

10. Michael Young, *The Rise of the Meritocracy* (Baltimore: Penguin, 1961), 108.

11. Rawls, *Theory of Justice*, 61.

12. Guttman, *Liberal Equality*, 131–32.

13. Soltan, *Causal Theory of Justice*, 182.

14. Rawls, *Theory of Justice*, 101–7.

15. Walter J. Blum and Harry Kalven, Jr., *The Uneasy Case for Progressive Taxation* (Chicago: University of Chicago Press, 1953).

16. Fred Hirsch, *Social Limits to Growth* (Cambridge: Harvard University Press, 1976).

17. Albert O. Hirschman, *The Passions and the Interests* (Princeton: Princeton University Press, 1977).

18. Charles Booth, *Life and Labour of the People of London* (London: Macmillan, 1902).

19. Friedman, *Capitalism and Freedom*, chap. 12.

20. Jenifer Hochschild, *What's Fair?* (Cambridge: Harvard University Press, 1981).

Chapter Eight

1. Four very different expressions of this view are E. F. Schumaker, *Small Is Beautiful* (New York: Harper, 1971); Barry Commoner, *The Closing Circle* (New York: Knopf, 1971); William Ophuls, *Ecology and the Politics of Scarcity* (San Francisco: Freeman, 1977); and Hazel Henderson, *The Politics of the Solar Age* (Garden City, N.Y.: Anchor, 1981). For overviews of the "deep ecology" movement, which is the form this persuasion took in the late 1980s, see George Sessions, "The Deep Ecology Movement: A Review," *Environmental Review* 11 (Summer 1987), 106–16 and Warwick Fox, "Deep Ecology: A New Philosophy for Our Time?" *Ecologist* 14 (1984): 194–200.

2. Aldo Leopold, *A Sand County Almanac* (New York: Oxford, 1949), 8–17. See also Roderick Nash, *The Rights of Nature* (Madison: University of Wisconsin Press, 1989).

3. David Stockman, "The Wrong War? The Case against a National Energy Policy," *Public Interest* 53 (Fall 1978): 3–44.

4. Schumaker, *Small Is Beautiful*.

5. Sustainability, as a prime attribute of rational enterprise, is an idea that continually reappears in the tradition of pragmatic liberal political economy. J. R. Stanfield notes that Karl Polanyi defined the economy as "an institutionalized process of interaction between man and his environment which results in a continuous supply of want-satisfying material

means." Veblen, of course, always thought of the economy in such terms. Economic institutions should be evaluated by their capacity to reproduce the means of social provision. Marc Tool, a contemporary institutional economist, sees the productive enterprise as "that which provides for the continuity of human life and the nonenvidious recreation of community through the instrumental use of knowledge." J. R. Stanfield, "Social Reform and Economic Policy," in Marc Tool, ed., *An Institutionalist Guide to Economics and Public Policy* (Armonk, N.Y.: M. E. Sharpe), 1984, 19–44; Marc Tool, *The Discretionary Economy* (Santa Monica, Calif.: Goodyear, 1979), 293.

6. Wendell Barry, *The Unsettling of America* (San Francisco: Sierra Books, 1977).

7. David Howard Davis, *Energy Politics* 3d ed. (New York: St. Martin's, 1982), chap. 3; Don Kash and Robert Rycroft, *U.S. Energy Policy* (Norman: University of Oklahoma Press, 1984).

8. Herman E. Daly, *Steady-State Economics* (San Francisco: Freeman, 1977), 17.

9. E. J. Mishan, *The Costs of Economic Growth* (Baltimore: Penguin, 1967).

10. Tribe, "Ways not to Think about Plastic Trees, 1315–33."

Chapter Nine

1. The clearest statement of this ideal of method is found in R. M. Hare, *Language and Morals* (Oxford: Clarendon, 1952).

2. As James Fishkin points out, very small differences in the specification of the idea of neutrality, or of the "original position," in rival liberal theories can result in enormous variation in the resulting principle, and in the moral and political implications of the theory, and there is no higher-order standard, in liberal philosophy, for adjudicating these differences. See Fishkin, *Beyond Subjective Morality*, 98ff., and idem., "Can There Be a Neutral Theory of Justice?" *Ethics* 93 (January 1983): 348–56.

3. Political scientists are most likely to be familiar with the criticisms of the rational ideal of deductive decision in Simon, *Administrative Behavior*, and Braybrooke and Lindblom, *A Strategy of Decision*. However, such analyses rested on a longer philosophical tradition that goes back to Peirce, at least, and eventually to Hume. See, for example, Thomas L. Thorson, *The Logic of Democracy* (New York: Holt, 1962), 34–50.

4. Rawls, *Theory of Justice*, 20ff., 48–51; Ronald Dworkin, "The Original Position," in Norman Daniels, ed., *Reading Rawls* (New York: Basic Books, 1976), 32.

5. A good example is Douglas T. Yates, Jr., "Hard Choices: Justifying Public Decisions," in Joel Fleishman, Lance Liebman, and Mark H. Moore, eds., *Public Duties* (Cambridge: Harvard University Press, 1981), 32–51.

6. Today, justification is less likely to be understood as formal Carte-

sian proof, a matter of deduction from indubitable principles, but rather as coherence, "a matter of mutual support of many considerations, of everything fitting together into one coherent view." Rawls, *Theory of Justice*, 21, 572.

7. Duncan MacRae, Jr., *The Social Function of Social Science* (New Haven: Yale University Press, 1976), 77–106. Also Brian Barry and Douglas A. Rae, Jr., "Political Evaluation," in Fred L. Greenstein and Nelson Polsby, eds., *Handbook of Political Science I: Scope and Theory* (Reading, Mass.: Addison, Wesley, 1975), 337–96. In fairness, MacRae is advocating a prescription for the development of policy science rather than a method of practical reason, but in the end, the implications are the same.

8. Frank Fischer, *Politics, Values and Public Policy* (Boulder, Colo.: Westview, 1980).

9. David C. Paris and James F. Reynolds, *The Logic of Policy Inquiry* (New York: Longmans, 1983), 255–70.

10. John Dewey, *Theory of Valuation* (Chicago: University of Chicago Press, 1939).

Chapter Ten

1. Bertrand de Jouvenal, *Sovereignty* (Chicago: University of Chicago Press, 1959), 17.

2. Braybrooke and Lindblom, *Strategy of Decision*. On meliorative reason, see 147–68. On the relationship of their thought to philosophic pragmatism, see 18–19.

3. John Stuart Mill, *A System of Logic* (London: Macmillan, 1898), 620–21.

4. Brian Barry, *Political Argument* (London: Routledge and Kegan Paul, 1965), 1–14.

Chapter Eleven

1. This is clearly consistent with the tradition from Hobbes, in which, failing proof of transcendental claims to knowledge, the individual becomes the final arbiter of moral worth and human purpose. However, the point could also be made within the idealist, Kantian tradition. Kant, after all, thought the uses of practical reason more fundamental than those of pure reason. See Onora O'Neill, "The Public Use of Reason," *Political Theory* 14 (November 1986): 523–51.

2. See the attack on Hobbes in this spirit at the beginning of Jean-Jacques Rousseau, "The Social Contract," in *The Social Contract and Discourses*, trans. G. D. H. Cole (New York: Dutton, 1950), 8.

3. This certainly seems to be the position of Richard Rorty. See both Rorty, *Philosophy and the Mirror of Nature*, and idem., *Consequences of*

Pragmatism. For the reflection of this attitude in institutional political economic thinking, see particularly the discussion of Clarence Ayers in Allan C. Gruchy, *Contemporary Economic Thought: The Contribution of Neo-Institutionalist Economics* (New York: Sentry, 1972), 90–94.

4. "Some philosophers have imagined that to start an inquiry it was only necessary to utter a question whether orally or by setting it down upon paper, and even have recommended us to begin our studies with questioning everything! But the mere putting a proposition into the interrogative form does not stimulate the mind to any struggle after belief. There must be a real and living doubt, and without this all discussion is idle." Charles Sanders Peirce, "The Fixation of Belief," in Justus Buchler, ed., *The Philosophical Writings of Peirce* (New York: Dover, 1955), 11.

5. Ibid., 5–22.

6. Charles Sanders Peirce, "How to Make Our Ideas Clear," in Buchler, *Philosophical Writings of Peirce*, 23–41.

7. John E. Smith, *Purpose and Thought: The Meaning of Pragmatism* (Chicago: University of Chicago Press, 1978), 18; Justus Buchler, "Introduction." in *Philosophical Writings of Peirce*, ix–xvi.

8. Smith, *Purpose and Thought*, 58.

9. Buchler, "Introduction," xiv.

10. See, in this connection, William Galston's argument that liberalism is not neutral among notions of the good but professes a very specific notion of human purpose and virtue. William A. Galston, "Liberal Virtues," *American Political Science Review* 82 (December 1988): 1277–93.

11. Lustig, *Corporate Liberalism,* 12–18.

12. Furniss and Tilton, *Case for the Welfare State*, chap. 6.

13. John Rawls, "Kantian Constructivism and Moral Theory," *Journal of Philosophy* 78 (September 1980): 518.

14. Elaine Spitz, "Citizenship and Liberal Institutions," in Alfonso Damico, ed., *Liberals on Liberalism* (Totawa, N.J.: Rowman and Littlefield, 1986), 198.

15. For an exemplary illustration of this form of argument, see Lester C. Thurow, "The Illusion of Economic Necessity," in Robert A. Solo and Charles W. Anderson, eds., *Value Judgment and Income Distribution* (New York: Praeger, 1981), 250–76.

Chapter Twelve

1. I do not go into greater detail here on this interpretation of the history of the discipline for I have written about it elsewhere. See Charles W. Anderson, "Political Theory and Political Science: The Rediscovery and Reinterpretation of the Pragmatic Tradition," in John S. Nelson, ed., *What Should Political Theory Be Now?* (Albany: State University of New York Press, 1983), 390–412.

2. A basic description appears in Lawrence Kohlberg, "From Is to Ought: How to Commit the Naturalistic Fallacy and Get Away with It in the Study of Moral Development," in T. Mischel, ed., *Cognitive Development and Epistemology* (New York: Academic Press, 1971), 151–235. For a full discussion of Kohlberg's approach, and an important study of liberal valuation based on it, see Fishkin, *Beyond Subjective Morality*.

INDEX

Adjudication, and political reason, 165–66, 201
Affirmative action, 33–34
Agriculture, as enterprise, 64, 108–11, 146
Airlines, deregulation of, 69–70
Amish, Old Order, 33
Argument, political. *See* Deliberation, political; Reason, practical political
Aristotle, 11, 163
Associations. *See* Enterprise
Augustine, Saint, 78

Barry, Brian, 159, 179
Braybrooke, David, 46, 159, 174
Buchanan, James, 7, 189
Burke, Edmund, 169

Cartesianism, 7, 25, 160
Citizenship, in polity and enterprise, 19–20, 51–54, 176, 178–79, 191–202
Cole, G. D. H., 91
Commons, John R., 56, 61
Community of practice and inquiry. *See* Enterprise
Compensation systems, 125–27
Competence, civic. *See* Education
Conservatism. *See* Tradition; Trusteeship
Contract: as basis of enterprise, 20–22; and legitimacy of enterprise, 85–86; and role of state, 61
Corporation: law of, 84–85, 88; municipal, 84

Corporatism, 90–97. *See also* Pluralism
Cost-benefit analysis, 65; and environmental policy, 149. *See also* Liberalism, utilitarian
Craftsmanship, 10–12, 27, 45–55, 187; and distributive justice, 130–34
Croly, Herbert, 56

Dahl, Robert, 31, 54
Daly, Herman, 148
de Jouvenal, Bertrand, 173
Deliberation, political, 31–32, 45–52, 58–59, 131–32, 155–79, 191–93; and purpose of enterprise, 82–85; and environmental policy, 149–51; teaching of, 194–202. *See also* Democracy; Reason, practical political
Democracy: theory of, 8–9; and government of enterprise, 23–24, 38–58, 86–88, 116–17; Industrial, 31–32, 49–52, 86–89, 131–32
Descartes, Rene. *See* Cartesianism
Dewey, John, 1, 2, 11, 46, 91, 173, 175, 185
Discrimination, and public policy, 62–63. *See also* Affirmative action
Durkheim, Emile, 91

Economic policy, 79–80, 101–20. *See also* Industrial policy; State; Enterprise

217